CHAOS THEORY

in the

FINANCIAL MARKETS

Applying Fractals,
Fuzzy Logic,
Genetic Algorithms,
Swarm Simulation &
The Monte Carlo Method
To Manage
Market Chaos & Volatility

Dimitris N. Chorafas

PROBUS PUBLISHING COMPANY
Chicago, Illinois
Cambridge, England

ISBN 1-55738-555-6

Printed in the United States of America

BB

1 2 3 4 5 6 7 8 9 0

To Dr. Heinrich Steinmann

■ Contents

List of Figures and Tables   xiii
Foreword by Richard Forsyth   xvii
Foreword by Masuteru Sekiguchi   xxi
Preface   xxiii
Acknowledgments   xxvii

PART 1   INTRODUCTION TO COMPLEXITY THEORY   1

1 Implementing Chaos Theory in Financial Markets   3

1 Introduction   3
2 Change, Order, and Non-Traditional Research   5
3 Time and the Concept of a Chaotic Market Behavior   9
4 Looking at the Origins of Chaos Theory   11
5 Concepts of a Chaotic Market Behavior   13
6 The Able Treatment of Time   17
7 Time Series, Nonlinearities, and Bifurcations   21
8 Why Are We Interested in Chaos Theory?   25
9 Efficient Market Hypothesis and Strange Attractors   28

2 Organization, Evolution, and the Edge of Chaos   33

1 Introduction   33
2 Understanding the Evolution of Systems   34
3 Learning Effects and the Edge of Chaos   37

Contents

4 Adaptive Agents and Critical Conditions   40

5 Edge of Chaos and Solution Space   43

6 A Grammar for Problems of Complexity   45

7 Is Equilibrium a Prerequisite to Organization?   49

8 Clues to the Origin of Dynamic Systems   52

9 Principles of Evolution and Risk Management   55

**3 Fundamental Notions Underlying the Theory
of Complexity and Its Mathematics**   **59**

1 Introduction   59

2 Macroscopic and Microscopic Concepts   60

3 Exploring the Macroscopic Viewpoint   64

4 Is Complexity Theory a Matter of Fashion?   68

5 The Need to Restructure Our Know-how   71

6 Learning from the Behavior of Other Systems   73

7 Entropy and Organization   77

8 Randomness, Probable States, and Prediction   81

9 Weeding Noise Out of Financial Data   86

**4 NonLinear Equations and Fractals
Underpinning Chaos Theory**   **89**

1 Introduction   89

2 Linear and Nonlinear Models in Forex Operations   91

3 Escaping the Linear Approaches   95

4 Developing Equations for Nonlinear Systems   98

5 Implementing Concepts from Physics
  in Financial Analysis   100

6 The Need to Rethink Time Series
  and Solution Spaces   104

7 Dynamic Equations, Forex Trading,
  and Fractal Concepts   108

8 An Introduction to the Theory of Fractals   112

9 Concepts and Processes in Fractal Geometry   118

PART 2   FROM GENETIC ALGORITHMS TO FUZZY ENGINEERING   125

5 The Essence of Genetic Algorithms and their Implementation   127

1 Introduction   127

2 What Is the Sense of Using a Genetic Algorithm?   128

3 The Mechanics of Genetic Algorithms   133

4 Selection, Mutation, and Performance
  in the Stock Market   136

5 The Process of Generation in Foreign
  Exchange Operations   140

6 Applying the Genetic Algorithm
  in Off-Balance Sheet Operations   143

7 Adaptive Agents and Research
  in the Capital Markets   146

8 Increased Returns and Positive Feedback   149

9 Biological Research and Genetic Algorithms   152

Contents

6 **Predictors, Simulators, and Artificial Life
at Santa Fe Institute**   **157**

1 Introduction   157

2 The Concept of Reasoning by Analogy   158

3 Modeling Community Intelligence   161

4 Can We Reflect a Pattern of Group Thinking?   165

5 Using Supercomputer Power
   to Face Processing Requirements   167

6 Swarms and Systems with Feedback   171

7 Competitive Advantages of an Ecological Approach   174

8 Problems and Opportunities
   in Developing Predictors   178

9 The Financial Industry's Achilles Heel   180

7 **Non-Traditional Financial Analysis at MIT**   **187**

1 Introduction   187

2 MIT Researchers Turn Away
   from Modern Portfolio Theory   188

3 Volatility and the Asynchronous Nature
   of Financial Data   191

4 Trying to Visualize Multiple Variable Data   194

5 Autocorrelation, Chaos, and Volatility   197

6 The Concept of Risk and Cumulative Exposure   200

7 Why Logistics Equations Need Memory Systems   204

8 Capitalizing on Computer Storage
   and Agile Algorithms   208

9 Bankers Trust Positions Itself for Greater
   Competitiveness in the Market   213

8 Using Fuzzy Engineering in Financial Environments 217

1 Introduction   217

2 Implementing Concepts in Fuzzy Logic   220

3 Financial Analysis through Fuzzy Sets   223

4 Advantages from the Implementation of Fuzzy Engineering   227

5 The Cyclical Nature of Financial Business   229

6 Benefits from a Fuzzy Cognitive Model for Financial Operations   233

7 Paying Attention to the Inference Method   236

8 Integrating Fuzzy Engineering and Neural Networks   240

9 Fuzzy Functions, Genetic Algorithms, and Fractals   243

PART 3   IMPLEMENTING ADVANCED FINANCIAL ANALYSIS   247

9 Dealing with Uncertainty in the Financial Markets   249

1 Introduction   249

2 Initial Conditions and Possibility Theory   251

3 The Meaning of Uncertainty in Financial Data   254

4 Can We Learn from Other Implementation Domains?   258

5 Improving the Scope of Analysis through Fuzzy Sets   261

Contents

6 Establishing the Customer's Profile
for Relationship Management   264

7 Using a Fuzzy Sets Graph to Judge
Customer Behavior   268

8 Automating Sensitive Aspects of Banking Work   272

9 Developing the Client Mirror
and Doing Sensitivity Analysis   276

10 Case Studies on How to Apply Fuzzy Engineering   281

1 Introduction   281

2 A Grading Procedure Involving Uncertainty
and the Defuzzification Concept   283

3 Capitalizing on the Power of Defuzzification   288

4 Quantification, Qualification,
and Fuzzification in Trading   290

5 The Evaluation of Collateral for Equities   293

6 More Accurate Ways for Pricing Collaterals   296

7 Visual Programming and Practical Results   299

8 A Fuzzy System for Bond Evaluation   303

9 Ways and Means of Estimating Cash Flow   308

11 Using the Monte Carlo Method in Financial Analysis   315

1 Introduction   315

2 Problems Connected to the Construction
of Stochastic Models   317

3 Concepts and Challenges in Implementing
Monte Carlo   320

Contents

4 Using Monte Carlo in a Financial Environment   324

5 Understanding the Business of Securitization   328

6 Making Home Mortgages a Marketable Product   333

7 Exploring the Business Opportunities
That Are Present   336

8 Developing Valid Models for Securities Pricing   339

**12 Can We Reach the Goal
of Managing Complexity?   343**

1 Introduction   343

2 Complexity, Adaptability, and Behavioral Patterns   345

3 The Process of Learning at the Edge of Chaos   350

4 Is Chaotic Behavior a Prerequisite to Renewal?   353

5 Pattern Formation in an Environment
of Complex Behavior   356

6 New Strategies in Financial Trading
and in Personalized Investment Services   360

7 Streamlined or Overlapping Research Interests?   363

8 Studies in Finance that Enhance
Competitive Advantages   366

9 Organizational Prerequisites
in Managing Complexity   369

Index   373

List of Figures and Tables

FIGURE 1-1 In a market environment, chaos theory helps in opportunity identification. The rest is management skill.   13

FIGURE 1-2 The theory of complexity interfaces between chaos and order, and addresses the problems of transition.   14

FIGURE 1-3 Terry's electrocardiogram presented a chaotic behavior.   20

FIGURE 1-4 Bifurcation diagram and chaotic solution spaces (attractors).   24

FIGURE 1-5 Infrastructure of a characteristic behavior with nonlinear systems, the way swap markets work.   27

FIGURE 2-1 From diversity to customization: sequential phases of a market development.   39

FIGURE 2-2 Growth, time, and complexity are interrelated concepts.   47

FIGURE 2-3 The inheritance of rules and information in a banking system and its business elements.   54

FIGURE 3-1 Complexity theory solutions support global and flexible viewpoints.   62

FIGURE 3-2 The theory of complexity uses metalevel and inheritance to pattern the characteristics of component parts.   65

FIGURE 3-3 Metalevels and detailed rules regarding derivative products.   67

FIGURE 3-4 Economics and finance have involved a significant number of interdisciplinary activities.   76

List of Figures and Tables

FIGURE 3-5   Organization and disorganization interact, a linkage
being provided through complexity theory.   84

FIGURE 4-1   A 3-D presentation of variation in gold price as a function of
Treasury bills rate and crude oil prices.   91

FIGURE 4-2   The simple equation $Z = \alpha \cdot x + \beta \cdot y$ gets complex as α
and β become variable, attenuating or amplifying x, y
or leading to bifurcation.   93

FIGURE 4-3   Discontinuity can be created due to many factors,
particularly so in nonlinear systems. This is an
example from microprocessor pricing.   104

FIGURE 4-4   Time series of market closing price at the stock
exchange.   105

FIGURE 4-5   A fractals graph of the equation $Z = Z^2 - 1$, which has been
the subject of 20,000 iterations on a parallel computer.   115

FIGURE 4-6   A closer look at one of the elements in Figure 4-5, clearly
distinguishing the fractal geometry.   116

FIGURE 4-7   Generating a Koch snowflake.   119

FIGURE 4-8   Developing Sierpinski triangles.   123

FIGURE 5-1   There are background reasons for wide fluctuations in
stock prices, the bottom line being profit and loss.   138

FIGURE 5-2   A coordinate system of tools that permits the exercise
of more accurate risk management.   149

FIGURE 6-1   Modern analytical reasoning manifested itself with scale
models but transited to digital simulation.   159

FIGURE 6-2   From linear, stand-alone models, economic analysts and
simulation proceed toward dynamic and flexible artifacts.   164

FIGURE 6-3   A free market is characterized by feedback, which permits
a process of regulation to take place.   172

FIGURE 6-4   Decentralized and federated organizations. Federation
provides for flexibility and timeliness.   184

FIGURE 7-1   Risk as a function of time and of cumulative exposure in
financial environments.   201

FIGURE 7-2   Efficient answer to market requirements has many sides
that should integrate into an aggregate.   207

List of Figures and Tables

FIGURE 7-3   Bifurcation in a logistics equation with two and many possible final values.   211

FIGURE 7-4   Non-traditional approaches to input and output requirements connected to computer systems.   215

FIGURE 8-1   Crisp and fuzzy functions in expressing size, from small to medium and large.   219

FIGURE 8-2   Expressing the variation in water temperature through possibility theory.   222

FIGURE 8-3   Using knowledge engineering to conceive, generate, and verify hypotheses in financial analysis.   226

FIGURE 8-4   Overview of a diagnostic system for operational support.   237

FIGURE 9-1   Imprecision in the expression of projected dollar inflation.   256

FIGURE 9-2   Fuzzy classification of client behavior in funds switching, for cash management purposes.   268

FIGURE 9-3   Grading customers A and B on how fast they move their cash balances from the bank.   271

FIGURE 9-4   Possible use of fuzzy engineering to calculate five different risks for bullet bonds ($100M represents capital and compound/interest for 20 years bonds).   275

FIGURE 10-1   Fuzzy sets to calculate degree of membership to different classes of college grades.   284

TABLE 10-1   Predicate matrix combining the inputs of Teachers A and B.   285

FIGURE 10-2   Input and output functions, predicate box combining the teacher's grades.   286

FIGURE 10-3   Defuzzification of the degree of membership to the medium and high membership sets.   287

FIGURE 10-4   Fuzzification of the Dow Jones Index considering ranges of the last 20 years and possible maxima, using today's perspective.   297

FIGURE 10-5   Fuzzification of stock value and combination of inputs into a market factor output function.   298

TABLE 10-2   Predicate matrix combining the absolute value of Dow Jones index and stock price variation.   299

TABLE 10-3	The knowledge bank of the fuzzy engineering expert system automatically generated by the shell after the predicate matrix was set.	300
FIGURE 10-6	Fuzzification of absolute market factor, as output of the Dow Jones Index and stock market price.	302
FIGURE 10-7	Defuzzification of variable: market factor.	303
FIGURE 10-8	Step-by-step combining of primary factors into a collateral evaluation.	305
FIGURE 10-9	Fuzzification of the acid test of current assets over current liabilities.	307
TABLE 10-4	Weighting factors connected to the CA&CL, cash flow and profitability inputs.	310
TABLE 10-5	Characteristics of A&L states leading to predicate matrix with three input variables.	311
FIGURE 10-10	Output function for collateral facilities, integrating the input from A&L cash flow and profitability.	311
FIGURE 10-11	Defuzzification of variable: collateral factor.	312
TABLE 10-6	Compilation into a knowledge bank of the predicate matrix defining the collateralization output.	313
FIGURE 11-1	Reliability curves of three components characterized by normal distribution.	321
TABLE 11-1	Calculating the life cycle of a mortgage pool in years.	326
FIGURE 11-2	Customer requirements analysis for securitized products: mortgage-backed financing.	331
FIGURE 12-1	Uncertainty in market trends is often misinterpreted as noise in the time series, while the reasons are different.	346
FIGURE 12-2	Segmenting seven levels of organization into two groups to better handle the issues of complexity.	348
FIGURE 12-3	Complexity can also be seen as interfacing between dynamic components and crumbling structures—characterizing a process of renewal.	354
FIGURE 12-4	Complex financial studies resemble a collection of overlapping research interests.	363

Foreword by Richard Forsyth

As we approach the twenty-first century a global marketplace is emerging that must be one of the most extraordinary monuments to human ingenuity and greed ever created. Every weekday, financial transactions amounting to a total value sufficient to buy the entire land area of France, and everything on it, take place during the hours when the banks are closed in Paris. This happens at the instigation of a relatively small number of people, who are employed to manage the assets of large corporations, governments, and pension funds by speculating in a wide variety of bonds, commodities, currencies, futures, options, and stocks.

The vast majority of this frenetic dealing does not directly involve the exchange of anything tangible, not even a bank note. It is all done electronically.

Some commentators have proposed that the world-wide communications network that makes such trading possible represents the emergence of some sort of "global consciousness" that marks a new stage in the evolution of intelligence. Others argue that it is, on the contrary, a cancerous growth, feeding on the "real economy," that will ultimately lead to a financial catastrophe so serious as to plunge western civilization into a new Dark Age.

Nobody can be quite sure which prognosis is correct, because nobody understands how this system works.

You might think that this is an excusable state of affairs, since the system has only been made possible by recent developments in computing and communications technology; but in fact the behaviour of the international financial market in the 1990s is remarkably similar to the behaviour of local markets in the 1890s—before computers, before geostationary satellites, before radio and television, even before the telephone—and nobody really understands how those old-fashioned markets worked either.

That this should be so is, in my view, an intellectual scandal, caused chiefly by a slavish devotion to the tenets of what is called the "efficient market hypothesis" on the part of academic economists. Briefly, this idealization of the real world requires instant, error-free processing of accurate information by well-informed rational investors to be the norm—which, apart from its inherent implausibility, has been empirically refuted on several occasions (e.g., Dimson, 1988).*

Until recently the situation could be summed up roughly as follows: while most academics clung to this implausible and discredited theory (because at least it was coherent and comprehensible) most practitioners grabbed at a hodge-podge of often bizarre ideas as long as they appeared to work in their own particular area (which at least was pragmatic). Indeed, Wall Street is one of the few places in the modern world where an astrologer can not only make a good living but also be taken seriously by a highly paid and highly educated audience.

In short, theorists and practitioners had very little of value to say to each other—which is where the book you hold in your hands, *Chaos Theory in the Financial Markets*, by Dimitris Chorafas, comes in. Here is a work that will help to bridge this unhealthy gulf of incomprehension between theorists and practitioners (though it is worth noting that the theorist in question, such as the free thinkers at the Santa Fe Institute, are more often

* Dimson, E. (ed.), *Stock Market Anomalies* (Cambridge University Press, 1988).

physicists, mathematicians, and computer scientists than economists). This work helps to show how we can use modern science to manage the chaos and complexity which, in part, it is responsible for plunging us into.

Dr. Chorafas, I am glad to say, gives the efficient market hypothesis short shrift. His book has a number of great merits: it is thoroughly pragmatic, it is free from dogmatism, and it is up to date. Above all, it is written by someone who is bold and open-minded enough to link ideas from many disciplines when that is necessary to illuminate his main field.

One of the main themes of this book is that we are forced to live at the edge of chaos—potentially a most uncomfortable position. It could be made more comfortable if we knew ways to apply some of the latest research into dynamic nonlinear systems. The trouble is that this research is carried on by different groups under a number of headings, such as

artificial life
chaos theory
complexity theory
fractal mathematics
fuzzy logic
genetic algorithms
stochastic simulation

and others.

Most of us have neither the time nor the mathematical sophistication to educate ourselves in these fields, exciting though they undoubtedly are. Professor Chorafas, however, has; and he has brought together the fruits of his investigations into these fields in an accessible fashion, which non-specialists can follow with ease.

Professor Richard Forsyth
Faculty of Computer Studies and Mathematics
University of the West of England, Bristol

Foreword by Masuteru Sekiguchi

Infrastructures to support the financial market used to imply the huge OLTP systems in banks and securities exchanges, or the payment network systems through which those systems were interconnected. However, due to the financial deregulations in the 1970s, the need for more precise customer information and profit management systems had increased, and the focus of information technology investment shifted to advanced DBMS and Expert Systems. Moreover, we experienced the explosion of money market and complex market instruments in the 1980s, which forced us to deploy more smart and dynamic applications.

It was early in the spring of 1981 that Dr. Dimitris N. Chorafas visited my laboratory in Tokyo for the first time, just when I was struggling to apply advanced technologies such as AI, IC card, and, later, neural networks, to financial systems. I gratefully recollect that, during the course of our discussions, he gave me a lot of suggestions on every topic.

Now, in the middle of the 1990s, the concerns about information technology applications in the financial markets is moving toward more sophisticated systems, which enable strategic decision making by utilizing analytic tools and models. Here, we must face difficult problems, forecasting the uncertain future and exploring optimal solutions under complex conditions, to which the traditional approaches, like stochastics and determinism, are proving inefficient.

Since the beginning of the 1990s, the new approaches based on complexity theory, such as chaos theory or genetic algorithms—the subject of this book—attract attention among researchers and analysts in the financial field, because of the expectation of a breakthrough to these new challenges. Considering today's rapid changes in the financial markets, I believe it is one of the most urgent tasks for financial engineers and analysts to develop innovative applications.

Dr. Chorafas has written not only a comprehensive but also a practical book on this advanced subject at this time. "There is no complete theory for complex systems," once said Takuma Yamamoto, chairman of Fujitsu Ltd., stressing the limitation of the theories and the importance of empirical know-how in systems design, when he was my boss and asked me to engage in the development of financial systems. But now, another respectable engineer named Dr. D. N. Chorafas is about to open a door to a new age, in which the substantial portion of complex systems might be elegantly described by theories.

In closing, let me express my hearty congratulation on this valuable publication to Probus of Chicago, the home of financial innovation, and my gratitude to the courtesy of Dr. Chorafas for giving me this honourable role of writing the foreword.

Masuteru Sekiguchi
Board Director
Fujitsu Research Institute
for Advanced Information Systems & Economics

■ Preface

Bernard Shaw's aphorism about England and America being separated by a common language certainly applies to financial analysts. They are separated by the mathematical tools they use. The tools we have employed so far in financial analysis have been linear and statistical. But neither linearity nor the hypothesis of a normal distribution can provide the support needed in a market that is more competitive than ever.

It comes, therefore, as no surprise that cutting-edge financial institutions have turned their attention to non-traditional means of research and analysis. Most of them come under the heading Complexity Theory and include such tools as nonlinearities, bifurcations, chaos theory, attractors, fractals, entropy, genetic algorithms, predictors, adaptive agents, swarms, fuzzy engineering, Monte Carlo, and patterning.

These are the themes this book covers. It does so in a comprehensive manner, with a bare minimum of mathematics. The presentation depends on visualization, rather than on equations, to explain concepts and to present practical examples.

The book is written for professionals in finance and in economics who wish to retool themselves in the trade. It can serve equally well in graduate classes in colleges and universities, as it covers topics the new scientists and businesspeople will need in order to analyze market behavior and to trade, develop trust, and communicate with each other.

Chapter 1 addresses the roots of the new challenges: How and why chaos theory is important in understanding trends and in gaining control of events in the financial markets. Organization, evolution, and the edge of chaos underpin this issue, and they are treated in Chapter 2.

Solutions in the new environment require concepts that are both broader, and therefore more comprehensive, and better focused than those we've used so far. These come under the term Theory of Complexity—which revolutionizes established fields from physics and engineering to finance—constituting the core issue of Chapter 3.

Nonlinear equations should be the preferred approach, advises Chapter 4, which explains how to develop and handle nonlinear algorithms. Another important topic in this chapter is the concepts and processes of fractal geometry.

One of the rather recent tools successfully used in financial analysis, as well as in scheduling, is genetic algorithms. This is the subject of Chapter 5. Specific applications examples are given, such as the use of genetic algorithms with off-balance sheet operations and their employment in connection to foreign exchange.

Chapter 6 focuses on the research projects done by the scientists of the Santa Fe Institute. It particularly treats those developments with predictive capabilities in the domain of finance. Chapter 7 does the same with sponsored projects at MIT that cover the most advanced aspects of non-traditional financial analysis.

Chapters 8, 9, and 10 address themselves to fuzzy engineering. Chapter 8 introduces the concept of fuzzy logic, applies it in the development of cognitive models for financial analysis, and demonstrates how and why fuzzy engineering integrates nicely with genetic algorithms and fractals.

Chapter 9 provides ways and means for dealing with uncertainty in the financial markets by capitalizing on fuzzy engineering. Plenty of practical issues are presented and these are further expanded in Chapter 10 through case studies on quantification and qualification in the evaluation of cash flow and of collateral. Bonds and equities are given as examples.

The subject of Chapter 11 is use of the Monte Carlo method in financial analysis. The concepts, tools, and challenges are explained by taking the case of securitization and examining all its aspects, both from a banking and from an analytical viewpoint. A case study on mortgage-backed financing further enriches this discussion.

Chapter 12 integrates what the preceding eleven chapters have presented into a comprehensive approach to the implementation of complexity theory. It explains why profits and even survival in the financial markets of the 1990s depends so much on personalizing trading and investment services, then shows in a convincing way that this can be done at an affordable cost by capitalizing on the new tools available to us.

Is all this happening because of the miracle of new tools? There are no miracles in finance, but there is *a different culture*. Paraphrasing Alexandre Dumas: There is neither truly new nor truly old in life. There is only a comparison between some other time and somewhere else—and the present time where we are living.

Let me close by expressing my thanks to everyone who contributed to making this text successful: to my colleagues for their advice, all of the organizations visited for their time and support, and a few selected friends who reviewed important parts of the text for their valuable comments.

Particularly my thanks go to Heinrich Steinmann, Executive Vice President and Member of the Group Executive Board of Union Bank of Switzerland for his imaginative ideas and the support he has provided to the research. In terms of new perspectives, special mention should be made to the Santa Fe Institute, specifically to Dr. L. Mike Simmons and the faculty who participated in the working meetings as outlined in the Acknowledgments. Also to Eva-Maria Binder for the artwork, typing of the manuscript, and the index.

Professor Richard Forsyth contributed an imaginative Foreword which both praises and gives hell to interactive computational finance; Dr. Masuteru Sekiguchi expressed the viewpoint of the research chief of a major technological corporation. Kevin Commins fathered this book and brought it to press; Pamela Sourelis did a fine editing job and Carol Klein has been instrumental in assuring an efficient publication. Without these collaborations the book the reader has in hand could not have been successfully completed.

Dimitris N. Chorafas
Valmer and Vitznau

■ Acknowledgments

The following organizations, their senior executives and system specialists, participated in the 1992 and 1993 research projects which led to the contends of the present book and its documentation.

UNITED STATES

1. BANKERS TRUST
    1. Dr. Carmine VONA, Executive Vice President for Worldwide Technology
    2. Shalom BRINSY, Senior Vice President Distributed Networks
    3. Dan W. MUECKE, Vice President, Technology Strategic Planning
    4. Bob GRAHAM, Vice President, Database Manager
    One Bankers Trust Plaza, New York, NY 10006

2. CITIBANK
    5. Colin CROOK, Chairman Corporate Technology Committee
    6. David SCHULTZER, Senior Vice President, Information Technology
    7. Jim CALDARELLA, Manager, Business Architecture for Global Finance
    8. Nicholas P. RICHARDS, Database Administrator
    9. William BRINDLEY, Technology Officer
    10. Michael R. VEALE, Network Connectivity
    11. Harriet SCHABES, Corporate Standards
    12. Leigh REEVE, Technology for Global Finance
    399 Park Avenue, New York, NY 10043

3. MORGAN STANLEY
   13. Gary T. GOEHRKE, Managing Director, Information Services
   14. Guy CHIARELLO, Vice President, Databases
   15. Robert F. DE YOUNG, Principal, Information Technology
   1933 Broadway, New York, NY 10019
   16. Eileen S. WALLACE, Vice President, Treasury Department
   17. Jacqueline T. BRODY, Treasury Department
   1251 Avenue of the Americas, New York, NY 10020

4. GOLDMAN SACHS
   18. Vincent L. AMATULLI, Information Technology, Treasury
       Department
   85 Broad Street, New York, NY 10004

5. J.J. KENNY SERVICES INC.
   19. Thomas E. ZIELINSKI, Chief Information Officer
   20. Ira KIRSCHNER, Database Administrator, Director of System
       Programming and of the Data Center
   65 Broadway, New York, NY 10002

6. MERRILL LYNCH
   21. Kevin SAWYER, Director of Distributed Computing Services
       and Executive in Charge of the Mainframe to Client-Server
       Conversion Process
   22. Raymond M. DISCO, Treasury/Bank Relations Manager
   World Financial Center, South Tower, New York, NY 10080-6107

7. TEACHERS INSURANCE AND ANNUITY ASSOCIATION/
   COLLEGE RETIREMENT EQUITIES FUND (TIAA/CREF)
   23. Charles S. DVORKIN, Vice President and Chief Technology
       Officer
   24. Harry D. PERRIN, Assistant Vice President, Information
       Technology
   730 Third Avenue, New York, NY 10017-3206

8. FINANCIAL ACCOUNTING STANDARDS BOARD
   25. Halsey G. BULLEN, Project Manager
   26. Jeannot BLANCHET, Project Manager
   27. Teri L. LIST, Practice Fellow
   401 Merritt 7, Norwalk, CN 06856

9. MASSACHUSETTS INSTITUTE OF TECHNOLOGY
    28. Prof.Dr. Stuart E. MADNICK, Information Technology and Management Science
    29. Prof.Dr. Michael SIEGEL, Information Technology, Sloan School of Management
    30. Patricia M. McGINNIS, Executive Director, International Financial Services
    31. Prof. Peter J. KEMPTHORNE, Project on Non-Traditional Methods in Financial Analysis
    32. Dr. Alexander M. SAMROV, Project on Non-Traditional Methods in Financial Analysis
    33. Robert R. HALPERIN, Executive Director, Center for Coordination Science
    34. David L. VERRILL, Senior Liaison Officer, Industrial Liaison Program
    Sloan School of Management, 50 Memorial Drive, Cambridge, MA 02139
    35. Prof.Dr. Kenneth B. HAASE, Media Arts and Sciences
    36. Dr. David ZELTZER, Virtual Reality Project
    Ames St., Cambridge, MA 02139

10. SANTA FE INSTITUTE
    37. Dr. Edward A. KNAPP, President
    38. Dr. L. Mike SIMMONS, Jr., Vice President
    39. Dr. Bruce ABELL, Vice President Finance
    40. Prof.Dr. Murray GELL-MANN, Theory of Complexity
    41. Prof.Dr. Stuart KAUFFMAN, Models in Biology
    42. Dr. Chris LANGTON, Artificial Life
    43. Dr. John MILLER, Adaptive Computation in Economics
    44. Dr. Blake LE BARON, Non-Traditional Methods in Economics
    45. Bruce SAWHILL, Virtual Reality
    1660 Old Pecos Trail, Santa Fe, NM 87501

11. SCHOOL OF ENGINEERING, UNIVERSITY OF CALIFORNIA, LOS ANGELES
    46. Prof.Dr. Judea PEARL, Cognitive Systems Laboratory
    47. Prof.Dr. Walter KARPLUS, Computer Science Department
    48. Prof.Dr. Michael G. DYER, Artificial Intelligence Laboratory
    Westwood Village, Los Angeles, CA 90024

12. SCHOOL OF BUSINESS ADMINISTRATION, UNIVERSITY OF SOUTHERN CALIFORNIA
   49. Dr. Bert M. STEECE, Dean of Faculty, School of Business Administration
   50. Dr. Alan ROWE, Professor of Management
   Los Angeles, CA 90089-1421

13. PREDICTION COMPANY
   51. Dr. J. Doyne FARMER, Director of Development
   52. Dr. Norman H. PACKARD, Director of Research
   53. Jim McGILL, Managing Director
   234 Griffin Street, Santa Fe, NM 87501

14. SIMGRAPHICS ENGINEERING CORP.
   54. Steve TICE, President
   55. David J. VERSO, Chief Operating Officer
   1137 Huntington Drive, South Pasadena, CA 91030- 4563

15. NYNEX SCIENCE AND TECHNOLOGY, INC.
   56. Thomas M. SUPER, Vice President, Research and Development
   57. Steven CROSS, NYNEX Shuttle Project
   58. Valerie R. TINGLE, System Analyst
   59. Melinda CREWS, Public Liaison, NYNEX Labs
   500 Westchester Avenue, White Plains, NY 10604
   60. John C. FALCO, Sales Manager, NYNEX Systems Marketing
   61. David J. ANNINO, Account Executive, NYNEX Systems Marketing
   100 Church Street, New York, NY 10007

16. MICROSOFT
   62. Mike McGEEHAN, Database Specialist
   63. Andrew ELLIOTT, Marketing Manager
   825 8th Avenue, New York, NY 10019

17. REUTERS AMERICA
   64. Robert RUSSEL, Senior Vice President
   65. William A.S. KENNEDY, Vice President
   66. Buford SMITH, President, Reuters Information Technology
   67. Richard A. WILLIS, Manager International Systems Design
   68. M.A. SAYERS, Technical Manager, Central Systems Development

69. Alexander FAUST, Manager Financial Products USA
(Instantlink and Blend)

40 E. 52nd Street, New York, NY 10022

19. ORACLE CORPORATION
    70. Scott MATTHEWS, National Account Manager
    71. Robert T. FUNK, Senior Systems Specialist
    72. Joseph M. DI BARTOLOMEO, Systems Specialist
    73. Dick DAWSON, Systems Specialist

885 Third Avenue, New York, NY 10022

20. DIGITAL EQUIPMENT CORPORATION
    74. Mike FISHBEIN, Product Manager, Massively Parallel Systems
    (MAS-PAR Supercomputer)
    75. Marco EMRICH, Technology Manager, NAS
    76. Robert PASSMORE, Technical Manager, Storage Systems
    77. Mark S. DRESDNER, DEC Marketing Operations

146 Main Street, Maynard, MA 01754 (Meeting held at UBS New York)

21. UNISYS CORPORATION
    78. Harvey J. CHIAT, Director Impact Programs
    79. Manuel LAVIN, Director, Databases
    80. David A. GOIFFON, Software Engineer

P.O. Box 64942, MS 4463 Saint Paul, MN 55164-0942 (Meeting held at UBS in New York)

22. HEWLETT-PACKARD
    81. Brad WILSON, Product Manager, Commercial Systems
    82. Vish KRISHNAN, Manager R+D Laboratory
    83. Samir MATHUR, Open ODB Manager
    84. Michael GUPTA, Transarc, Tuxedo, Encina Transaction
    Processing
    85. Dave WILLIAMS, Industry Account Manager

1911 Pruneridge Avenue, Cupertino, CA 95014

23. IBM CORPORATION
    86. Terry LIFFICK, Software Strategies, Client-Server Architecture
    87. Paula CAPPELLO, Information Warehouse Framework
    88. Ed COBBS, Transaction Processing Systems
    89. Dr. Paul WILMS, Connectivity and Interoperability
    90. Helen ARZU, IBM Santa Teresa Representative

91. Dana L. STETSON, Advisory Marketing IBM New York
Santa Teresa Laboratory, 555 Bailey Avenue, San José, CA 95141

24. UBS SECURITIES
92. A. Ramy GOLDSTEIN, Managing Director, Equity Derivative Products
299 Park Avenue, New York, NY 10171-0026

25. UNION BANK OF SWITZERLAND
93. Dr. H. BAUMANN, Director of Logistics, North American Operations
94. Dr. Ch. GABATHULER, Director, Information Technology
95. Hossur SRINKANTAN, Director, Telecommunications
96. Roy M. DARHIN, Assistant Vice President
299 Park Avenue, New York, NY 10171-0026

UNITED KINGDOM

1. BARCLAYS BANK
1. Peter GOLDEN, Chief Information Officer, Barclays Capital Markets, Treasury, BZW
2. Brandon DAVIES, Director of Financial Engineering
3. David J. PARSONS, Director Advanced Technology
4. Christine E. IRWIN, Group Information Systems Technology
Murray House, 1 Royal Mint Court, London EC3N 4HH

2. BANK OF ENGLAND
5. Mark LAYCOCK, Banking Supervision Division
Threadneedle Street, London EC2R 8AH

3. ASSOCIATION FOR PAYMENT CLEARING SERVICES (APACS)
6. J. Michael WILLIAMSON, Deputy Chief Executive
14 Finsbury Square, London EC2A 1BR

4. ABBEY NATIONAL BANK
7. Mac MILLINGTON, Director of Information Technology
Chalkdell Drive, Shenley Wood, Milton Keynes MK6 6LA

8. Anthony W. ELLIOTT, Director of Risk and Credit
Abbey House, Baker Street, London NW1 6XL

5. NATWEST SECURITIES
9. Sam B. GIBB, Director of Information Technology

10. Don F. SIMPSON, Director, Global Technology
11. Richard E. GIBBS, Director, Equity Derivatives
135 Bishopsgate, London EC2M 3XT

6. ORACLE CORPORATION
   12. Geoffrey W. SQUIRE, Executive Vice President, and Chief Executive
   13. Richard BARKER, Senior Vice President and Director British Research Laboratories
   14. Giles GODART-BROWN, Senior Support Manager
   15. Paul A. GOULD, Account Executive
   Oracle Park, Bittams Lane, Guildford Rd, Chertsey, Surrey KT16 9RG

7. VIRTUAL PRESENCE
   16. Stuart CUPIT, Graphics Engineer
   25 Corsham Street, London N1 6DR

8. VALBECC OBJECT TECHNOLOGY
   17. Martin FOWLER, Ptech Expert
   115 Wilmslow Road, Handforth, Wilmslow, Cheshire SK9 3ER

9. CREDIT SWISS FINANCIAL PRODUCTS
   18. Ross SALINGER, Managing Director
   One Cabot Square, London E14 4QJ

10. CREDIT SWISS FIRST BOSTON
    19. Geoff J. R. DOUBLEDAY, Executive Director
    One Cabot Square, London E14 4QJ

11. E. D. & F. MAN INTERNATIONAL
    20. Brian FUDGE, Funds Division
    Sugar Quay, Lower Thames Street, London EC3R 6DU

SCANDINAVIA

1. VAERDIPAPIRCENTRALEN (VP)
   1. Jens BACHE, General Manager
   2. Aase BLUME, Assistant to the General Manager
   61 Helgeshoj Allá, Postbox 20, 2630 Taastrup, Denmark

2. SWEDISH BANKERS' ASSOCIATION
   3. Bo GUNNARSSON, Manager, Bank Automation Department

4. Gosta FISCHER, Manager, Bank-Owned Financial Companies Department
5. Gøran AHLBERG, Manager, Credit Market Affairs Department

P.O. Box 7603, 10394 Stockholm, Sweden

3. SKANDINAVISKA ENSKILDA BANKEN
   6. Lars ISACSSON, Treasurer
   7. Urban JANELD, Executive Vice President Finance and IT
   8. Mats ANDERSSON, Director of Computers and Communications
   9. Gosta OLAVI, Manager SEB Data/Koncern Data

   2 Sergels Torg, 10640 Stockholm, Sweden

4. SECURUM AB
   10. Anders NYREN, Director of Finance and Accounting
   11. John LUNDGREN, Manager of IT

   38 Regerings, 5 tr., 10398 Stockholm, Sweden

5. SVEATORNET AB of the Swedish Savings Banks
   12. Gunar M. CARLSSON, General Manager

   (Meeting of Swedish Bankers' Association)

6. MANDAMUS AB of the Swedish Agricultural Banks
   13. Marie MARTINSSON, Credit Department

   (Meeting of Swedish Bankers' Association)

7. HANDELSBANKEN
   14. Janeric SUNDIN, Manager, Securities Department
   15. Jan ARONSON, Assistant Manager, Securities Department

   (Meeting of Swedish Bankers' Association)

8. GOTA BANKEN
   16. Mr. JOHANNSSON, Credit Department

   (Meeting of Swedish Bankers' Association)

9. IRDEM AB
   17. Gian MEDRI, Former Director of Research at Nordbanken

   19 Flintlasvagen, 19154 Sollentuna, Sweden

AUSTRIA

1. CREDITANSTALT BANKVEREIN
   1. Dr. Wolfgang G. LICHTL, Director of Foreign Exchange and Money Markets

2. Dr. Johann STROBL, Manager, Financial Analysis for Treasury Operations

3 Julius Tandler-Platz, 1090 Vienna

2. BANK AUSTRIA
   3. Dr. Peter FISCHER, Director of Treasury
   4. Peter GABRIEL, Deputy General Manager, Trading
   5. Konrad SCHCATE, Manager, Financial Engineering

   2 Am Hof, 1010 Vienna

3. ASSOCIATION OF AUSTRIAN BANKS AND BANKERS
   6. Dr. Fritz DIWOK, Secretary General

   11 Boersengasse, 1013 Vienna

4. AKTIENGESELLSCHAFT FUER BAUWESEN
   7. Dr. Josef FRITZ, General Manager

   2 Lothringenstrasse, 1041 Vienna

5. MANAGEMENT DATA of CREDITANSTALT
   8. Ing. Guenther REINDL, Vice President, International Banking Software
   9. Ing. Franz NECAS, Project Manager, RICOS
   10. Mag. Nikolas GOETZ, Product Manager, RICOS

   21-25 Althanstrasse, 1090 Vienna

GERMANY

1. DEUTSCHE BUNDESBANK
   1. Eckhard OECHLER, Director of Bank Supervision and Legal Matters

   14 Wilhelm Epstein Strasse, D-6000 Frankfurt 50

2. DEUTSCHE BANK
   2. Peter GERARD, Executive Vice President, Organization and Information Technology
   3. Hermann SEILER, Senior Vice President, Investment Banking and Foreign Exchange Systems
   4. Dr. KUHN, Investment Banking and Foreign Exchange Systems
   5. Dr. Stefan KOLB, Organization and Technological Development

   12 Koelner Strasse, D-6236 Eschborn

3. DRESDNER BANK
    6. Dr. Karsten WOHLENBERG, Project Leader Risk Management, Simulation and Analytics Task Force Financial Division
    7. Hans-Peter LEISTEN, Mathematician
    8. Susanne LOESKEN, Organization and IT Department
    43 Mainzer Landstrasse, D-6000 Frankfurt

4. COMMERZBANK
    9. Helmut HOPPE, Director Organization and Information Technology
    10. Hermann LENZ, Director Controllership, Internal Accounting and Management Accounting
    11. Harald LUX, Manager Organization and Information Technology
    12. Waldemar NICKEL, Manager Systems Planning
    155 Mainzer Landstrasse, D-60261 Frankfurt

5. DEUTSCHER SPARKASSEN UND GIROVERBAND
    13. Manfred KRUEGER, Division Manager, Card Strategy
    4 Simrockstrasse, D-5300 Bonn 1 (Telephone interview from Frankfurt)

6. ABN-AMRO (Holland)
    14. Mr. SCHILDER, Organization and Information Technology
    (Telephone interview from Frankfurt)

7. MEDIA SYSTEMS
    15. Bertram ANDERER, Director
    6 Goethestrasse, D-7500 Karlsruhe

8. FRAUNHOFER INSTITUTE FOR COMPUTER GRAPHICS
    16. Dr.Ing. Martin GOEBEL
    17. Wolfgang FELBER
    7 Wilhelminerstrasse, D-6100 Darmstadt

9. GMD FIRST—RESEARCH INSTITUTE FOR COMPUTER ARCHITECTURE, SOFTWARE TECHNOLOGY AND GRAPHICS
    18. Prof.Dr.Ing. Wolfgang K. GILOI, General Manager
    19. Dr. BEHR, Administrative Director
    20. Dr. Ulrich BRUENING, Chief Designer
    21. Dr. Joerg NOLTE, Designer of Parallel Operating Systems Software
    22. Dr. Matthias KESSLER, Parallel Languages and Parallel Compilers

23. Dr. Friedrich W. SCHROER, New Programming Paradigms
24. Dr. Thomas LUX, Fluid Dynamics, Weather Prediction and Pollution Control Project

5 Rudower Chaussee, D-1199 Berlin

10. SIEMENS NIXDORF
    25. Wolfgang WEISS, Director of Banking Industry Office
    26. Bert KIRSCHBAUM, Manager, Dresdner Bank Project
    27. Mark MILLER, Manager Neural Networks Project for UBS and German banks
    28. Andrea VONERDEN, Business Management Department

27 Lyoner Strasse, D-6000 Frankfurt 71

11. UBS GERMANY
    29. H.-H. v. SCHELIHA, Director, Organization and Information Technology
    30. Georg SUDHAUS, Manager IT for Trading Systems
    31. Marco BRACCO, Trader
    32. Jaap VAN HARTEN, Trader

52 Bleichstrasse, D-6000 Frankfurt 1

SWITZERLAND

1. BANK FOR INTERNATIONAL SETTLEMENTS
    1. Claude SIVY, Director, Controllership and Operational Security
    2. Frederik C. MUSCH, Secretary General, Basel Committee on Banking Supervision

2 Centralbankplatz, Basel

2. CIBA-GEIGY AG
    3. Stefan JANOVJAK, Divisional Information Manager
    4. Natalie PAPEZIK, Information Architect

Ciba-Geigy, R-1045, 5.19, 4002 Basle

3. EURODIS
    5. Albert MUELLER, Director
    6. Beat ERZER, Marketing Manager
    7. B. PEDRAZZINI, Systems Engineer
    8. Reto ALBERTINI, Sales Engineer

Bahnhofstrasse 58/60, CH-8105 Regensdorf

JAPAN

1. BANK OF JAPAN
   1. Harry TOYAMA, Councel and Chief Manager, Credit and Market Management Department
   2. Akira IEDA, Credit and Market Management Department
   2-1-1 Kongoku-Cho, Nihonbashi, Chuo-ku, Tokyo 103

2. DAI-ICHI KANGYO BANK
   3. Shunsuke NAKASUJI, General Manager and Director, Information Technology Division
   4. Seiichi HASEGAWA, Manager International Systems Group
   5. Takahiro SEKIZAWA, International Systems Group
   6. Yukio HISATOMI, Manager Systems Planning Group
   7. Shigeaki TOGAWA, Systems Planning Group
   13-3 Shibuya, 2-Chome, Shibuya-ku, Tokyo 150

3. FUJI BANK
   8. Hideo TANAKA, General Manager Systems Planning Division
   9. Toshihiko UZAKI, Manager Systems Planning Division
   10. Takakazu IMAI, Systems Planning Division
   Otemachi Financial Center, 1-5-4 Otemachi, Chiyoda-ku, Tokyo

4. MITSUBISHI BANK
   11. Akira WATANABE, General Manager, Derivative Products
   12. Akira TOWATARI, Manager, Strategic Planning and Administration, Derivative Products
   13. Takehito NEMOTO, Chief Manager, Systems Development Division
   14. Nobuyuki YAMADA, Systems Development Division
   15. Haruhiko SUZUKI, Systems Development Division
   7-1 Marunouchi, 2-Chome, Chiyoda-ku, Tokyo 100

5. NOMURA RESEARCH INSTITUTE
   16. Tomio ARAI, Director, Systems Science Department
   17. Tomoyuki OHTA, Director, Financial Engineering Group
   18. Tomohiko HIRUTA, Manager, I-STAR Systems Services
   9-1 Nihonbashi, 1-Chome, Chuo-ku, Tokyo 103

6. MITSUBISHI TRUST AND BANKING
   19. Nobuyuki TANAKA, General Manager, Systems Planning Division

20. Terufumi KAGE, Consultant Systems Planning Division
9-8 Kohnan, 2-Chome, Minato-ku, Tokyo 108

7. SAKURA BANK
21. Nobuo IHARA, Senior Vice President and General Manager, Systems Development Office VIII
22. Hisao KATAYAMA, Senior Vice President and General Manager, System Development Office VII
23. Toshihiko EDA, Senior Systems Engineer, Systems Development Division
4-2 Kami-Osahi, 4-Chome, Shinagawa-ku, Tokyo 141

8. SANYO SECURITIES
24. Yuji OZAWA, Director, Systems Planning Department
25. K. TOYAMA, Systems Planning Department
1-8-1 Nihonbashi, Kayabacho, Chuo-ku, Tokyo 103

9. CENTER FOR FINANCIAL INDUSTRY INFORMATION SYSTEM SYSTEMS (FISC)
26. Shighehisa HATTORI, Executive Director
27. Kiyoshi KUMATA, Manager, Research Division II
16th Floor, Ark Mori Building, 12-32, 1-Chome Akasaka, Minato-ku, Tokyo 107

10. LABORATORY FOR INTERNATIONAL FUZZY ENGINEERING RESEARCH (LIFE)
28. Prof.Dr. Toshiro TERANO, Executive Director
29. Dr. Anca L. RALESCU, Assistant Director
30. Shunichi TANI, Fuzzy Control Project Leader
Siber Hegner Building, 89-1 Yamashita-Cho, Naka-ku, Yokohama-shi 231

11. REAL WORLD COMPUTING PARTNERSHIP (RWC)
31. Dr. Junichi SHUMADA, General Manager of RWC
32. Hajime IRISAWA, Executive Director
Tsukuba Mitsui Building, 1-6-1 Takezono, Tsukuba-shi, Ibarahi 305

12. TOKYO UNIVERSITY
33. Prof.Dr. Michitaka HIROSE, Dept. of Mechano-Informatics, Faculty of Engineering
34. Dr. Kensuke YOKOYAMA, Virtual Reality Project
3-1, 7-Chome, Hongo Bunkyo-ku, Tokyo 113

13. TOKYO INTERNATIONAL UNIVERSITY
    35. Prof.Dr. Yoshiro KURATANI
    9-1-7-528 Akasaka, Minato-ku, Tokyo 107

14. JAPAN ELECTRONIC DIRECTORY RESEARCH INSTITUTE
    36. Dr. Toshio YOKOI, General Manager
    Mita-Kokusai Building—Annex, 4-28 Mita, 1-Chome, Minato-ku, Tokyo 108

15. MITSUBISHI RESEARCH INSTITUTE (MRI)
    37. Masayuki FUJITA, Manager, Strategic Information Systems Dept.
    38. Hideyuki MORITA, Senior Research Associate, Information Science Dept.
    39. Akio SATO, Research Associate, Information Science Dept.
    ARCO Tower, 8-1 Shimomeguro, 1-Chome, Meguro-ku, Tokyo 153

16. NTT SOFTWARE
    40. Dr. Fukuya ISHINO, Senior Vice President
    223-1 Yamashita-Cho, Naka-ku, Yokohama 231

17. RYOSHIN SYSTEMS (Systems Developer Fully Owned by Mitsubishi Trust)
    41. Takewo YUWI, Vice President, Technical Research and Development
    9-8 Kohman, 2-Chome, Minato-ku, Tokyo 108

18. SANYO SOFTWARE SERVICES
    42. Fumio SATO, General Manager, Sales Department 2
    Kanayama Building, 1-2-12 Shinkawa, Chuo-ku, Tokyo 104

19. FUJITSU RESEARCH INSTITUTE
    43. Dr. Masuteru SEKIGUCHI, Member of the Board and Director of R+D
    44. Takao SAITO, Director of the Parallel Computing Research Center
    45. Dr. Hiroyasu ITOH, R+D Department
    46. Katsuto KONDO, R+D Department
    47. Satoshi HAMAYA, Information Systems and Economics
    9-3 Nakase, 1-Chome, Mihama-ku, Chiba-City 261

20. NEC
    48. Kotaro NAMBA, Senior Researcher, NEC Planning Research
    49. Dr. Toshiyuki NAKATA, Manager, Computer System Research Laboratory
    50. Asao KANEKO, Computer System Research Laboratory
    3-13-12 Mita, Minato-ku, Tokyo 108

21. TOSHIBA
    51. Dr. Makoto IHARA, Manager Workstation Product Planning and Technical Support Dept.
    52. Emi NAKAMURA, Analyst Financial Applications Dept.
    53. Joshikiyo NAKAMURA, Financial Sales Manager
    54. Minami ARAI, Deputy Manager, Workstation Systems Division
    1-1 Shibaura, 1-Chome, Minato-ku, Tokyo 105

22. MICROSOFT
    55. James LALONDE, Multinational Account Manager, Large Accounts Sales Dept.
    Sasazuka NA Bldg, 50-1 Sasazuka, 1-Chome, Shibuya-ku, Tokyo 151

23. APPLE TECHNOLOGY
    56. Dr. Tsutomu KOBAYASHI, President
    25 Mori Bldg, 1-4-30 Roppongi, Minato-ku, Tokyo 106

24. DIGITAL EQUIPMENT JAPAN
    57. Roshio ISHII, Account Manager, Financial Sales Unit 1
    2-1 Kamiogi, 1-Chome, Suginamiku, Tokyo 167

25. UBS JAPAN
    58. Dr. Peter BRUTSCHE, Executive Vice President and Chief Manager
    59. Gary P. EIDAM, First Vice President, Regional Head of Technology
    60. Charles UNDERWOOD, Vice President, Head of Technical Architecture and Strategy
    61. Masaki UTSUNOMIYA, Manager, IT Production Facilities
    Yurakucho Building 2F, 1-10-1 Yurakucho, Chiyoda-ku, Tokyo 100

PART 1

Introduction to Complexity Theory

Implementing Chaos Theory in Financial Markets

1 INTRODUCTION

The last three years have seen a significant increase in the number of financial analysts who look at the theory of complexity to understand the market environment in which they operate and to foresee future events affecting the profitability of the institutions for which they work. The role of the financial analyst is to contribute *insight* and *foresight* regarding market movements. That is why he tries to predict the future. Financial analysts do so through personal ingenuity, assisted by mathematical tools and computers. Recently, this effort has included the application of:

- *Chaos* theory by Dr. Edward Lorenz and Dr. Mitchel Feigenbaum,
- *Fractals* theory by Dr. Benoit Mandelbrot,
- *Fuzzy Engineering* by Dr. Lotfi Zadeh and Dr. Richard Bellman
- *Nonlinear* approaches to simulation of financial systems.

Nonlinearity simply means that effect is not proportional to cause. Financial markets are nonlinear, which is partly but not exclusively due to the fact that financial data have lots of noise. Because of nonlinearities:

- The same-sized cause can have different effects, depending on the circumstances.

For instance, a ten base point rise in interest rates will affect in the same way different financial markets. The impact may, for example, depend on how the market interprets the authorities' objectives.

- This makes the mathematics of cause and effect quite complex, but also provides lots of profit-making opportunities.

The aim of studying nonlinearity as well as fractals is in the market, therefore, in their prediction. The background goal of non-traditional research projects is that of forecasting fluctuations and trends in financial markets.

An overriding need in any business is the ability to represent problem information in such a way that the full complexity and dynamic nature of the underlying structures is captured. *Financial systems* are no exception. Business problems need to be encoded in order to help in the comprehension and management of

- Market movements and
- Strategies by counterparties*

Among the most critical types of problems are price clusters that include informal or temporary groupings of traders,

* *Counterparty* is a very common term in banking. Any deal involves two or more parties: The one who initiates the transaction and the other(s) with whom the deal is done. These are the counterparty or counterparties—and may be a person, a manufacturing company, merchandising firm, or another (corresponding) bank.

commodities, and money rates; and pricing schedules with conditions or dependencies.

These are typically *nonlinear problems*. They are characterized by distribution networks of dynamically changing configurations of market forces. The behavior of many financial services and products falls into this category.

The real question in price movements is related to how people make decisions. Securities specialists, for example, have a common tendency to make overconfident predictions. But in case of major market twists such confidence can be fatal.

Do we have the methodology and the tools to face the developing market perspectives in a timely manner? To unlock important information? To reposition ourselves against current and latent market forces?

Benoit Mandelbrot was right when he stated that almost all our statistical tools are obsolete and we might eventually need to consign centuries of work to the scrap heap. Worn-out technology and its déjà vu tools help neither the managers nor the traders. Hence the interest leading institutions now have *non-traditional means for financial analysis*.

2 CHANGE, ORDER, AND NON-TRADITIONAL RESEARCH

Visions are conceptualizations designed to be projected onto the future. Their existence helps in forecasting performance by creating a plausible picture of future events. They give a general direction in which pragmatic *predictions* might be made.

But valid predictions are not that easy. Though it is not always recognized, typical business problem information has multiple layers of complexity. These include networks, dependencies, and feedback loops. Changing conditions affect the pattern or flow of a financial process.

- Over time, there is a steady evolution of problem characteristics, while

- Temporary or permanent deviations affect not one but many parts of a larger problem.

The pattern given by a forecast should be realistic, while visions may exist that are so far out they might never mature. It takes a great deal of effort to keep projections in a practical track, but this can be assisted through mathematical modeling, provided we have the appropriate tools.

One of the principal reasons why many visions dwell in a totally abstract and theoretical domain is that they have been generated by people without the necessary practical experience. Hence, the hypotheses being made are not plausible. On the other hand, one reason a large majority of people are unable to visualize great events is their *inability to deal with diversity and change*:

- There are people who see diversity as unsettling, even if its rationale is deep rooted in market forces.

- Others reject diversity outright because they fear it is not possible to reconcile the existing differences and contradictory trends.

Yet diversity, not monolithic standardization, is the sense of life. *Diversity is deep and wide in the financial markets; it is precisely its existence that permits the making of profit,* provided we can predict the trend of events and reposition our bank in the right side of the balance sheet.

As the information and the tools needed to solve prediction problems becomes more complex, it is increasingly more challenging to foresee and represent the evolving real-world situation. From risk management to the generation of profits, flexibility is the cornerstone to a successful prediction process.

When we have to force market information into a format that fits the available mathematical tools, programming languages, or database constructs, the result is an inadequate or even distorted representation of the real problem.

- Distortions due to the inadequacy of our culture, information, and tools are responsible for lower-quality projections, which time and again prove to be out of context, but also
- Since the representation of forthcoming events is not obvious, we find it virtually impossible to reuse in any meaningful sense the hypotheses and models we have constructed.

The new mathematical tools currently under development, generally known as *complexity theory*,* are designed to change this situation. Specifically, they are made to accommodate the dynamic nature of real-world problems, providing algorithms, heuristics, and information elements associated with them.

The goal is to do away with an inadequate representation that scales back the scope of financial analysis. Also targeted is the ability to provide traders and other decision-makers with the means to make their actions more competitive than ever before.

One of the major shortcomings of the process of making financial decisions is the lag between the reception of market information, the cognition of the new trends under development, and subsequent response to them. Taken together, these references make up the ability of *repositioning to face market forces*, but in the typical case

- People do not recognize trends until they are well established—which means until it is too late.

* The underlying concept of complexity theory is discussed in Chapter 3.

- The majority of financial specialists do not begin to extrapolate a phenomenon like rising inflation unless it rises for some time.

- The mathematical tools at our disposal work in a linear function, and are not able to account for market discontinuities.

After irrefutable statistical evidence is at hand, people react in large numbers to information that may have been ignored until that time. By overreacting to it, they create *panics*.

Panics develop because the market psychology can change very rapidly from a situation in which there are no sellers to one in which there are no buyers. Both selling and buying are driven by expectations and therefore overreactions show up:

- When the California residential property bubble burst in 1889, land prices plunged to a quarter of their peak value by the time the market stopped falling.

- In 1974 share prices in Britain fell to little over a quarter of their peak value in 1972—as if to confirm that shares are inherently risky, particularly in panic selling.

Bubbles and panics do have a mathematical shape familiar to *rocket scientists.** The bubble follows the line of an explosive curve. The panic usually shows a vertical drop at a given point in time, after the growth curve passes beyond the point at which it can be sustained.

Can chaos theory and other new tools help to manage a changing financial environment in a more orderly sense?

---

* *Rocket Scientists.* The term came up in Wall Street in the mid-1980s and identifies engineers, physicists, and mathematicians who have been working with the aerospace industry, nuclear research, and other advanced sectors—subsequently hired by banks to use their skills and knowhow in non-traditional financial analysis.

---

3 TIME AND THE CONCEPT OF A CHAOTIC MARKET BEHAVIOR

Behind the new tools available for non-traditional research are developments in the physical sciences, which can have a direct impact on financial trading and portfolio management.

An underlying characteristic of the new theories that come into the financial world from the physical sciences is the fact that all forms of organization simultaneously map themselves into two states that are at odds with each other:

- *Change* and
- *Order*

Change is characterized by the freedom to move away from the status quo by altering things in a manner reflecting new developments and by taking full account of the forces behind the process of *innovation*.

Not only is the representation of change complex, but *the transition between change and order* involves a great number of uncertainties as well. It is precisely this transition that is full of surprises and makes predictability so difficult to realize.

By contrast, *order stems from the status quo*, using efficiency and rationality as its justification. Order is represented by simpler and settled paths to regulation and is often expressed in a structured, hierarchical manner.

In the early 1960s, Donald Schön, an American organization expert, argued that *creativity*—particularly scientific creativity—comes from change, which leads to the displacement of concepts. That is, taking concepts from one field of life and applying them to another brings *fresh insights*.

- New concepts are signalled by a more representative language, which is as important as a new theory.
- New theory without the appropriate language can go unnoticed because language forms our minds.

Precisely along this frame of reference, leading-edge American financial institutions are now financing non-traditional economic research and market forecasting projects, like those by Bankers Trust at MIT and by Citibank at the Santa Fe Institute (SFI) in New Mexico.

An integral part of this research is the analysis of the behavior of pricing mechanisms, including the development of theories able to fit the market in a better way than the existing ones do. Novel approaches are being used. For instance,

- Exposure and risk are studied over short time periods, such as holding a deal for a couple of hours.

- The effects of volatility are micromanaged in connection to the pricing of interday options, rather than at the more leisurely pace usually followed.

It is precisely in this micromanagement that the effects of a *chaotic market behavior* become visible, as we will see in subsequent sections. The tools employed in the past in connection with financial analysis have been incapable of detecting chaotic behavior because they were not fine enough—apart from the fact that the concepts supposed to underlie different situations were not present.

This attention to the minute impact of market forces is *non-traditional* and contrasts to the bulk of the work being done in the majority of institutions, which address closing market data that may be meaningless. "God is in the detail," Mies van der Rohe once said.

"The key issue," suggested Patricia McGinnis, Executive Director, International Financial Services, of MIT, "is what can you find out by analyzing transactional data. A focused study of realtime market information puts you at better than 50 percent in position to face market risk." What does it take to make such a focused study?

4 LOOKING AT THE ORIGINS OF CHAOS THEORY

In the 19th century the physicist Sadi Carnot and other researchers realized it was both tedious and impractical to describe every interaction taking place in physical systems. They also discovered that they could predict the statistical behavior of an aggregate if they simplified its structure.

Based on Newtonian concepts, system predictions became the laws of thermodynamics. Their existence could explain the increase in temperature and pressure when gas molecules are heated in a container. But at the same time, thermodynamics did not provide a complete description of the most complex interactions as, for instance, in the case of gas molecules strongly attracted to one another.

Subsequently, Henri Poincaré (1854–1912) realized that *if a system consisted of a few parts that interacted strongly, it could exhibit unpredictable behavior.** This concept is at the origin of *chaos theory.*

Both in physics and in finance, *the object of chaos theory is to study the irregular behavior of simple deterministic equations* by providing more sophisticated tools that are closer to real life. This is an appealing notion to financial analysts confronted with a dynamic system that exhibits *aperiodic fluctuations* because it implies that

- These fluctuations might be explained in a relatively simple manner in terms of only a few dynamic equations of motion.

- Models able to reflect dynamic behavior make it possible to predict future fluctuations, at least in the short term.

---

* Quite interestingly, this is also the reason why tightly coupled systems like mainframes have a lower reliability than networked loosely coupled computers.

What is done with this prediction once it has been made is of course a different issue. Alternative strategies are reflected in Figure 1-1, with the outlined alternatives being problem solution and problem avoidance; both are managerial not analytical qualities:

- Chaos theory is no substitute for management or trader skill.
- It is simply a means for making valid opportunity identifications.

There have been many attempts to solve nonlinear problems, and the 19th century developments we have seen in this section are only a few examples. Classically, the modeling of a dynamic system has proceeded along the following path:

- Deterministic equations of motion are derived from first principles.
- Initial conditions are measured, and the equations of motion are integrated in time.
- When a first-principles model is unavailable or initial conditions are not accessible, the dynamic system is modeled as a random process.
- Typically, such modeling is done by using non-deterministic but linear laws of motion.

The mathematical properties of dynamic, nonlinear equations have been studied since the time of Poincaré but the physical and, to an even greater extent, financial implications of chaos have not been appreciated until the work of Lorenz, Feigenbaum, and Ruelle. This new formulation of chaotic conditions provided researchers with both tools and examples of chaos.

Though the scientists who restructured and modernized chaos theory have been physicists and mathematicians, both the

FIGURE 1-1   In a market environment, chaos theory helps in opportunity identification. The rest is management skill.

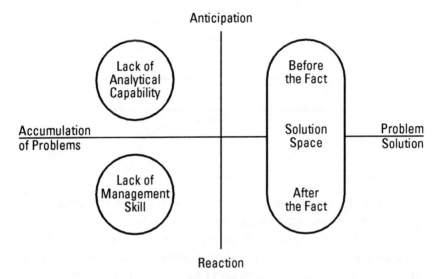

concepts and the analytics of complexity rapidly penetrated other domains. Finance is one example; control engineering is another; medicine is a third example, as we will see in section 6.

The hypothesis advanced by a new breed of rocket scientists is that it is possible to extend analytic and computational methods in finance, by combining them with concepts from modern physics. This interdisciplinary approach helps to develop prediction models with performance beyond that of current applications.

5 CONCEPTS OF A CHAOTIC MARKET BEHAVIOR

Both change and order are essential, though they are contradictory to each other. Their incompatibility is best expressed through modes of complexity that account for phenomena that, at first sight, don't even seem to fit together.

FIGURE 1-2   The theory of complexity interfaces between chaos and order, and addresses the problems of transition.

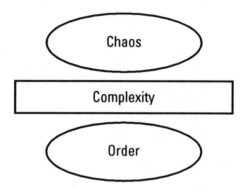

Here is exactly the domain where the new scientific discipline termed *complexity* is emerging and where its practitioners believe a real revolution is brewing. That revolution is both *conceptual* and *analytical*, addressing interface problems as well as the transition between chaos and order shown in Figure 1-2.

Chaotic systems are essentially periodic. What makes them appear random is *a continual transition from one periodic orbit to another*. The study of chaos reveals hidden patterns of order fluctuations that quite often characterize complex systems such as the following:

- The stock market
- Weather patterns
- Epidemics
- Heartbeats

In the past, the perceived state of randomness was thought to be due to *chance*. But as Dr. David Ruelle advises, beyond the problem of chance we should try to understand something of the triangular relation between

- The strangeness of mathematics,

- The physical world,* and
- Our own mind.

Whether guided by market laws or by physical laws, *chaos is a time evolution with sensitive dependence on initial conditions.* Its study is a nonlinear science, and the solution spaces, also known as *attractors,* may themselves be chaotic.

Chaos, lack of *equilibrium,* and the fundamental concept of *instability* have gone beyond the confines of their 19th century definition. They are beginning to acquire formal aspects based on mathematical relationships. These three terms, however, are not necessarily synonymous:

- A chaotic system could be stable if its particular irregularity persisted in the face of small disturbances.

In other terms, *in spite of its unpredictability, chaos may be globally stable* even if it exhibits a pattern of irregularity and is locally unpredictable.

- There exist, therefore, patterns with disturbances, which some people think reflect an orderly disorder.

The standard theory of chaos deals with time evolutions that repeat themselves and by so doing open new horizons in scientific and business research.

The implementation of chaos theory rests on a few *simple principles.* The essence of studies in chaotic behavior lies in the way in which patterns change over time:

- The pattern we make of chaos pulls the data into shapes that are visible and therefore detectable.
- Such pattern also tends to indicate that of all possible pathways of disorder, nature and the markets favor only a few.

* As well as the financial world.

Chaos is a state of vitality and at the same time of decay. In a paper in the *Journal of the American Medical Association*,* Lewis Lipsitz suggests that aging is marked by a loss of complexity in measures such as heart rate, blood-pressure changes and brain-wave patterns. In old age, they all become less chaotic. The same is true of financial markets.

In a dynamic environment, there can be no equilibrium conditions in the transition that is steadily characterizing the alterations of change and order. The concept of equilibrium is based on the assumptions of Newtonian mechanics that conditions gravitate toward a certain state of stability.

Albert Einstein challenged this Newtonian concept to its roots. But it is really the post-World War II physicists who advanced laws radically altering the hypothesis that systems gravitate toward stability.

The same principles characterizing chaotic behavior and, therefore, instability are applicable to the model of the economy and of society at large. As it will be seen in subsequent sections,

- Healthy capital markets and money markets are characterized by turbulence and volatility, rather than by efficiency and fair price.

- Like any dynamic system, a healthy economy does not tend to equilibrium but is, instead, in steady change.

- That is why economists who are currently using equilibrium theories to model market systems are likely to produce dubious results.

Though they have been used for nearly 50 years, simplifying approaches, such as the equilibrium theory and the efficient market hypothesis, utterly ignore *the proper treatment of time*. Yet no dynamic system can be correctly modeled if the analysts

* April 1992.

ignore time or, at best, treat time as a controllable variable—which could not be further from the truth.

6 THE ABLE TREATMENT OF TIME

Time is a unique resource. It cannot be accumulated like wealth, yet without it we can accomplish none of our tasks. In spite of this, of all available resources, time is the one least understood and most mismanaged.

- If the steam engine were the prime mover of the industrial age, the clock is central to post-industrial society.

- Managers and traders who learn how to live by the clock concentrate on the development of better and more flexible plans and strategies.

Time is the particular instance at which a process occurs or a structure *exists*. It is also the instance in which the structure *endures*, the process *continues*, a measurement is made, or an act takes place. For instance, a financial commitment is made.

One of the truly restrictive assumptions in traditional financial analysis involves the way time affects different events. In finance today there is a concept of *Intrinsic Time*. For instance, seconds are shorter during the Asian lunch break than during the American lunch break, because American traders eat lunch at their desks while continuing to trade.

By redefining the width of time units, computer software draws graphs incorporating assumptions about how different traders in the market might react to a price movement in an intrinsic time sense. These graphs may present a similar overall shape, but have different slopes according to each trader's

- time horizon, or
- risk profile.

Each trader is assumed to react in a nonlinear way. At first, with a minor response to a price rising above its moving average, then with increasing interest, and finally with major response as the trader thinks a clear trend has developed.

The computer adds up these different reaction models and arrives at an estimate of how the whole market could react to an event. Or the output can be a history of market behavior over the past day or hour:

- The computer can forecast what the market *might* do in the days or hours ahead, and

- The model provides the forecast with an increasing width to illustrate a growing margin of error.

A flashing point can indicate the present moment. When the tolerance of the line goes below that point, the computer alerts to an *overbought* opportunity; hence go short. When it goes above that point to an *oversold* opportunity, go long. Both are treated as advice.

The concept of intrinsic time changes the long-held beliefs regarding time behavior, which have been based on Newtonian physics, where time is considered invariant as it is not important to its problems.

- In a theoretical framework, the motion of bodies in space can be undone by simply reversing the algorithm.

- When financial analysis borrows heavily from Newtonian physics, it tends to treat time as relatively unimportant to its problems.

- Yet time is tremendously important. What we do today is conditioned both by yesterday and by tomorrow, hence by a time function.

We will see in subsequent sections what this means in terms of the equations we should be using. Markets, economies, and financial systems are dynamic; therefore, time is at the focal point of interactions and of their effects.

The concept of the importance of time helps to reduce the lag between decision and execution. It also assists in the appreciation of the changes time brings. The concept assures that the dynamic aspects of change are perceived earlier, permitting the framing of decisions and actions necessary to handle a quickly evolving situation.

No better example can be given of chaotic behavior as a function of time than heartbeats prior to a terminal event. Based on an electrocardiogram of Terry (my guard dog), who died shortly thereafter of cardiomyopathy, a type of primary myocardial disease, Figure 1-3 shows *the dramatic changes in rhythms* that have been recorded.

In a show of significant interdisciplinary spirit, control engineers at the U.S. Naval Surface Warfare Center have discovered that the behavior of the heart during a heart attack is actually *a case of chaotic dynamics* rather than a completely random breakdown. This can have profound medical implications, opening the door to the possibility of controlling heart attacks with *intelligent pacemakers.*

Already on the market, pacemakers incorporating programmable microchips that head off heart attacks have followed a brute-force approach. They deliver a major electrical jolt to the heart if it gets out of control, which can be extremely painful. But with a computational subsystem based on chaos theory, navy researchers hope to spawn a new generation of intelligent pacemakers:

- These will be able to analyze and control the heart in realtime as if it were a conventional dynamic system.

- When an arrhythmic condition indicating a transition to chaos occurs, the pacemaker would then deliver control pulses to steer the heartbeat back to normal rhythms.

FIGURE 1-3   Terry's electrocardiogram presented a chaotic behavior.

D1

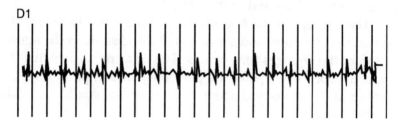

D2

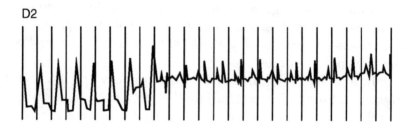

D3

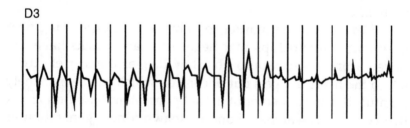

The fact that heart tissue enters a chaotic dynamic state during a heart attack is a new medical finding in itself with implications in many other fields, including finance. The new strategy is to

- Work with continually altered parameters to keep the system from wandering between periodic orbits and

- Put in place real-time response, incorporating all critical constraints in the algorithms.

No better description can be made of what is required with financial systems in order to micromanage market movements. If Mitchel Feigenbaum, Edward Lorenz, Benoit Mandelbrot, and David Ruelle are at the forefront of modern market theory, the projects currently under way at the Santa Fe Institute, MIT, and Naval Research Surface Warfare center are talking examples of time-dependent applications fields.

7 TIME SERIES, NONLINEARITIES, AND BIFURCATIONS

From physics and mathematics to financial analysis, much of the modeling processes aim at the study of *time series* of values resulting from measurements attributed to specific events. These may be stock market prices, the measurements of a process control instrument, or heart pulses shown on an oscilloscope.

The changing values of any one variable have been traditionally displayed as a function of time. Different algorithms—mostly linear—are being used to exploit and visualize the relationship that may exist between time series values.

There is a reason for displaying time series in a graphic form or using statistical tools for their analysis. This reason is to make possible some foresight of future events:

- Past is past, but what might be the next value?
- What amount of confidence can be placed in this projection?

Both linearity and randomness have been used for predictive reasons. Probabilistic approaches both contrast to and are an improvement upon the notions of determinism. As a result, *determinism* and *randomness* have been seen for many years as opposites and therefore as separate subjects.

Based on this line of reasoning, it has been assumed that complex phenomena have resulted from systems with many degrees of freedom that were analyzed as random processes. Simple phenomena, however, were modeled deterministically even if they belonged to dynamic constructs.

- In the longer run this procedure ends by producing unpredictable behavior.

- In contrast, under the influence of nonlinearity only a few degrees of freedom are necessary to generate chaotic motion.

Precisely for these reasons, mathematicians and physicists have worked on methods and tools for nonlinear modeling. Their usage has already led to a number of applications where nonlinear approaches motivated by chaotic dynamics provide superior prediction capabilities as compared to linear models.

A financial example helps in appreciating this reference. Since interest rates are not stable, banks have to hedge them, and the same is true of exchange rates. If banks are to manage risk and be competitive in their pricing, they have to have a good view of the correlation, if any, between

- Movements in short-term interest rates and

- Movements in the exchange rate of currencies.

Typically, financial analysts apply correlation of covariance to the interplay of two currencies and their interest rates. But no one has yet come up with a model that can comfortably predict how an interest movement in one currency relates to the exchange and interest rate of another—and for good reason. The relationship between these factors is nonlinear.

During the European Exchange Rate Mechanism (ERM) crisis of October 1992, for example, historical correlations proved to be totally misleading. The correlation between Deutschmark interest rates and the movement in the mark-dollar is normally about 0.3 and 0.4. Therefore, increases in interest rates have only a marginal effect on the strength of the mark. But

- When the ERM burst with the British pound, the Italian lira and other currencies dropping out, those correlations went wild, in some cases approaching 1.
- This produced a very positive correlation between the downward direction of sterling and the downward direction of sterling interest rates, and banks got hurt.

As financial institutions know by experience, the volatility of the correlation is a problem, and it cannot be predicted through classical analytic tools. As a result, in contrast to the first 80 years of this century when chaotic behavior in dynamic systems has often been viewed with dismay, it is now beginning to be regarded as presenting business opportunities.

The most important of these opportunities lies in understanding market movements and in *predicting changes over the short term*. This is the outcome of mathematical breakthroughs that took place during the last 20 years and are now becoming popularized:

- Rather than the classical analysis of time series as linear processes, recent studies have used chaos theory to examine *the information content of time series*.
- They reconstruct multidimensional *attractors*, that is solution spaces helping to define a temporary equilibrium of the system.

The process of analyzing solution spaces helps in constructing vector fields for the purpose of short-term forecasting. It assists in noise reduction as well as in finding unstable periodic motions for understanding structure in the space of phase variation.

A basic concept in connection to the behavior of dynamic systems is that of *bifurcation*. With nonlinear dynamics, this identifies the split of possible solutions after a given situation has passed the *critical stage*.

- A critical stage is connected to values of *control parameters*.

- Such parameters have a *threshold* at which the nature of the dynamic behavior itself changes.

In a bifurcation the sum of energy carried by the resulting tracks can be less than the energy of the original track. This is a good example of interchangeability between energy and matter.

The system can bifurcate, as shown in the X, Y coordinate axes of Figure 1-4, or it can make the transition from stable to turbulent and eventually chaotic behavior. *Turbulence* is easy to see but hard to understand. As David Ruelle aptly suggested: "To see means to be able to guess what is true and what is false, what is useful and what is not."

FIGURE 1-4   Bifurcation diagram and chaotic solution spaces (attractors).

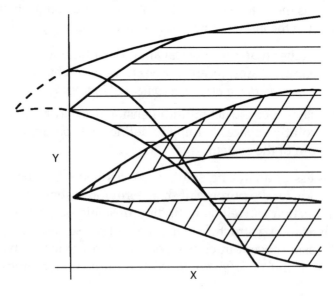

8 WHY ARE WE INTERESTED IN CHAOS THEORY?

Nonlinear approaches to short-term forecasting employ chaotic attractors, making it possible to predict incipient crises. It is doing so by dynamically examining time series taken near the catastrophic bifurcation threshold.

This explains where chaos theory can be of help. It presents the possibility that systems that seemed to be random might actually be described by simple rules and, might therefore, be predictable:

- The aim is to develop models that generate rather accurate predictions, in spite of prevailing turbulence.
- This is doable provided that we have methods for devising nonlinear models directly from data streams.

The aim is to apply prediction capabilities to financial markets and financial instruments, making it possible to reach a high degree of significance in terms of predictability:

- The goal of integrating complexity theory and prediction technology into trading systems is not novel.
- What is novel is the type of tools now beginning to be used, which make the study of complexity feasible.

The implementation of chaos theory in financial trading essentially embraces the dynamics of nonlinear solution spaces. A chaotic system can produce random-looking results, which however are not truly random, each chunk of values being limited within a given region. This gives the impression of a stochastic behavior and at the same time makes long-term forecasting impossible.

The successive bifurcations we have seen in Figure 1-4 exemplify the discontinuities that do not permit long-term forecasting. Within the region defined by a given bifurcation, there exists a sensitive dependence on initial conditions:

- Nonlinear dynamics do not only describes how complex systems change.
- They also suggest that a change in one input possibly has an effect out of all proportion to its size.

Chaos affects any system that has some sort of sensitive dependence on initial condition, be it a financial market or a weather pattern. Any small change or uncertainty in conditions at a starting point will eventually make predictions about the system and its behavior extremely difficult, if not impossible.

The point many people trained in traditional financial analysis fail to appreciate is that *discontinuous changes require a sort of discontinuous thinking*. Because of its upside-down characteristics, discontinuous thinking has never been popular with the upholders of continuity and the status quo—nor with mathematicians tied to the classical theories.

The recent appreciation that both natural and human-made systems are characterized by many discontinuities theoretically changes nothing except *the way we think*. But for all practical purposes this different way of thinking affects everything on which much of our economic future depends.

Discontinuous thinking is an invitation to consider the unlikely, if not the absurd. Nothing should be dismissed out of hand in a time of transition from stability to chaos—and vice versa—when discontinuities, not equilibria, are the rule.

Figure 1-5 shows the infrastructure of a characteristic behavior with nonlinear systems. This is *the* way swap markets work and the reason why *avalanches* occur:

- Minor fluctuations at the bottom of the tightly knit structure
- Lead to significant impact at the final load level.

The basic concept underlined by this statement is that the world is not orderly, and this is as true of financial systems as it

FIGURE 1-5   Infrastructure of a characteristic behavior with nonlinear systems, the way swap markets work.

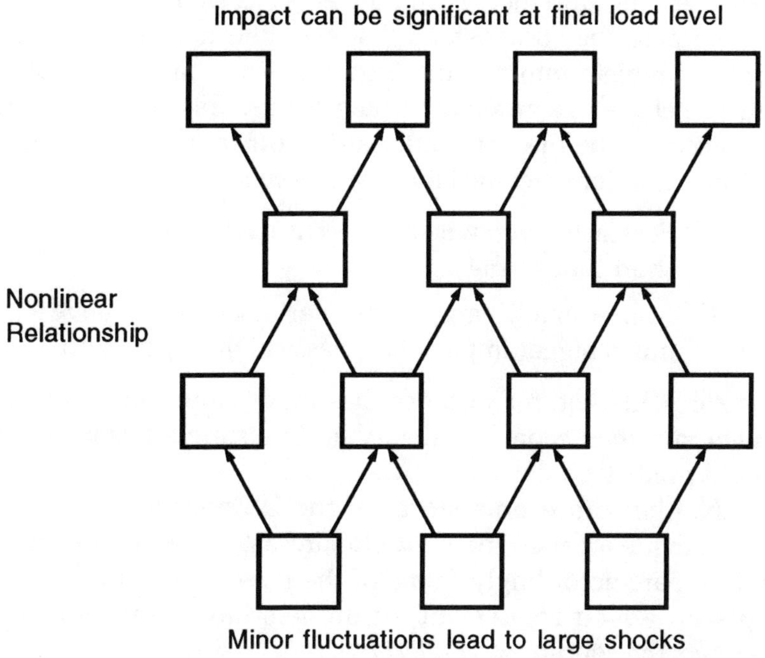

Impact can be significant at final load level

Nonlinear
Relationship

Minor fluctuations lead to large shocks

is of other human-made artifacts and of natural systems. The financial markets are not orderly even if, superficially, within a limited time frame market behavior seems to be so:

- Money markets and capital markets are human creations, even if we find it difficult to understand how they work.

- Precisely in order to enhance understanding, traders and financial analysts have typically proceeded with oversimplification of reality.

- Deterministic and stochastic models used so far have improved upon guesswork performance, but have been too much based on simplifying assumptions.

Whether working only through guesswork or by means of simple models, economists have led themselves to serious forecasting errors. And there is an echo effect as well.

Because they understand that simplifications lead to disregard of problem information, economists and financial analysts tend to behave as a group at turning points. This in no way takes into account the discontinuities and bifurcations embedded in real-life situations, yet the latter see to it that

- Forecasts, even when correct, are relevant in only a short time frame.

- Even a small change in one variable tends to have a much bigger impact than classical theory suggests.

The stock market, for instance, has more large changes in the longer run than economic theory and its simple linear models would predict.

Neither did econometrics of the Leontief Input/Output type provide a persistent ability to forecast our economic future and prepare accordingly. Some of the reasons lie with the concepts on which Input/Output models have been built (for instance, the concept of *equilibrium*).

9 EFFICIENT MARKET HYPOTHESIS AND STRANGE ATTRACTORS

Classical econometric analysis assumes that if there are no outside or *exogenous* influences, the system is at rest. Internal or *endogenous* factors are thought to balance out. This rests on the hypothesis that supply equals demand and therefore an *efficient market* comes into play. Nothing could be further from the truth.

Both endogenous and exogenous factors can shift a financial system away from equilibrium. As the market reacts, it moves away from the stable conditions associated with order and tidiness. Disequilibria rather than equilibria are the characteristic properties. Living systems behave that way.

Financial markets are dynamic, evolving structures and do not respond kindly to attempts to control an economy and keep it at equilibrium, no matter how good the intentions may be:

- Stability implies a lack of sensitivity to emotional forces, such as lust, greed, and fear.

- That is why the concept of an efficient market in which assets are fairly priced according to available information is utopian.

Even at the foundations of the efficient market hypothesis, a lack of dynamic movement takes the life out of the system. When this happens, it has negative aftermaths on the functioning of markets—as the Marxist experience has shown.

- Extended over a longer period, low volatility is an unhealthy sign.

- But it is not the intention of chaos theory to correct market behavior.

- Rather, the goal is that of mapping what there is—making short-term predictions possible.

Since the characteristic of free capital markets and money markets is dynamic behavior, we need models able to represent—without undue simplification—disorderly systems that move by fits and starts. Underlying turbulence is *flow*, which involves

- Shape and change,
- Motion and form.

Complex systems are not inherently efficient. Instead, they can give rise to turbulence *and* coherence at the same time.

Turbulence in fluids might have something to do with an infinitely tangled solution space, which David Ruelle called *strange attractor*.

A strange attractor is a mathematical portrait of order within a chaotic environment. It is a solution space that traces the behavior of a complex system over time, revealing how it is attracted to an ideal state—essentially revolving around it.

Flow dynamics assume that change in systems reflects some reality independent of a particular instant. It is like seeing liquid penetrating a liquid or a solid growing crystals. Both create a state of turbulence, and we are interested in its shape.

We can look into this same issue from an information technology viewpoint. As a system becomes chaotic, it generates a steady stream of information.

- Because of its unpredictability, each new observation is a new entry.
- The channel transmitting the information upward is a strange attractor.

In the domain of strange attractors, initial small uncertainties are magnified into large patterns. Their initial condition might have been due to randomness.

Making predictions under these conditions is *as if* we are trying to guess the evolution of shape in space and in time. This concept has significant practical importance because we can think of flows in many ways, including flows in economics and finance:

- At first, such flows may be linear.
- Then they can bifurcate to a complex state.
- Subsequently, they oscillate.
- Finally, they may be chaotic.

Flow dynamics are characterized by a universality of shapes with similarities and dissimilarities across scales. Flows within flows are part and parcel of dynamic systems in market dynamics, among other domains.

These are the notions on which the new breed of rocket scientists is now working. Financial analysts who understand chaos theory look at strange attractors as engines of information. Their domain is characterized by both *order* and *disorder*. Our perception of its nature gives a challenging twist to the question of measuring the system's entropy—as we will see in Chapter 2.

Order does in fact arise out of complex behavioral processes, through successive transitions. Chaos theory and other modern modeling techniques aim to represent these transitions:

- For dynamic systems with simple attractors, the solution space may contain in its behavior sufficient information to make chaos predictable.

- It is always important to know in advance when catastrophes may occur, in order to be prepared for their consequences.

We can effectively study the behavior of a financial system by following decay and uplift. It is a process that, in James Hutton's famous words (stated back in 1788), shows "no vestige of a beginning and no prospect of an end."

Hutton belonged to the polymath breed of eighteenth century thinkers who took all knowledge for their province, moving freely between philosophy and science. Nonconformists today do practically the same thing in order to provide direct evidence for multiple cycles of uplift and erosion—not only in terms of the classical seven years of plenty and seven years of scarcity, but also

- Within the daily transactional scheme of financial operations.

- In an environment characterized by movements in and out of phase locking.

Phase or mode locking is a phenomenon in which one regular cycle of a certain behavior, for instance of the Deutschmark-dollar exchange rate, locks into another. Also known as *entrainment*, it explains why satellites tend to spin in some whole-number ratio.

Both in physics and in finance, mode locking also accounts for the ability of oscillators to work in synchronization, though in an economic environment this raises some interesting questions:

- How well can a system withstand small jolts, i.e., how *robust* is the system?

- How well can it function over a range of frequencies, i.e., how *flexible* is the system?

- How well can the aggregate and its components adapt to *change*, avoiding enslavement?

The primary characteristic of living systems is their ability to respond to circumstances that vary rapidly and often unpredictably. This being said, some requirements have contradictory aims. Robustness reflects consistency, but flexibility calls for an ability to increase the range of behavior, broadening the system's spectral dimension.

Physicists have brought these notions into financial analysis, which can be easily recognized if one appreciates the fine print of the message they carry. The major contribution of the new discipline in the financial domain is conceptual. To those willing to place field observations before preconceptions, this theory makes it possible to break through the classical constraints.

2 Organization, Evolution, and the Edge of Chaos

1 INTRODUCTION

Any system goes through a phase transition from order to chaos and back, if the interaction between interconnected agents is strong enough to hold it together. This process repeats itself if the construct is able to perform at the *boundary between order and chaos*—known as the *edge of chaos*.

Complex adaptive systems tend to evolve toward this boundary through a natural process that might be defined as the chance that the underlying structure will survive long enough. As we saw in Chapter 1, while it may be unpredictable, this behavior is not completely random.

Studying the transition from order to chaos and back again has been shown to provide better insight than dealing in a linear fashion with nonlinear real-life situations.

- Economists and financial experts start to look for non-linear patterns in the markets because

- From biology to physics, processes have gradually been revealed to be chaotic.

As we have seen in the preceding chapter, the concepts behind chaos theory help to understand highly dynamic systems, and financial markets are a case in point. At least we have come

---

to appreciate that, because of a sensitive dependence on initial conditions, any error fed into the system can grow exponentially.

The fact that dynamic systems, and therefore markets, move at the edge of chaos is one of the basic reasons why in an environment like the economy, trying to make medium to long-range forecasts* is a process prone to error. But we can use concepts from chaos theory in short-term trading and investment decisions.

Taking nonlinearity into account, we could outperform competitors by reflecting on indicators able to provide messages on how reliable market information is. This permits shorter-term forecasts about the direction of the economy and whether it may turn from a stable to a turbulent state—or vice versa.

Still, it is wise to keep in mind that the nonlinear theory of how financial markets work, and the associated algorithms, are at the formative stage. In market economics there is an understanding of price equilibrium but not of price adjustment, which is necessary in projecting new stability levels, even if we know that these are bound to be temporary.

Within the domain implied by these constraints, chaos theory could be useful in helping to study the behavior of financial markets. At least it can provide some understanding of why certain factors are not predictable in the long term, thus helping to formulate hedging strategies to face a coming time of instability.

2 UNDERSTANDING THE EVOLUTION OF SYSTEMS

"The main thrust of chaos theory and of the mathematics of complexity is to understand the evolution of systems as opposed to galactic evolution where there is no learning," suggests Dr. Murray Gell-Mann. Terrestrial systems are based on

---

* For instance beyond six months.

chemical reactions that gave rise to life, but animals evolute through learning:

- Cultural evolution has made humans what they are and gave rise to different civilizations.
- The evolution of languages permitted the structuring of societies and of organizations.

Language has been developed for communications and therefore for cultural transmission—a process that exists with all animals. Through the written word, the printing press, and now communications networks there has been a wiring of society, beyond what language alone can accomplish.

Precisely this transmission of rules and information, inherent in cultural as well as in trading processes, sees to it that a dynamic system can be chaotic—and it is chaotic if it displays sensitive dependence upon initial conditions. As we have seen in the preceding chapter, this happens in the sense that

- Small differences in initial conditions that may be random
- Are magnified by iteration within the system boundaries.

Therefore, the understanding of system evolution can be an instrumental process in appreciating why certain key parameters display volatility. For example, in financial markets expectations seem to play an important role in generating volatility.

Contrary to more or less generalized beliefs, complex systems can be both spontaneous and disorderly. But at the same time their dynamic behavior has a pattern. It is not made of unpredictable gyrations.

During the last twenty years, chaos theory has brought to the foreground the realization that simple dynamic rules can give rise to extraordinarily intricate behavior. In a literal sense

- Chaos by itself does not explain the structure, coherence, and self-organizing characteristics of systems.

- But understanding the dynamic process makes us aware of the balance point that we called *the edge of chaos*.

At the edge of chaos, system components never quite lock into place, but never quite dissolve into turbulence either. A living system has enough stability to sustain itself and enough creativity to steadily evolve.

It is precisely because of the existence of the edge of chaos that new ideas and innovative issues are challenging the status quo, seeing to it that the entrenched "old guard" will eventually be overthrown—whether it consists of people or rules. *This is what makes complex, dynamic systems spontaneous and adaptive— therefore alive.*

It is conceivable that such behavior might be coded in a data stream at a certain level of detail, as with DNA in living organisms. We don't really know the answer, but, as Murray Gell-Mann suggests,

- If it is coded, then some of the fluctuations can be due to regularities, even if the pattern seems to be irregular.

- Other fluctuations, however, do originate from totally random events.

Regularities can be compressed and mapped into algorithms, which is not true of random behavior. Examples of compressed regularities are myths, rites, schemata, laws, customs, and institutions.

Regularities discovered in the financial marketplace can lead toward a structural model that is instrumental in giving insight into the prevailing economic forces. But this does not necessarily mean that economic forces will not generate nonlinearities (they often do) or lead to chaotic conditions.

Any structural model can experience endogenous discontinuous changes while it is still in an apparent equilibrium. That is why economists are keen on developing and studying asset pricing models that can generate better returns than might otherwise be the case:

- Rocket scientists try to find ways and means for variations to be analytically tractable.
- This allows us to speak of the presence of economic forces causing abrupt changes in terms of returns.

Detected regularities and irregularities help to describe the financial environment and to express possible behavioral patterns. Once developed, such a model can be enriched with inference rules to be used for

- Description and
- Prediction.

A feedback loop can be incorporated as well, to help in judging the resulting schema(ta). In the event that there are alternative representations, the feedback process sees to it that one schema survives, though its turn will eventually be demoted or die out. This is the basis of the genetic algorithm we will study in Chapter 5.

The process of model *promotion* and *demotion* can be absolute or relative, but, in a manner reminiscent of natural living organisms, it is always present. Promotion and demotion are phases of survival, and their existence is necessary to complete the feedback loop that substantiates an adaptive system.

3 LEARNING EFFECTS AND THE EDGE OF CHAOS

One of the critical elements introduced by chaos theory is the notion of a systems trajectory and the associated learning effects. Learning effects often account for one species, product, or technology getting ahead of the others. Evolution fascinates the biologist, Dr. Stuart Kauffman suggested, because of the dual effect that comes into play:

- Death: drive out
- Birth: drive in

Many issues are connected to this concept. In the technological domain, for instance, when the horse and carriage disappeared the blacksmiths did also. In came the cars with their supporting professions: exploration specialists, oil engineers, refiners, gas station attendants, mechanics, and so on.

In an evolutionary process emulating nature, a network of niches has become extinct, but new ones have been born. Economists observe similar processes in the behavior of markets and financial products—and they need a language to express this type of complementarity.

The importance of learning effects is that they see to it that the work done by economists and financial experts has to integrate concepts of *market customization*. This, too, is a process in full evolution and in many ways resembles the fitness of organisms. Their evolutionary curve typically has

- A few well-defined peaks of high fitness and
- A large, flat valley of low fitness.

Both high fitness and low fitness are stages in transition. The former represents the survival advantage of a market, technology, or species; the latter is a prelude to decay.

Within the perspective we have been considering, we can take market evolution as an example. Markets are restructuring themselves all the time. As seen in Figure 2-1, they move from the diversity of local, limited structures to mass concepts. But then they become segmented, develop niches, and respond to

FIGURE 2-1   From diversity to customization: sequential phases
of a market development.

| Local Markets | Mass Market | Segmented
Mass Market | Development
of Market
Niches | Customized
Products and
Markets |

requirements for customizations—which brings diversity back again.

This steady restructuring and patterning of evolutionary concepts is a good example of learning at the edge of chaos. By doing away with mass market concepts, product and market customization overcomes one of the traditional contradictions in our post-industrial economy, but the process of transformation does not stop at any specific point.

Until rather recently, consumers were served by the mass market, and those people asking for individualized services were thought to be occupying opposite ends of the economic spectrum.

- To satisfy mass market consumers, the production and distribution processes must be characterized by low cost.

- But the No. 1 criterion of customers of individualized services is high quality.

There seems to be a bifurcation in goals, but in reality we have come to appreciate that the two underlying concepts are not that incompatible. They have a common origin, which, if properly exploited, permits us to simultaneously provide high quality and low cost, and to do so with very short *time-to-market*.

Consumers need products and services in the time frame that serves them best, not in the more leisurely time frame of most producer organizations. Financial institutions that deliver their products in real time have a significant advantage over their competitors and stand a better chance to make profits as well as to survive.

The dynamics of the system become much more complex if the fitness characteristics—and therefore solution spaces—of different entities, artifacts, or organisms are coupled. That is, in Malthusian* terms, if elderly men living alone depend on cats for companionship, and cats depend on mice as a food source,

- As the mice develop new strategies, they will alter the resources available to cats, thereby influencing the latters' fitness.

- To survive, cats also have to develop new strategies, therefore influencing the elderly men's fitness.

- A change in strategy means a change in the contours of the surface of the solution space, which affects the players of the game.

In other terms, the dynamics of a behavioral system are a function of how strongly mice, cats, and elderly men interact. If the coupling is very strong, any slight change in strategy is likely to change the character of *the whole fitness surface*.

4 ADAPTIVE AGENTS AND CRITICAL CONDITIONS

Something similar happens with the response of financial markets. How tightly coupled are the traders and the salespeople with the investors and the speculators? Operating with very

---

* After Thomas Robert Malthus (1766–1834), British economist.

short lag in terms of time-to-market increases the interdependency. The result is no lag between the identification of a market need and its fulfillment.

As it turns out, in a wide variety of coupled systems *the highest mean fitness is at the phase transition between order and chaos*. The relevant unit of time with which response should be measured varies with each type of economy:

- When agriculture was dominant, it took a relatively long time to produce goods, and people had little or no influence on nature's cycles.

- The age of manufacturing focused on wide mechanization as a way to reduce costs, not on time compression.

- Time-to-market is the characteristic of the post-industrial economy and identifies how fast an organization can adjust to the rapidly changing market perspectives.

This is precisely why the fitness surface of a dynamic market behavior has many short hills separated by valleys and will always be generating new ones as its contours are changing. The tight cat-and-mouse coupling is in a supercritical state.

Interestingly enough, if the coupling is neither too strong nor too weak, the dynamics become more complex. In this case, the mice may develop a successful strategy that works for a long time before the cats also find a different strategy causing a major change in the fitness surface.

In any dynamic system, the fitness surface of each organism—natural or of human construction—will change over time, displaying peaks as well as valleys that vary greatly in frequency and size. This makes the market system nonlinear and complex, with critical states that chaos theory aims to uncarth.

Within the perspective of a complex system and its critical states, adaptive agents can be anything from a single-cell organism to the whole human society. In short, any construct capable of forming and altering strategies is learning to capitalize on changing conditions in the environment within which it lives and with which it interfaces.

Whether a natural system or a financial market, a larger aggregate consists of many adaptive agents. Each one of them interacts with other agents that have the same or different strategies:

- The resulting behavior largely depends on the sophistication of the mechanism of change that is available.

- Through an ingenious optimization, adaptive agents can develop good solutions to rather difficult problems.

An integral part of these strategies is the search for a solution space. By so doing, they create competitive moves within a given environment or new economic web. In response to stimuli they generate new conditions.

Many of these conditions-to-be cannot be foreseen, much less planned, even under the assumptions of some economic theorists about an efficient market hypothesis. For instance, no one predicted in any basic sense, prior to their becoming a mass market, the effects of cars or computers.

We do not even have a mathematical language to express the underlying concept of new product/market couplings and their aftermaths. What we know, though, is that to analyze the behavior of such systems we must heavily rely on computer simulation.

We need analytical reasoning, simulation and knowledge engineering, because the laws and rules that describe the forces underlying complex processes prove too difficult to tackle otherwise. For this purpose, logistics equations and generic algorithms have been developed, as we will see in Chapter 4.

5 EDGE OF CHAOS AND SOLUTION SPACE

Very often we observe a data flow that has fewer variables than we need to describe the dynamic system we are dealing with. The time series available to us may consist only of a sequence of scalar values, leading to the need of constructing a better defined solution space.

A set of information elements constitutes a state of the solution space fully or partially describes the system at a fixed instant in time. An example is the equilibrium that might exist in the cat and mouse universe:

- *If* such equilibrium is known with accuracy, and if the system is deterministic,
- *Then* the state contains sufficient information to project the future of the system.

This, however, is not the case with dynamic systems. Hence the goal of solution space reconstruction is to use the immediate past behavior to map the current state of the system, at least to a level of accuracy permitted by noise. An alternative approach is to approximate the future state through nonlinear function(s) that

- Maps the current state
- Into a future state.

In both cases this is a modeling exercise, and the risk associated to it is that we may be at the edge of chaos without really knowing it. The paradigm of a hill of sand can help explain this reference.

If we pour sand over a hill that is in a steady state, the mass will continue to grow, though for awhile its slope may remain constant. With further additions to the sand pile, the slope becomes steeper, eventually reaching the critical value (critical state). Adding a few grains of sand will trigger an avalanche.

As the mass of sand increases, it grows out of the subcritical or orderly phase. Then, when placed under supercritical conditions, it collapses. As long as energy is added to the system by dropping grains of sand, the system will be dynamic—but eventually it reaches the edge of chaos.

Similar paradigms exist with living systems from financial markets to natural organisms. By selecting an appropriate strategy—which, however, accounts mainly for the current not the future solution state—organisms tune their coupling to their environment to whatever value suits them best:

- By adjusting the coupling to their own advantage, players reach the boundary between order and chaos; this is the peak average fitness.

- The hypothesis is that complex systems are able to adapt up to a point. After the edge of chaos has been reached, adding a grain of sand can create an avalanche.

In this switch from apparent equilibrium conditions to the edge of chaos and beyond comes the *theory of complexity*.* It aims to bring forward the general principles for a system whose many parts interact to produce a sophisticated behavior pattern.

Work on the theory of complexity began with describing conditions in the physical universe or parts of it, but now proceeds with market environments and other adaptive systems. This field is going to take off, but not like a rocket because there are still many things we don't know both about nature and about artifacts.

"Adaptive systems are complex because they consist of many relatively independent parts that are highly interconnect-

* Which we examine in Chapter 3.

ed and interactive," suggests Dr. George Cowan. "The systems of interest are not in thermodynamic equilibrium. They metabolize, absorbing energy from an external source and are dumping back waste."

Metabolism, energy consumption, and waste management characterize many constructs, not only physical systems. Markets evolute; cultures can reverse under conquest and decay. Generally, however, if an aggregate survives, as time goes forward its complexity increases.

In the natural sciences, for instance, more and more irregularities appear to be coming from sources that are not necessarily under our control, such as:

- The basic laws of physics, and
- The shared events of the past

A quantum mechanics accident might give innumerable twists to the future. If one is able to change that accident, creating a different set of initial conditions, he or she may change a lot of things down the line with it. But this is not the role of complexity theory; the role is that of studying systems and agents whose behavior has desirable or undesirable effects.

6 A GRAMMAR FOR PROBLEMS OF COMPLEXITY

Solutions to the challenge of complexity provided for physical systems can be conceptually ported to human-made environments. "Think of a protein and enzyme as strings of symbols," advises Stuart Kauffman. Phase transitions characterize the emergence of a system. Once we are able to map it into a program we can translate

- Proteins into goods and services, and
- Catalysis into a production process.

What we need is a *grammar model* to help express such relationships as well as the diversity that would be embedded into the behavior of a dynamic system.

Diversity is one of the agents that leads the behavior of natural constructs and artifacts toward the edge of chaos. It is also the characteristic that underpins complexity:

- If it is a simple economy without diversity, nothing will happen in terms of development, only stagflation.*
- In a complex economy diversity gives rise to growth and brings about the edge of chaos effects.

This relation between growth, time, and complexity is shown in Figure 2-2. A growth economy is a complex one which after takeoff expands at a wide margin, though eventually it will reach a state equilibrium and then, if it continues to be dynamic, it will move to a new state:

- Growth leads to the edge of chaos because of the forces underlying complex processes and the unknowns these involve.
- The new expansion, too, will search for an equilibrium after it transits from order to chaos and back.

This is a cycle that repeats itself over time. The financial crisis of 1929–1932 was neither the first nor the last the capitalist system has gone through. But it was a milestone, and after the negative effects were overcome it led to a new prosperity.

- During the transition which has taken place, some of the things that were central in the old economy became only peripheral to the new one, or died out.

---

* Stagnation and inflation.

FIGURE 2-2   Growth, time, and complexity are interrelated concepts.

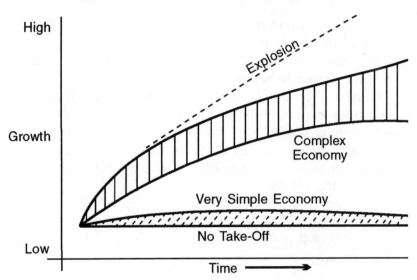

- But new products, markets, and issues came up, propelled in a dynamic manner. Eventually they take the place of the old and help in expanding the economy.

Models of economic evolution suggest that an environment which is characterized by slow or no growth is stagnant and never really takes off. As seen in Figure 2-2, even if there is a minor pickup this rather slow-rising curve will likely bend. A static system has no explosions but plenty of stagnation.

The difference between the two states—dynamic and stagnant economies—suggests that we can attack complexity in an able manner *only if we can provide at length a concise description of regularities and irregularities*. Paraphrasing Dr. John von Neumann and his statement about errors:

- Irregularities are no unwanted, extraneous, or misdirected events by any means;

- They are an integral part of a dynamic process.

The contribution of peaks, valleys, and irregularities in modern economies is fully comparable to other intended and critical factors of a system in operation, for example, comparable to those known in biology, physics, and engineering.

What is important is our ability to describe the prevailing irregularities in order to be able to detect in advance the corresponding signals. When this is done, we can position ourselves for their aftermaths well before events actually happen. In managing a dynamic environment in an able manner, much depends on the level of

- Detail
- Language used, and
- Context

that we are able to address. Real-world complexity needs appropriate tools for its description and an agile grammar we can use in a polyvalent sense. This is the role of language.

Such grammar should address both rules and information. Because dynamic problems become more complex not only in their solution but also in their description, the classical hierarchical structures lead to cumbersome forms of representation:

- As interactions and dependencies multiply, the need to track events increases dramatically.
- It becomes nearly impossible to maintain referential integrity as the problem changes both in its edges and in its details.

The grammar we use must permit us to create dynamic but perishable classification hierarchies able to represent initial structure and current and future states, as well as handle nonlinear inputs and produce nonlinear outputs. The problem information may be fuzzy or crisp, as the representation evolves, but it must be

- *Flexible,* being modified without risk of missing a dependency,
- *Complete* and *accurate,* yet easy to maintain and extend,
- Able to offer the possibility of *exploring alternatives* to be reflected in the solution.

The grammar and language we choose should see to it that the application itself can modify the representation at run time, so that developers and users can impact on rules as well as add or alter information elements as the environment itself changes.

7 IS EQUILIBRIUM A PREREQUISITE TO ORGANIZATION?

The reason why we need powerful descriptive languages and an agile grammar, as section 6 has underlined, is that only a combination of theory and practice can produce profitable technology. But we should not feel wed to a linguistic solution when it reaches its limits of the description of complexity, or remain attached to theories when it is demonstrated that they no longer reflect real life.

One of the best examples on the need to renew our theories has already been presented: In economics and in the financial markets we have long used the assumption that a system left alone tends to equilibrium. This derives from Newtonian mechanics but, as it has been demonstrated, it is no longer true:

- Equilibrium has been classically tied to a body at rest.
- Motion is achieved by disturbing the system with a force.

We can apply this concept to money markets and capital markets, accounting for the fact that the system they represent is naturally in motion—not equilibrium. It is perturbed by endogenous and exogenous shocks.

Stated in a different manner, *there is no natural balance between supply and demand, because steady new inputs change the supply and demand equation.* They cause the economic and financial system to seek a new equilibrium by passing through the edge of chaos.

Even the long-held view that nature maintains a balance in which organisms compete but coexist in an ecological setup whose workings are stable over time is now being seriously questioned. This "natural balance" hypothesis is being replaced by acknowledgement that nature is in a continually fluctuating state with peaks, bumps, and valleys.

Whether in nature or with human-made systems, static equilibrium is not a natural state—and we must face the fact that *in dynamic environments, chaos and order coexist.* It is therefore irrational to think of efficient markets and linear relationships. The new market hypothesis suggests that

- Nonlinearities offer rich possibilities in the study of system interactions,
- But they do not necessarily provide easy answers for planning and control.

It is not surprising that Newtonian concepts dominated the world of economics for so long and by extension capital market and money market theories. Many people consider curious the fact that in any system complexity increases with time, as demonstrated by the evolution of the species, but it is true.

A significant number of the dynamic evolutionary characteristics of living systems are shared by financial markets. But whether we talk of organizations or molecules, *dynamic characteristics have fuzzy properties* that are notoriously difficult to pin down—even if they look obvious enough in many cases.

What we do understand is that no system can function, or even exist, unless *the whole is presupposed by all its parts.* This means there is the presence of an in-built ingenuity that gives the appearance of the aggregate having been designed throughout for a purpose. Hence the supposition of the existence of a *creator.*

Since natural and human-made systems satisfying the foregoing prerequisites evolute, dynamic behavior is not some absolute quality that would have suddenly appeared. It is a process that has emerged gradually during evolution and helps in distinguishing:

- Living organisms that are active, developing, and behaving quite near the edge of chaos, from

- Constructs that do not participate in the process of evolution because they are dying or are ossified.

From markets to molecules, living organisms are full of an evolutionary machinery that organizational principles try to regulate. But in structural matters, too, there is plenty of scope for accidental discoveries of effective new combinations of components and subsystems, with every major change bringing closer a state of chaotic behavior.

As a chaotic system changes cycles and becomes more stable, the aggregate fitness seems to go up. Therefore, Stuart Kauffman suggests: "Organisms have gotten more complex since life began."

- Can we learn why organisms become more complex?

- What is the competitive advantage they gain?

- What is the sense of changing structure and organization?

Nobody yet knows the answer to these queries. The search for an answer in fact might well start with *the origin of life* and the model of an autocatalytic polymer, then proceed with a theory of complexity and organization. Can this hypothesis represent the initial conditions and the aftermaths?

If this hypothesis were valid, it could lead not only to a better prediction theory on which current research efforts focus, but to a better appreciation of two processes that, by all indications, are *complementary* not contradictory to one another,

- Chaos and
- Organization.

"The more random things happen, the more they are turned into laws," says Murray Gell-Mann. "Life itself is an accident and so is the fact that it is based in right-handed molecules. It is an ancestor accident that became *a law of evolution.*"

8 CLUES TO THE ORIGIN OF DYNAMIC SYSTEMS

There exist two primary reasons why complexity theory is so much interested in the origins of life. Both have to do with the fact that there is no better example of dynamic systems than that of natural, living organisms.

One reason connects to the initial conditions, whose importance to chaos and order has been demonstrated in Chapter 1. The other has its origins in the role information plays in an evolutionary process:

- No creator can know in advance which parts and pieces of even a relatively simple dynamic system will be relevant.
- In the longer run it is the whole machine that makes sense of its components, and it does so during its functioning.

This sorting out of what is necessary and what is not is done through a process that has plenty of small print to be scrutinized. What we know is that careful analysis is sure to alter first impressions.

In dynamic systems *the whole is presupposed to exist for all its parts*, not just for some of them, as first impressions usually say. The interlocking is tight and critical:

- Just as there can be no traders and no financial instruments without a market,

- There can be no complex living organisms or even molecules without a system common to all life.

At the aggregate level everything depends on everything else. Hence, it is no surprise that market systems are so conservative. When everything depends on everything, it is difficult for anything to be changed at random, even if the aggregate as a whole shows a random behavior.

Just as molecules are not just clumps of atoms, a trading center is no random collection of dealers, and a clearing house is no heap of transactions. Both trading centers and clearing houses can best be described as *machines* that depend on organization and information for the performance of their functions.

The block diagram in Figure 2-3 shows the inheritance of rules and information in a banking system. Most of the business elements shown in the graph are endogenous to the bank, reflecting its bylaws and procedures but also the agreements it has signed with its clients.

The execution rules have an exogenous element, which concerns the instructions by the Federal Reserve to be observed. Also exogenous to the bank's procedural system are issues associated to client orders, which start the transactions rolling. The whole process is information centered; there is no movement of goods.

In its fundamentals, this diagram corresponds to information transfer in natural organisms. As A.G. Cairns-Smith aptly

FIGURE 2-3 The inheritance of rules and information in a banking system and its business elements.

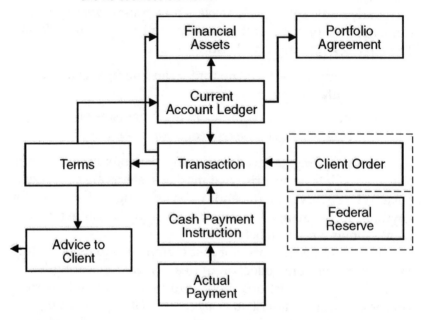

suggests:* "The distinction between goods and information is a case of the ancient distinction between substance and form." The message, as such, is form and it involves both *rules* and *data.*

Another vital characteristic of both biological and human-made systems is *inheritance.* But there is an important distinction to be made between two issues which with organisms act as pillars though they are subject to evolution:

- The inheritance of goods
- The inheritance of information

* *Seven Clues To The Origin of Life* (Cambridge: Cambridge University Press/Canto, 1985).

It is the messages, their content, and the pattern they create, that are the most important inheritance. In biology, these messages persist over millions of years. In financial markets, they are more ephemeral—yet they make the market tick.

Every living organism has genetic information stored in itself. That is a set of instructions about how the organism is to be made and maintained. Quite similarly, clearing houses and trading centers have rules compiled into manuals, outlining procedures and protocols. The protocols imply terms of behavior to be observed by all participants in the game.

Like every dealer should know, these manuals and their protocols are indispensable to trading action. They also underpin the process of life. Every cell in a multicellular organism, which constitutes a natural system, has a complete set of genetic information. In it are stored the facts. All known living creatures and all dynamic artifacts are at root the same because the coded messages are so similar.

9 PRINCIPLES OF EVOLUTION AND RISK MANAGEMENT

Life as we know it is a chemical phenomenon and molecules can spontaneously undergo complex chemical reactions with one another. This paradigm is just as right for financial markets, but right after this statement the limits of the unknown begin.

Can we learn from nature? What is it that permits molecules to do what quarks and quasars can *not* accomplish? The more clear-eyed scientists think there may be two reasons:

1. Chemistry's power is simple variety.

Unlike quarks, which can only combine to make protons and neutrons in groups of three, atoms can be arranged and rearranged to form a huge number of structures. This sees to it that the space of molecular possibilities is effectively limitless, but it also suggests that organization imposes constraints.

2. Another source of power is reactivity.

A structure X can manipulate structure Y to form a new structure Z. It does so with the help of catalysts, in an environment characterized by constraints, rates, temperatures, and other dependencies.

A large number of factors are critical in understanding real chemical reactions. The outcome is a concept that actually applies to a wide variety of complex systems, including financial markets.

- Ideas interact with ideas to produce new concepts, which we turn into products and services involving both *opportunity* and *risk*.

- Financial products and services interact with other financial products and services to produce new business perspectives.

Lack of interaction leads to stagnation as the lower part of Figure 2-2 helped to demonstrate. But when economic factors dynamically interact with other economic factors they produce the growth curve we have seen in the upper half of Figure 2-2.

A sound procedure of risk management does not center on the random trivia of the day but addresses the fundamental problems involving one or more of the many phases of risk, as well as the compound exposure.

- It is concerned not with trades as they are but with outcomes as they *might be*.

- It does not just record or photograph, but creates and projects—exactly the way a living system operates.

This is the sense of projections and extrapolations from currently ongoing trades and events, aiming to define the risk a financial organization is taking from its day-to-day operations as well as from longer-term commitments management makes.

To properly evaluate risk, responsible managers require information about income and expense performance, balance sheet and off-balance sheet levels, statistical volumes, and key indicators such as market volatility, liquidity, and other sensitivities. Such information must be presented in such a way that exposure can be managed, making it possible to run the bank's business in a properly controlled manner.

In all this activity, account is taken of the fact that a dynamic system, and therefore life, does not reflect some absolute quality that has suddenly appeared. Life emerged gradually during evolution; a dynamic economy emerges gradually through successive deals.

That is why in the post–World War II years the boom in world trade has gradually brought a major growth to First World economies engaged in it. Eventually, after it reached the necessary critical mass, it developed in a dynamic, aggressive manner.

The background factors of evolution we have seen in this section also help to explain why in the past two decades, since flexible exchange rates have been instituted there is a major boom in financial products, particularly

- Swaps,
- Futures,
- Options, and
- Derivatives.

Not only is a state of equilibrium unnecessary for systems to function, but it might create exactly the opposite result—leading to stagnation. By contrast, living at the edge of chaos improves upon performance by creating higher-level, and therefore more sophisticated, structures.

Such a creation has its own momentum and cannot be micromanaged. But, with human-made systems, developments can be directed, and this is done through control action based on *reporting*. The problem is that traditional financial reporting tools rarely, if ever, provide the type or level of detailed of information needed to make critical decisions in a timely manner.

This reference is valid all the way from market sensitivity to product pricing, risk management, costing, resource allocation, and so on. What is necessary is

- Quick access to very current information, and
- Powerful algorithms permitting manipulation of data streams in a meaningful sense.

The result must be a consistent view of performance across legal entities, product lines, customer groups, market sectors, or any other defined business criterion. With this consistency, decisions can be made based on a clear perspective about where and when to invest resources and capitalize on new opportunities.

In every one of these examples, risk management involves a thorough evaluation of strategic and tactical decisions made both on a consistent and an exception basis. The concept is no different than that of good management, but it is focused on all issues involving profitability and associated risks.

In conclusion, like living organisms, financial markets are effectively active at the edge of chaos, yet they have an underlying order. The management of the transition between order and disorder, or instability, requires people able to live—and even thrive—with vagueness and with uncertainty.* Otherwise, panics will result.

---

* Two concepts we will elaborate on in Chapters 8, 9, and 10.

3 Fundamental Notions Underlying the Theory of Complexity and Its Mathematics

1 INTRODUCTION

A *complex system* is typically composed of several strongly interacting components and subsystems, the way it has been described in Chapter 2 by taking living organisms as an example. Complex systems require an analytical study of their behavior; complex human-made constructs call for advanced management skills, which are not always available.

Many scientists share a belief about complexity, which is not necessarily documented by the nature of things. This belief is that simple constructs behave in simple ways that can be reduced to a few well understood, rather deterministic laws. When this is done, their long-term behavior is taken as being stable and predictable—which may be true but only up to a point.

By contrast, it is generally accepted that complex behavior implies complex causes that make the system *unstable* and *unpredictable*. It may not be out of control but

- It is governed by a multitude of independent factors, and
- It is subject to random external influences.

The irregular side of nature, the discontinuities and erratic behavior, have been puzzles that scientists have tried to solve by perfecting their own conceptual, analytical, and computational tools. Complexity theory is one of the conceptual approaches toward this end, and its evolution demonstrates how our mind proceeds in the cognition and interpretation of new facts.

Because the applications of complexity theory occur in so many different fields, it would be foolish to try to study them all. Instead, we will focus on examples that illustrate the methods of analysis.

This will not be done in a "How-to" way which, while valuable on a level of lower skills, does not prepare a scientist or financial analysts to tackle new complex problems. It is possible to develop the necessary conceptual and analytical skills

- By concentrating upon the methods of analysis and
- By keeping the principles constantly in view.

In turn, conceptual and analytical skills permit us to elaborate macroscopic views based on the results of both macroscopic and microscopic evaluations. Complexity theory is *not* an automatic mechanism that sees to it that when some things are introduced at the bottom, results will emerge at the top.

2 MACROSCOPIC AND MICROSCOPIC CONCEPTS

It is quite possible to develop a logical system that uses only the concepts and procedures generally accepted as "self-evident." Such truths are held by some persons to be the only proper ones, but is this approach sound?

The argument runs in this manner: We may take the laws of physics (or of any other science) as axioms, since experimentation shows that they have never been violated. Then we can construct an emulator of other systems. Yet

- The detailed motion of particles is not verifiable and
- The axioms of statistical mechanics cannot be checked in detail.

Therefore there is a counterargument that deductions made through this process are less likely to be in error. A closer examination of complexity issues, however, demonstrates that it is the counterargument rather than the original hypothesis that is unsuitable for the study of dynamic systems.

What we should be ready to admit is that we know very little about the constructs nature has made, and any axioms or theories that we use are bound to be tentative. The same is true about the artifacts we create.

- Euclid's geometry, for instance, is not suitable for relativistic studies of very large or very small distances.
- This and other examples suggest that the inviolability of principles is not an argument to prove the uniqueness of rules.

Neither are the theories, axioms, and rules of different scientific disciplines able to interpret the complex behavior of a compound system. Like chaos itself, phase transitions involve a kind of macroscopic behavior that seems hard to predict by looking only at microscopic details. That is why Dr. Toshiro Terano* suggests the use of a *macroscope*.

An old Hindu proverb talks about the blind men who felt the elephant. They all described it differently, for each of them touched only a small part of the animal. None of them had a system-wide concept or view able to grasp global effects, and none of them was correct.

* Professor at Hosei University and director of the Laboratory for International Fuzzy Engineering (LIFE), Yokohama, Japan.

- Typically, a specialist will address himself or herself in a detailed manner to a small issue concerning only part of the problem.

- She or he will not take a polyvalent and multifunctional approach to the problem and its compound effects.

Figure 3-1 suggests the wisdom of using a *metalevel*, above the level of detail that constitutes the object of our examination. Supported by the metalevel, the macroscopic view permits us to both focus on the component parts (through zooming) and to examine the integrative view of the detailed elements.

Sure enough, studying what there is in terms of detail is a very important function, and someone has to do it. But at the same time too much specialization and narrowing of the field of investigation results in tunnel vision cutting out parts of the big picture which are no more kept in view.

- The metalayer is based on macroscopic knowledge, which is conceptual and often fuzzy.

FIGURE 3-1 Complexity theory solutions support global and flexible viewpoints.

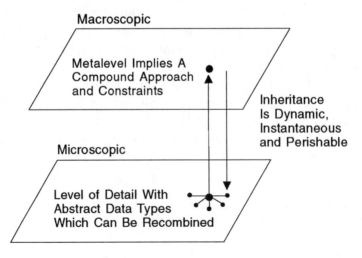

- The lower layer will reflect microscopic knowledge. The finer grain tends to be crisp and analytical.

Several finer grains at the microscopic layer will correspond to a coarser grain at the metalayer. Both the lower layer components and the metastructures need to be networked— among themselves and trans-layer.

This is precisely what past, discrete island approaches have been missing. Therefore, Toshiro Terano suggests *building a macroscope* that permits us to look at the grand design, avoiding tunnel-vision traps. There exists a lot of differences between macroscopic and microscopic cultures and mentalities, as well as tools:

- *Microscopic* knowledge is focused on one domain in which there is little or *no contradiction*.

An example is the handling of a specific financial product, such as letters of credit. The specialist's microscopic knowledge is very important to assure not only the proper debits and credits but also to calculate the risk being taken by the bank.

The variables entering into a microscopic landscape are exact, logical, and systematic. They are more or less objective, as are all cases with analytical and largely quantitative expressions. Hence they can be easily processed by computer. Furthermore

- *Microscopic* knowledge is often considered "obvious" to persons with experience in a given limited domain.

Yet, though microscopic knowledge typically addresses a narrow field, there are several difficulties in data and knowledge acquisition. Also, while there is only one or at most very few established patterns, there exist at times less than realistic reasoning. Finally,

- *Microscopic* knowledge is fixed in several ways. By consequence, it is *crisp*.

Crisp means a yes or no, black or white, 0 or 1 type of answer. The data such reasoning presents is often impressive because we try to fit a time series into crisp patterns that are not known to represent the majority of natural and human-made processes.

Crisp representation is in a way similar to the simplifications made in order to map nonlinear processes into linear forms, of which we have spoken in Chapter 1. A similar concept exists in patterning financial data when we try to express in the form of a normal distribution information elements that are usually unevenly distributed.

3 EXPLORING THE MACROSCOPIC VIEWPOINT

The formalisms applied to data representing market behavior result in microscopic rules of calculation. These rules lead to predictions about the important trends in the behavior of a financial market, without considering such behavior as a whole.

Our work can be more accurate if instead of only concentrating on detail and forgetting the compound effects, we focus on both financial data and metadata. The latter are generalizations of the former, aimed at revealing patterns and trends.

- Zooming in on greater details requires the use of two-way layering, with access that is general to specific and specific to general.
- Layering permits us to see each level of detail in an orderly node-by-node manner.
- This process can be repeated through different layers, each of a still-finer grain.

Figure 3-2 makes this point, suggesting that once we are able to appreciate the global view, we can understand the general pattern and its interpretation at a metadata level. Detail can be sub-

FIGURE 3-2   The theory of complexity uses metalevel and inheritance to pattern the characteristics of component parts.

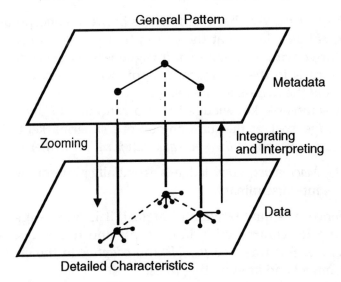

sequently analyzed through zooming. The macroscopic view is in essence an integrated set of microscopic views, but

- *Macroscopic* knowledge is, by and large, fuzzy and so are the models it uses.

An example is 24-hour banking, with the financial markets operating around the clock. From New York to Tokyo, Zurich, and London, the sun never sets on financial transactions. Seen from a macroscopic viewpoint, 24-hour banking is a reality, but it is a fuzzy concept as well.

Macroscopic knowledge concerns not only the grand design but also projections, extrapolations, inference, deductions, abductions, and inductions. By consequence, it deals with *soft-data*—which sometimes is vague and uncertain, therefore not crisp.

- *Fuzziness* characterizes the goals and constraints of *macroscopic* knowledge.

One of the two basic differences between conceptual and analytical people is that the conceptual people can live and even thrive with uncertainty and vagueness. The second major difference is in the macroscopic approach conceptual people take—and the two issues are related.

Macroscopic knowledge is not a collection of microscopic knowledge, such as the summing-up of a supermarket bill. It is *a long experience crystallized into qualitative rules.* Furthermore

- *Macroscopic* knowledge is essentially philosophical and interdisciplinary.

Since it is qualitative and logical, it is often suggestive, allowing for contradiction in concepts and references—even vagueness. But it is also *flexible* and *adaptive* to the changing environment and its evoluting rules.

Taking a paradigm from business life, ideally a customer relationship will be examined from the macroscopic viewpoint, while detailed information elements will be at the microscopic plane—in customer files, billing, references, and general ledger accounts. As every bank knows,

- All of these files deal with the same information elements, but they are often scattered and difficult to interrelate.

- Hence the need of networking the microscopic views providing an integrative approach that permits interpretive action.

This relatively simple concept is the basis of all integrative procedures. It is also a cornerstone to relationship banking and to able customer account management at large.

The layered structure we have seen is the way the theory of complexity approaches the problems it confronts. A complete specification methodology is one that produces conceptual schemata that are correct and executable. In the three-layered structure shown in Figure 3-3:

- The top schema (metaschema) is that of an architectural specification for *derivative products*.

- The second level holds the specifications for implementing transactions in specific applications areas: *Swaps*, *Futures*, and *Options*.

- The third, and lowest, level handles the details for each transaction in that application area—atomic level rules and corresponding information elements.

Consecutive analysis through zooming provides significant advantages not only in terms of studying in an orderly manner the details embedded in complex financial products,

FIGURE 3-3 Metalevels and detailed rules regarding derivative products.

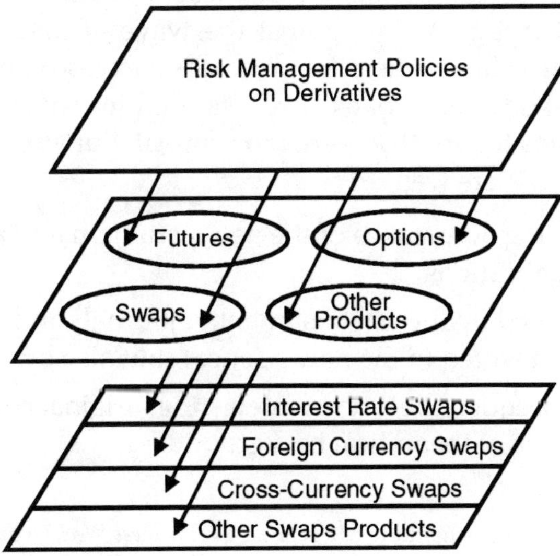

but also in terms of subsequent integration. Level by level, knowledge engineering constructs can profitably be used both in analysis and in synthesis.

One of the practical applications of the layered strategy of macroscopic and microscopic views is in *concurrent engineering*. Concurrent engineering gets products to market faster and does so at lower cost, its concepts being applicable all the way from manufacturing to finance.

Companies can cut development cycles by up to 40 percent, and knowledge engineering can help to compound the savings. "Our goal is to reduce time to market another 50 percent," for a total of 70 percent, says Harold J. Raveche* in connection to a major project his institution has recently undertaken. "The key is artificial intelligence."

4 IS COMPLEXITY THEORY A MATTER OF FASHION?

The evolution of complexity theory teaches some lessons on how difficult it is to swim against the wave of preconceived ideas—as well as how, when the process is successful, fashion is then established. Years back, professional journals rejected papers on chaos theory that were too original. But after the field gained ground, there was

- Growing acceptance of the new paradigm and a swarm of publications,
- Followed by the establishment of journals and institutes devoted to the new science—but also by
- A consequent decline in interesting, original concepts in terms of theoretical background.

* President of the Stevens Institute of Technology. *Business Week* (April 5, 1993).

"The discovery of new ideas in science cannot be programmed," advised David Ruelle.* "That is why revolutions and other social cataclysms often have a positive influence on science. By temporarily interrupting the routine of bureaucratic chores and putting the organizer of scientific research out of commission, they give people the opportunity to think."

That's how controversial ideas of old become interesting topics and then fundamental ideas. That is also how fashions develop favoring "this" or "that" theory or analytical approach over another, eventually displacing the latter with the former.

Fashions always play an essential role in business as well as in the funding of projects. A specialized subject comes into fashion for a few years, and either it succeeds in delivering results or it is dumped. In the meantime, a swarm of people comes to the new field, attracted by the possibility of making a name and a career.

While a number of new scientific disciplines do come into fashion, a larger number of new and old ideas, theories, methodologies, and tools fall by the wayside. Some are discarded because their time is gone; others never really received any appreciable recognition; still others had merits but found a level of resistance they have not been able to overcome.

Leon Tolstoi once made a penetrating statement: "I know that most men, including those at ease with problems of the greatest complexity, can seldom accept even the simplest and most obvious truth if it be such as would oblige them to admit the falsity of conclusions which they have

- "Explained to colleagues,
- "Taught to others, and
- "Woven, thread by thread, into the fabric of their lives."

* *Chance and Chaos* (Princeton, NJ: Princeton University Press, 1991).

This resistance to ideas and solutions that go beyond the beaten path surely will be faced by complexity theory. That is why it is so important to relate basic principles to known facts and do so in connection not only to one but to many sciences. As we will see in the next section, there is a great deal to be learned—as well as demonstrated—from the behavior of other systems.

The reason why new theories, principles and methods that can help explain complex behavior—due to their structure and organization—is so important, is that we know we will be confronted by increasingly complex situations. The economic paradigms promoted by our epoch require new approaches to the development of companies and of people as well as in the interpretation of patterns prevailing in business: from design, manufacturing, and marketing to finance.

We should also be able to appreciate that a field of study as wide as complexity theory must of necessity develop broad and powerful methods of attack for problems. Methods, underlying theories, and the mathematical tools they bear form the subject of this and the following chapters. Examples are introduced to illustrate the issues of complexity, but both the methods and the examples should be remembered.*

The study of complex systems is an exercise in logic requiring significant qualifications, to be carried on in an able manner. In its fundamentals, this study essentially falls into two parts:

- The first concerns definitions and is essentially a semantic effort.

- The second is the actual manipulation of concepts and principles, as well as the inquiring of the deeper meaning of the words being used.

* Remembering the examples *only* narrows the field's or theory's understanding, as new cases are never the same with the old ones used as examples.

The wisdom and skill necessary for analyzing and designing complex systems is not available to people who would have knowledge without understanding or who would not like to spend the necessary effort. There are no magic formulas for attacking the problems of complexity.

5 THE NEED TO RESTRUCTURE OUR KNOW-HOW

Some of the most basic concepts all of us learned in universities and in practice are now up for reevaluation and restructuring. For instance, we now come to appreciate that the hierarchical organization model developed 70 years ago by Alfred Sloan produced

- Very few creative individuals and
- A large majority of non-creative persons

This was acceptable in an industrial economy of rather static conditions and more or less limited dimensions, which characterized the first hundred years after the Industrial Revolution, from the mid-19th century to the mid-20th century. Hierarchical models even served during the next two decades until around 1985, when they started falling apart.

We now have enough experience with the new economic paradigms to appreciate that the rational treatment of market facts can be done best by computers enriched with knowledge engineering, while people should be taught how to use their imagination, where they can excel. Concentrating on conceptual tasks places a new emphasis on thinking ability as well as on the management of change—and also brings up new challenges.

Not the least among these challenges is the question "Why does disorder increase in the same direction of time in which an organization or the universe as a whole expands? Other queries are just as complex and demanding. Answers have to be factual and documented—and they are not forthcoming without insight, foresight, and the powerful means complexity theory aims to provide.

Complexity theory is not a matter of fashion but of need. We have to get away from the limited viewpoints that have frequently been favored. This requires breaking some conceptual barriers. As

- Interdisciplinary thinking becomes the prevailing rule when we approach new systems,
- There is much to be learned from the behavior of complex aggregates that have been successfully studied in the past.

Much of Edward Lorenz's work in the study of weather patterns was concerned with equations able to model their inherent world of complexity. One of the dominating concepts has been the near-circular motion of a fluid rising up and around like an asymmetrical wheel. His model took into account

- The velocity of motion and
- The transfer of heat.

The two physical processes interacted and, as Lorenz discovered, over long periods the spin can reverse itself time and again. In essence it never settles to a steady state—but neither does it repeat itself in a predictable manner. Financial markets have a similar pattern of behavior.

To the early explorers of chaos, Lorenz's attractor resembled a butterfly's wings* or, in a different metaphor, an owl's

---

* The schema of the butterfly's wings used to describe Lorenz's attractor should not be confused with the *butterfly effect* often referred to as a metaphor. A butterfly beating its wings in Haiti *might* create a cyclone in the Carolinas *if* an innumerable number of often chaotic amplification effects take place.

face. This became a good way to visualize the hidden structure of a stream of data:

- To make a picture from chaotic information, Edward Lorenz used each set of three numbers as coordinates to specify the location of a point in three-dimensional space.
- The sequence of these numbers produced a sequence of points tracing a continuous path, which helped in recording the system's behavior.

If this path leads to one place and stops, the message is that the underlying behavior has settled down to a steady state. But if the path forms a loop, then it has entered a pattern of behavior that will repeat itself periodically.

One of the basic conditions is that the system displays a sort of infinite complexity, staying within certain bounds but never repeating itself. This gives a strange distinctive shape, a double spiral in three dimensions like the owl's face. Such pattern reflects disorder, since no point or points ever recur. Yet it also gives an impression of underlying order. These are the basic characteristics of chaotic systems.

6 LEARNING FROM THE BEHAVIOR OF OTHER SYSTEMS

Traditionally, physics has been used as the laboratory for advances in modeling that can be implemented in the study of the behavior of capital markets and money markets. But other sciences can play that role, too, an example being developments that have taken place in engineering, and more recently, in biology.

The trillions of neurons in the human brain, electrically firing their chemical neuro-transmitters across synaptic gaps, can

be viewed as a process that turns complexity into ordered, predictable reactions to stimuli.

- Within a finite time frame, the very nature of ever-
  changing system conditions can generate order.
- But each system has its own definition of what is
  "finite," and each definition should be kept dynamic.

Biologists working on economic models are basing their
approach on the principles of biological evolution. They are
looking at the real-world situation they are confronted with, as
combinatorial optimization problems whose solution, however,
is enriched through the presence of *adaptive agents*.

How can adaptive agents evolve? According to Dr. Stuart
A. Kauffman,* self-organized criticality occurs in models of
coevolution. What can we learn from that model that is applicable in finance?

- Communities with a subcritical diversity of organisms
  lack the momentum to explosively develop into a new
  breed.
- By contrast, supracritical communities expand so rapidly that they consume all their available food and die off.

It is precisely at the edge of chaos** that mutations, crossovers, and innovation occur. Something similar happens with
other dynamic systems. In fact, as recent non-traditional
research starts documenting, capital markets and money markets are good examples on this evolutionary reference.

One of the interdisciplinary lessons worth recording concerns the dimension of system dynamics. This dimension indicates the number of irreducible degrees of freedom.

* Biochemist, professor at the University of Pennsylvania School of Medicine
and the Santa Fe Institute.
** Which has been discussed in Chapter 2.

- Complex aperiodic behavior can result from deterministic physical systems with only a few degrees of freedom.

- But a dissipative dynamic system has many nominal degrees of freedom we should consider.

These degrees of freedom might settle down after an initial transient. Dimensioning counts the number of degrees of freedom necessary to describe such motion, helping to quantify the difficult issues of modeling behavior.

The notion of dimensioning is important as the available constructs for the implementation of chaos theory apply to *a low dimensional structure*. While the exact number depends on the amount of data we have available, it is wise to keep this rule in mind:

- We have to find a structure that is *tradeable*, and this may have really nothing to do with mathematics.

- In terms of a financial implementation, the structural analog helps to define *how close to real life* the resulting model will be.

Proceeding by means of analogical reasoning is nothing new in economies. The evolution of the whole field has involved interdisciplinary activities, as illustrated in Figure 3-4. Any functional similarities will pass over

- *Analogies,* that is similitudes in structures and/or thinking

- *Homologies* and the ability to record taxonomies of descend.

Analogies teach us about the limits of variety when separate physical or logical lineages evolve structures for similar functions. A good paradigm is the attraction toward an ideal state that has been briefly mentioned in connection to strange attractors.

FIGURE 3-4 Economics and finance have involved a significant number of interdisciplinary activities.

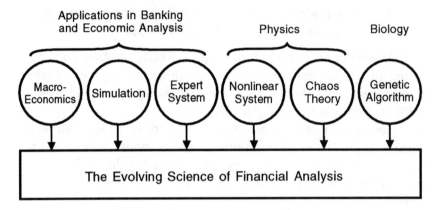

Inferences on the behavior of the financial system under study can often be made through analogical reasoning from projects in physics and biology where experience accumulates over the years.

- The reasonableness of results often depends on understanding the solution space.

- Study of the possible types of catastrophic bifurcations is vital.

- Able approaches require understanding of the types of unstable basic sets and their leading to crises.

A different strategy from the handling of complexity issues is followed by examining how new classes of organisms arise. What conditions would have been present at the beginning of time to produce contemporary classes of organisms? Such conditions are of course abstractions, not realities—but the organisms themselves and their values may be real.

This reference is just as valid in terms of financial markets and products as it is in physics and in biology. The same is true of the query: "What other conditions have arisen in the course of development that shaped a specific path or paths?"

By trying to model the interactions entering into our evaluation, it is possible to understand better the origin of the fittest. A vital issue is, for instance, how stock market players learn while

- The character of their business is changing,

- The weaker players are eliminated from the game, but

- System dynamics are not well described by classical economics.

In conclusion, there is evidence that analogical reasoning provides concepts and tools useful to the study of complex systems. This is part and parcel of the development of new analytical approaches, much stronger than their predecessors, which help to raise the level of understanding and modeling of economic and financial systems.

7 ENTROPY AND ORGANIZATION

In 1824, Sadi Carnot published the first statement of what would much later become known as *the second law of thermodynamics*: Heat will not spontaneously flow from cold objects to hot ones. This simple evident fact placed severe limits on how efficient a steam engine could be but had other, much more important, repercussions as well.

It was known for considerable time that heat flows from a higher to a lower temperature, but never in the reverse direction except through the action of an agent external to the system. What Sadi Carnot essentially did was to consider this phenomenon and deduce that heat would not be converted to work without the existence of a temperature difference.

The transformation function underpinning the second law of thermodynamics is *entropy*, expressed in terms of the heat and temperature of the system. With time

- Temperature and heat have been pictured in terms of the kinetic energy of the molecules comprising the system.

- Thus, entropy became a measure of the probability that the velocities of the molecules and other variables of the system are distributed in a certain way.

Etymologically, the word entropy was first coined by Rudolf Clausius.* Some 40 years after the law by Carnot, Clausius intended to use it to mean *transformation*, but it evolved as a concept to include *uncertainty*—a concept to which Chapter 8 is dedicated.

Information is the negative of uncertainty. It is not accidental that the word "form" appears in the middle of this word, since the able exploitation of information leads to patterning. But meaningful information decreases as entropy progresses.

Since, according to the second law of thermodynamics, *a system tends to increase in entropy over time*, the information it provides decreases. There is no principle of conservation of information as there are principles of the conservation of matter and energy:

- The total information can be decreased in any system without increasing it elsewhere.

- But it cannot be increased without decreasing the entropy in the system.

This is what many data processors do not understand because they keep on thinking in old accounting machine terms. The curious thing is that even some nuclear engineers turned data processors repress, losing their appreciation of the meaning of entropy.

Entropy measures the amount of randomness present in a given construct. In a way, a system entropy tends to be propor-

* In his book *Abhandlungen über die mechanische Wärmetheorie* (Brunnswick: 1864).

tional to its size and to the prevailing organization or disorganization.

- In thermodynamics, entropy measures the *amount of energy* unavailable for useful work in a system undergoing change (second law of thermodynamics).
- In computers, communications, and heuristics, entropy is a measure of the *information content of a message* evaluated as to its uncertainty.
- In organizations, entropy is the *degree of disorder* in a structure or a substance of any kind.

It is a matter of common experience that disorder will tend to increase if things are left by themselves. At a technical level, of information technology for instance, *filtering* aims to decrease the amount of entropy.

Increase in entropy is interpreted as the passage of a system from probable states. The ratio of the actual to the maximum entropy is known as *relative entropy*. A high ratio of relative entropy indicates redundancy of information, and a similar statement can be made about redundancy and bureaucracy—hence entropy in organizations?

As Dr. Stephen W. Hawking suggests,* the laws of science do not distinguish between forward and backward directions of time. But three arrows of time tend to point to the forward direction:

- A thermodynamic arrow describes the time direction in which disorder increases,
- A psychological arrow sees to it we remember the past and try to predict the future.
- A cosmological time arrow points to the direction the universe expands rather than contracts.

* *A Brief History of Time* (New York: Bantam, 1988).

In this text we are principally interested in the first and second of the three arrows. *Entropy in organizations* measures the degree of disorder and points to the direction this disorder can expand until it reaches the edge of chaos.

In any structure, project, or personal life, disorder will tend to increase if matters are left to their own without the proper planning, organization, and control. To create order out of disorder requires expenditure of effort or energy, thus decreasing the amount of available energy in the system.

Scientists have tried to visualize a measure of *entropy per unit time*. They have done so by means of a geometric representation of pictures or surfaces stretching and folding them in phase space. The concept of this approach lies in

- Drawing an arbitrarily small box around some set of initial conditions and
- Calculating the effect of various expansions or twists on the box.

The geometric figures, for example, might stretch in one direction, while remaining narrow in the other. Area changes corresponded to an introduction of *uncertainty* about the system's past, translated through a gain or loss of information—a switch from unpredictability toward some sort of predictability.

These are relatively recent entropy concepts relating in large measure to information technology.* They can be seen as an extension of the meaning of the word *entropy* in thermodynamics. One of the reasons entropy is so important to the theory of complexity is that it constitutes a dynamic entity:

- *Thermodynamics* problems involve time, hence dynamic considerations.

* And the work done by Dr. Claude E. Shannon at Bell Telephone Laboratories in the 1950s.

- By contrast, *thermostatics* is concerned with equilibrium processes that do not depend upon time as an explicit variable.*

Usually in literature the term *thermodynamics* is used when one means both processes, that is including statics, but what particularly interests complexity theory is the dynamic aspects.

Since every physical event is accompanied by an energy transformation, the study of thermodynamics—like that of complexity theory—embraces all sciences: from physics to engineering and finance. In physics and engineering energy transformation is done in separate fields such as mechanics, electromagnetics, chemistry, and the properties of materials, with theories best expressed and in a way interconnected through axioms, propositions, and conclusions.

8 RANDOMNESS, PROBABLE STATES, AND PREDICTION

The reason entropy is greatest when temperature is constant throughout a body is that this distribution of temperatures is the most probable. Increase of entropy is therefore interpreted as the passage of a system from less probable to more probable states.

Indeed, *the second law of thermodynamics* results from the fact that there are always many more disordered states than ordered states. This is true of any system:

- The second law of thermodynamics states that the entropy of an isolated system always increases.

- When two distinct systems are joined, the entropy of the aggregate is greater than the arithmetic sum of the entropies of the individual components.

* Myron Tribus, *Thermostatics and Thermodynamics* (Princeton, NJ: D. Van Nostrand, 1961).

The statistical explanation of the second law is that atoms are constantly trying to randomize themselves, but this concept came some 70 years after Carnot's original publication—as did *the first law of thermodynamics.*

(Interestingly enough, the earliest known attempt at a theory of atoms was made in ancient Greece by Democritos (455–370 B.C.). It is Democritos who suggested that the properties of *matter* were determined by the properties of the *atoms* of which they were composed.)

In the 1840s the English brewer and scientist James Joule led the experiments that created the foundations for the first law, also known as *the conservation of energy.* The first law of thermodynamics underpins the fact that energy can change from one form to another—chemical, thermal, mechanical, electrical—but can never be created or destroyed.

While it was in the 1850s that the two laws of thermodynamics were stated in explicit, mathematical form, the deeper meaning embedded in them continues to be discovered. As we have seen in the previous section, entropy, for example, is a measure of

- Disorder,
- Disorganization,
- Lack of patterning, and
- Randomness.

All this is written in regard to the organization of a system and its antithesis: lack of organization, which is linked to an increase in the amount of entropy.

Thus the reduction of entropy embedded in a given system indicates the amount of progress from improbable to probable states. The unit in which it is measured empirically is *ergs* and *joules* per degree absolute.

In terms of thermal energy, Myron Tribus aptly suggests, it is completely misleading to speak of "heat stored in a body."

Only energy can be stored. Heat is energy in transit—therefore, in a process of transition and transformation.

Most significant in an information sense is the measure of the content of a message. As Claude E. Shannon has underlined, the statistical measure is the *negative entropy*, or negentropy. Information measure can be used to evaluate any kind of organizational entropy, since any organization is based upon the interrelations among its components. If two parts are interrelated

- Quantitatively or
- Qualitatively,

knowledge of the state of one can yield information about the state of the other. Information measures can demonstrate when such relationships exist and whether there is a tight or lose linkage.

Apart from other implications, complexity theory is greatly interested in the two laws of thermodynamics because they address system implications that run deeply in the behavior and structure of constructs. Because of the second law of thermodynamics, for example, death is a process inherent in every system and will come sooner or later.

It was nearly 100 years ago when J.W. Gibbs formulated the law of the degradation of energy, which added to the second law of thermodynamics. The basic concept is that thermodynamic degradation is irrevocable over time (a burned log cannot be unburned). Even though there is an equivalence between

- A certain amount of work and
- A certain amount of heat,

when a system is restored to its original state, there can never be a net conversion of heat into work, though the reverse is possible. All these are fundamental concepts in understanding the background of complexity theory.

Just as we cannot convert an amount of heat into its equivalent amount of work without other changes taking place in the system, we cannot move from chaos to organization without the contribution of other factors. Expressed statistically, *changes constitute a passing of the system*

- From ordered arrangement into more chaotic or random distribution and

- Back again from chaotic to more orderly conditions and structures, as we have seen in Chapter 2.

With complexity theory in evolution and due to the impact of the knowledge engineering, we might be moving toward a point in self-organization, though the process of organization turns out to be much more difficult to understand than that of disorganization.

Figure 3-5 presents this concept with the key players complexity, entropy, and diversity. The underlying pattern has

FIGURE 3-5 Organization and disorganization interact, a linkage being provided through complexity theory.

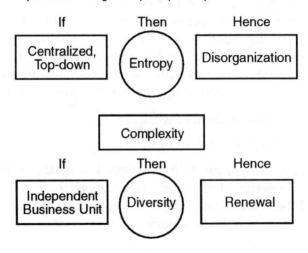

important implications for organizational flexibility and structure:

- *If* the organization is awfully centralized and fully top down, *then* the entropy increases, leading to disorganization and chaos.

- *If* the organization is composed of independent business units with a sort of inverse delegation, *then* diversity dominates—and therefore renewal is feasible.

The passage from diversity to entropy and vice versa is done *through complexity*, but as Dr. J. Doyne Farmer suggests: "We are still missing the key idea, at least in a clear and quantitative form. We need something we can pull apart to get a nice, clear description of what makes it tick. But we cannot do that yet. We only understand little pieces of the puzzle, each in its own isolated context."

A physicist by training, Doyne Farmer works in this domain in an effort to develop a prediction theory for the behavior of financial systems. The puzzle presented by traders, markets, and price changes has some of the characteristics of a jigsaw puzzle.

- There is only one arrangement in which the pieces give a complete picture.

- But there exists a large number of compositions in which the pieces are disordered and do not make sense.

There are still many unknown linkages we have to examine, though we have a good understanding of nonlinearities and fractals, which even in simple systems can generate very complex behaviors.

In biology we know quite a bit about gene regulation, but we do not have many specifics regarding market behavior. The hope is that complexity theory and its tools might create the infrastructure necessary for understanding what really makes markets tick and what keeps them going.

9 WEEDING NOISE OUT OF FINANCIAL DATA

One of the issues requiring appropriate attention in terms of financial analysis is that of *noise*, which may be embedded in a time series of market data. *Noise is any unwanted input*, either because it is irrelevant or because it distorts the presentation of values and/or their interpretation.

Noise embedded in financial information has to do not only with data collection procedures, though the measurement of values and their registration is by no means perfect. A major contributor to noisy financial data is explained by principles borrowed from servo theory, most particularly the so-called *stationary random processes*.

When the statistics of the values, or the probability distribution functions, do not change with time, the random process is termed *stationary*. For instance, the statistics of radar input with system searching may differ radically from the statistics with system tracking. Considering only the searching time, however, the radar signal is ordinarily a member function of a stationary random process.

Ergodicity is the property of stationary random processes. It is particularly important in the development of statistical design theory, as it is applied in economics and other sciences. The ergodic hypothesis involves the assumption that

- The time average over one member function of a stationary random process is equivalent to an average over the ensemble of functions.

- Essentially, ergodicity implies that after a sufficient length of time the effect of initial conditions is negligible.

In other words, if one function of the aggregate is inspected over a sufficiently long period of time, all salient characteristics of the system of functions will be observed. Any one function, then, can be used to represent the ensemble.

Under the new light cast by chaos theory, the ergodicity hypothesis is *patently false*.* Yet practically all traditional studies done today in economics and finance are using ergodicity properties—just as they employ the distorted concept of linear behavior in financial systems.

In whichever domain it is applied, the concept of a linear system is truly valid only when both values and noise possess as well as demonstrate normal distributions:

- In a wide variety of practical financial problems, however, the values definitely do not represent a normal distribution, nor are the relationships linear;

- Therefore, marked improvement can be realized if the linear hypothesis is replaced by a nonlinear hypothesis.

The registration of values in the presence of random noise is perhaps the most important example in which *nonlinear characteristics* can be used to advantage. The limited efficiency of the linear system arises because optimization utilizes only the auto-correlation function of the input.

The validity of superposition indicates that the linear system can only separate two values. By contrast, a nonlinear system—such as power density or energy density—may be able to effect a certain amount of filtering, even if the signal and noise possess proportional spectra.

The reference to a power density spectrum is taken from automatic feedback control systems in engineering, and helps introduce the concept of *white noise*, which is more generally

* As we have seen with the butterfly effect.

applicable. White noise is ordinarily defined as noise with a flat frequency spectrum, for instance, a spectrum that is a constant.

The importance of properly understanding the types of noise affecting a time series of financial information rests on the fact that the able implementation of chaos theory requires low noise. The problem is that financial data often have lots of it:

- Dynamic noise disturbs the information obtained on the states of the system.

- Observation noise makes the measurements less accurate than is desirable.

We can handle in a more agile manner those cases where the dynamic and observational noise are relatively small, and where much of the apparent randomness is caused by low dimensional behavior in the financial system.

One of the reasons for lower accuracy when a dynamic market operates creating a noisy environment is that near an area of instability it will appear to be very sensitive to excitation at certain frequencies. The precise way this may happen will depend on the type and nearness of bifurcation parameters.

There may, for instance, be a progressively weaker damping of transients as an instability region is approached, or characteristic bumps in the power spectrum. We will talk of these conditions in Chapter 4 in connection with the mathematics of chaos theory.

4 Nonlinear Equations and Fractals Underpinning Chaos Theory

1 INTRODUCTION

One of the questions I posed to Dr. Murray Gell-Mann has been: "Is complexity something we do not yet quite understand?" His answer was: "Yes! But also multiplication was complex under Roman numerals." And the same is true with all mathematical tools until we comprehend and master the proper signs and rules:

- Mathematics is a game of signs and rules.
- A basic characteristic of a mathematical system is that its rule-based structure is complete and consistent.
- This means that the rules must be non-contradictory.

Mathematics (noun, singular) groups tools and methods from many branches of science. It includes geometry, trigonometry, arithmetic, algebra, calculus, logic, algorithms, and heuristics. Its equations and models are linear and nonlinear; deterministic and stochastic; probabilistic and possibilistic.* The entities and values they handle can be crisp or fuzzy.

Mathematics, as a process, is the formalization of the abstraction of thought. In this conceptual frame, it does not belong to any other branch of science, but constitutes a branch of its own with methods and tools for modeling objects, processes,

---

* Probabilistic measures address randomness, while possibilistic measures concern the fuzziness of a system.

---

and interactions in a systems sense. Mathematics is as well a valid means for establishing general methods of reasoning.

- Since mathematical concepts and tools operate cross-science their applicability is wide.
- At the same time, different sciences and professions have their own preferred breed of mathematical reasoning and tools.

Mathematical methods and the tools they put at our disposition can be instrumental in challenging the "obvious" because they contribute to a process of clarification and *visibilization*:

- Visibilization helps us to visualize very large entities, such as the universe, and very small ones, such as the atom.

We have spoken of this concept in Chapter 3, where emphasis was placed on the macroscopic and microscopic views of a system.

- Visibilization is very important in scientific research and is becoming quite so in finance.

Mathematics is not just a collection of theorems and formulas. It is also the visualization of ideas, a process we refer to as *visistraction*. This basically means the ability to visualize ideas and concepts as points, lines or n-dimensional constructs in space, trying to derive some concrete meaning out of them.

Three-dimensional graphics are an example of *visualization* not necessarily of the more sophisticated visibilization and visistraction. However, as shown in Figure 4-1, good 3-D graphics produce an excellent sensation of market trends:

- Figure 4-1 presents a 3-dimensional graph of gold price vs. Treasury bills rate and crude oil prices.
- Such a dynamic presentation in color graphics can be scaled not only to the closing price but also to hourly or any other price movements.

FIGURE 4-1   A 3-D presentation of variation in gold price as a function of Treasury bills rate and crude oil prices.

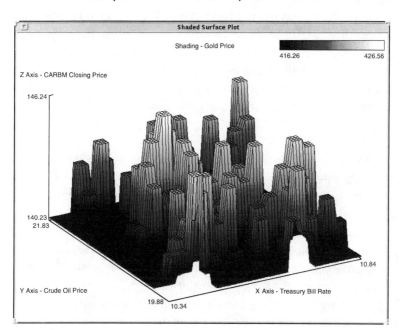

* Contributed by Eurodis Technology, and plotted through PV Wave, a registered trademark of Visual Numerics.

The shading indicates transaction price. Compare the clarity of this figure to the number of cumbersome tables needed to convey the same information to the trader or executive of the brokerage firm.

2 LINEAR AND NONLINEAR MODELS IN FOREX OPERATIONS

Once the concepts underlying chaos theory and its practical implementation are understood, the mathematics are relatively simple to apply. This is true all the way from the examples discussed in the following paragraphs to the genetic algorithms and the fuzzy engineering tools we need in non-traditional financial analysis.

Say that we wish to study the dollar/yen exchange rate. In the opinion of forex experts interviewed with the objective of identifying the variables, two factors are the most important: The exchange rate of the two currencies will depend on the rate of inflation, X, and the money supply, Y.* If Z stands for exchange rate, the simplest possible equation will be:

$$Z = a \cdot X + b \cdot Y \qquad (1)$$

When coefficients "a" and "b" are fixed, exchange rate Z depends solely on current levels of X and Y. This evidently forgets the qualitative aspects of *market psychology:* from rumors and trends to lust and greed.

Foreign exchange dealers are influenced by what has happened in the past, and their recent experiences have an impact on their expectations of the future. There is also a feedback effect. The market as a whole may have no long-term memory, but some individual persons who burned their fingers or made a fortune from past events have lots of it.

In a financial market setting, the feedback system is always in operation and sees to it that neither "a" nor "b" is fixed. They will themselves be variable with an effect of *attenuation, amplification,* or *bifurcation,* as shown in Figure 4-2.

- The speculation on dollar/yen exchange rate may attenuate, as it did in October 1992, when the attack on the French Franc versus Deutschmark parity took all of the market's attention.

- It may amplify, finally forcing a discontinuity in the parity trend, as it did in the same period with the

* Which itself is the product of the monetary base M and the velocity of circulation of money v:

$$Y = M \cdot v$$

FIGURE 4-2   The simple equation $Z = \alpha \cdot x + \beta \cdot y$ gets complex as α and β become variable, attenuating or amplifying x, y or leading to bifurcation.

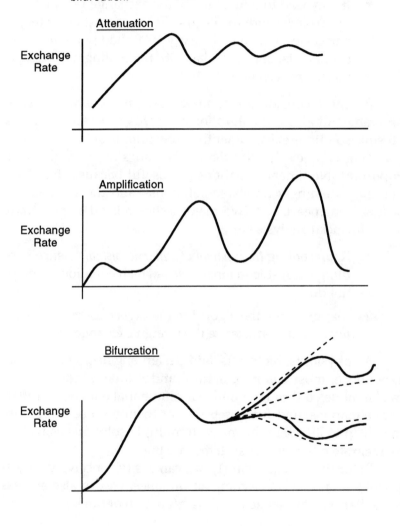

British pound and the Italian lira respectively devalued by 20 and 30 percent,* or

- It may lead to bifurcation of the exchange rate price, as for instance with the Belgian Franc against other major currencies, which in the early 1980s had two values: commercial and financial, both fluctuating according to market movements.

All these considerations make foreign exchange markets profitable but also difficult to forecast. This is because multiple possible solutions exist, rather than one unique one.

That is precisely why the mathematics of chaos theory is important. Nonlinear equations are useful because they have multiple, seemingly unrelated solutions—and the same is true of fuzzy engineering.** Two major issues related to non-traditional financial analysis are

1. Representing *the behavior of dynamic systems,* hence handling in an able manner *time*—which equation (1) does not do.

2. Mapping into the algorithm the *vagueness and uncertainty* that characterize the foreign exchange markets.

As physicists, biologists, and design engineers know from experience, most complex natural and human-made systems can be modeled through nonlinear differential equations, difference equations, and fuzzy sets. All of them are useful because they help to attack problems with multiple solutions as well as to integrate other similar systems into them.

Returning to equation (1), we can easily conceive the coefficient "a" and "b" to be complex variables. We can also express the dollar/yen exchange rate Z as a function of time:

* After the pound and the lira dropped out of the ERM.
** See also D.N. Chorafas, *New Information Technologies: A Practitioner's Guide* (New York: Van Nostrand Reinhold, 1992).

$$Z_{(t+1)} = f \cdot Z_t \tag{2}$$

The future value of the dollar in terms of yen will increase or decrease in function of "f", which is itself a variable influenced by bid and ask—hence by buyers and seller. This is a simple linear model. But is it realistic?

Theoretically, of course, linearity has several advantages. Linear functions are both much better known and have a unique representation. Also, they are relatively easy to approximate. But dynamic linear systems are rather exceptional since real life situations contain nonlinearities.

These are the fundamental notions underpinning the implementation of mathematical notions in connection with dynamic financial systems. But prior to moving forward with the example we just saw, it would be wise to briefly return to the fundamentals.

3 ESCAPING THE LINEAR APPROACHES

From arithmetic expressions to business statistics, present-day applications in finance largely target linear approaches in an attempt to solve complex problems that defy such tools. By contrast, what complexity theory teaches is that

- Instead of establishing and trying to solve very complicated equations,
- We should take a good look at the problem and the tools until we find something more appropriate to deal with.

The solutions suggested by complexity theory incorporate many of the principles we know from simulation: that we should look for background factors, the main ingredients, and the idealized solution. A sound notion is that *we must deal with complexity as plainly and as simply as we can.*

- What's the simplest method of representation?
- How much refinement is needed to make the approach realistic?
- What's the practical effect of our assumptions?

We know that whether change takes place incrementally or in large steps, some effects can be lasting. Can we map the rules that create these effects and embed them into our model?

The result of modeling—as in equations (1) and (2)— should be steadily checked against our own intuition about what constitutes reasonable behavior. When the output of a simulation or experimentation reveals disagreement, one or more of five conditions may lie in the background:

- The mathematical model includes mistaken assumptions.
- A degree of oversimplification has prevailed.
- Initial assumptions were correct, but some factors in the real world changed.
- The artifacts themselves were inadequately developed.
- The level of iteration has been low, permitting no penetrating insight into the problem.

One of the reasons mathematics can be a powerful tool is the insight it provides into the problem, as well as the foresight it makes feasible even by default. Some people believe, for instance, that Einstein's success was attributable in part to the fact that he recognized that space is not Euclidean.

Along the same frame of reasoning, non-traditional financial analysis has taken off on the realization that algorithms similar to equation (1) are too simple to represent real life. The algorithm of equation (2) is an improvement, but we should not be satisfied, for predictive reasons, with its current status.

To make the model more realistic, we can express it by means of a quadratic equation. In the early 1980s, due to two-digit number interest rates, the dollar appreciated significantly against the yen. While the dollar price increased at $f \cdot Z_t$, sellers further pushed up the price by $f \cdot Z_t^2$. Hence, the equation became:

$$Z_{(t+1)} = f \cdot Z_t + f \cdot Z_t^2 \qquad (3)$$

or

$$Z_{(t+1)} = f \cdot Z_t \cdot (1 + Z_t) \qquad (4)^*$$

This is not an accurate model for dollar/yen exchange rates, but it helps explain two issues. First, that sellers can have a compound effect on prices adding to (as in the foregoing case) or subtracting from a *time function* that might otherwise have been simpler.

Second, equation (4) demonstrates that nonlinear effects are indeed realistic. In this case, dollar buying pressure rises by a factor "f", but at the same time selling pressure increases the dollar price at a rate $f \cdot Z_t^2$.

If these factors and trends are not changed due to *market psychology, fundamental* or *technical* reasons, or intervention by the reserve banks, *then* amplification of system output will continue. Eventually, it will reach a *critical level*, which will be expressed through an abrupt change such as exchange rate discontinuity.

(The terms *fundamental* analysis and *technical* analysis date back to the 1920s. In a simplified form, the difference lies in the fact that fundamentalists assume that investors are rational and that the market is efficient. Technical analysts presume the market to be driven by emotions, which *quantitative analysts* (Quants) try to express in an algorithmic form.)

* Equation (4) will be further expressed in a later section.

4 DEVELOPING EQUATIONS FOR NONLINEAR SYSTEMS

Chaos theory is served by many different mathematical tools, rather than only one. But, in practice, the mathematics of nonlinear dynamic systems are often seen as both underpinning and being nearly synonymous to the implementation of chaos theory.

The study of nonlinear dynamic systems is practically indivisible from the study of *turbulence*, or more precisely the transition from a stable state to a turbulent state and back. This has been discussed in Chapter 1 as represented by the edge of chaos and therefore by complexity.

- In this transition, a very small cause that typically escapes our notice determines a considerable effect that becomes visible.

- Because of our unawareness of the small cause, or our inability to observe it, we think that the major effect is due to chance.

The practical meaning of this reference, as far as the financial markets are concerned, is that in essence very small differences in *initial conditions* might produce quite significant outcomes in final phenomena. A small error in the input may lead to an investment error in the final result—or, according to a popular paradigm, a butterfly flapping its wings in Haiti *might* create a typhoon in Florida.

This is the concept underlying *sensitive dependence* to initial conditions and that is why leading-edge financial institutions now pay so much attention to *sensitivity analysis*. Sensitivity analysis

- Targets the important characteristics of dynamic systems and

- Focuses on the characteristics that make them unpredictable in the long run.

The signature of a chaotic time series, for example, is that prediction accuracy falls off with increasing prediction time. By contrast, with a noisy limit cycle *prediction accuracy* might be more or less independent of prediction time.

This issue can be further corroborated by comparing the accuracy of predictions obtained from the nonlinear model with predictions made through a linear model. Recent research tends to confirm that if data is chaotic, the nonlinear predictions should be significantly better.

Mechanical vibrations provide a good test bed for nonlinear input and output modeling.* The input is a force or acceleration, which may be a single pulse, an irregular oscillation, or a continuous random signal:

- Experimentation along this line of reference in structural mechanics involves vibrating a structure with an input and measuring the output.

- The aim is to predict the response from a known input and extrapolate on statistics such as average or maximum amplitude of the response.

Obtained measurements permit us to plot a power spectrum of the mechanical system being examined. Studies regarding the effects of vibrations and oscillations of matter—from frames to mass—are the classical predecessor of the implementation of nonlinear equations in financial markets.

The theory of *measurements* and the exploitation of the obtained results is generally applicable from physics and engineering to finance. Measurements can never be perfect. Quite often very small influences are neglected—yet, as we have seen in the preceding paragraphs, they can have significant effects.

A great deal of what science has learned over the centuries

---

* Today we also have the tools to study mechanical vibrations through fuzzy engineering. Volkswagen, for example, does so. The same tools are applicable in financial engineering.

---

in terms of measurements and forecasts has come from work with mechanics, particularly concerning mass and energy. That's why so much attention has been paid in Chapter 3 to thermodynamics—as both the underlying concepts and the algorithms now find their way into finance.

The concept of energy arose in mechanics, where it was found that it helped to solve certain very difficult problems. Christiaan Huygens (1629–1695) and Isaac Newton (1642–1727) have been credited with recognizing that the decrease in gravitational energy when a mass "m" descends a distance "h" under attraction per unit mass "g" is equal to the increase in *kinetic energy*:

$$1/2\,m \cdot v^2$$

where v stands for velocity. Newton concentrated his attention upon *momentum*:

$$m \cdot v,$$

while Huygens felt that *the force of liveliness*:

$$m \cdot v^2,$$

was the most important characteristic of the motion. The algorithm: $m \cdot v^2$ is also known as twice the kinetic energy.

This is an instructive example because it helps demonstrate that two great physicists have followed two different approaches: The one chose a linear equation to express energy, while the other thought that a quadratic—hence nonlinear—algorithm might be more accurate.

5 IMPLEMENTING CONCEPTS FROM PHYSICS IN FINANCIAL ANALYSIS

If Newton's laws of motion put an end to the idea of absolute position in space, Einstein's theory of relativity gets rid of absolute time. What Albert Einstein established is that

- There is no unique absolute time.

- Instead, each person has her or his own personal measure of time.

This measure of time depends on where that person is and how he or she is moving. With these two contributions, *space and time have become dynamic entities.* When a body moves or a force acts, it affects the curvature of space and time. Something similar can be stated about behavior in the financial markets.

The background issue with non-traditional economic and financial analysis lies precisely in the abandonment of the beaten path of linear equations, simple time series, and the normal distribution hypothesis in statistics. The overriding need is for new departures capitalizing on breakthroughs in other sciences.

What could be a better field to learn from than physics, where the concepts of chaos and complexity have originated? It is no strange coincidence that many rocket scientists are physicists by background.

- The focal points are the models developed by leading scientists regarding energy and matter.
- But this is also a domain that helps demonstrate how scientists might take the wrong path, particularly if they are unable to tear down their theories.

Aristotle believed that matter was continuous. One could continue dividing a piece of matter into smaller bits with practically no limit. Yet, much earlier, Democritos had already advanced the hypothesis of the atom, as we saw in Chapter 3.

Up until a quarter century ago, it was taught that protons and neutrons were elementary particles. However, experiments in which protons were collided at high speed with other protons or electrons indicated that they were made up of smaller particles. These particles were named *quarks* by Murray Gell-Mann.*

---

* There is thought to exist at least six flavors of quarks: up, down, strange, charmed, bottom, top.

CHAPTER 4

The theories we have are not cast in stone. They are simply *models* of a universe or a restricted part of it. They typically reflect our hypotheses in a set of rules that relate quantities in the model to the observations and measurements we make. Both in physics and in economics,

- These models exist in our minds and do not have any other reality.

- However, they help in making predictions about future measurements and other observations.

In physics, for instance, whether we look at it in a microscopic or in a macroscopic sense, *matter* is anything which has mass "m" and occupies physical space, while *energy* is defined as the ability to do work. The principle of conservation of energy says that it can neither be created nor destroyed, but it can be converted from one form to another.*

It is not the modern rocket scientists, but Pierre Simon Laplace (1749–1827) who first assumed that there are laws similar to the physical laws governing everything else, including human behavior. This belief has been further strengthened by Dr. Werner Heisenberg's famous *uncertainty principle*—which is a fundamental property of the world in which we live.

Physics teaches that, as a matter of principle, mass and energy are equivalent. One can be converted into the other in accordance with the algorithm we have seen in the previous section. This can be seen as predecessor to models used in economics, given that the better established mathematics of physical systems often serve as guidelines.

Whether natural or human-made, such as financial markets, living systems need specific types of matter and energy in adequate amounts. As a living system,

* See also the discussion in Chapter 3 on the laws of thermodynamics.

- Financial markets can nicely use this paradigm to create similar principles through analogical reasoning.
- And let's never forget that one of the most important lessons we can be taught from physics concerns the importance of *time*.

The study of physical systems also teaches a great deal about *discontinuities* and their impact. Discontinuity is an apparent jump in distance, which may be caused by a sudden increase in size of the main attractor (solution space).

Discontinuities usually happen because of an interior crisis. Since a large jump occurs, any attempt to predict it using values derived from linear approaches would be doomed to failure. This is true in many sciences and most particularly in economics.

- The large jump may be caused by an unstable period, touching off a chaotic attractor, or
- The discontinuity may occur, as in Figure 4-2, and lead to bifurcation.

Nonlinear mathematics suggests that there are in fact infinitely many possibilities for discontinuities, that is combinations of factors causing jumps, though many of these jumps can be of small magnitude.

The example of the discontinuity shown in Figure 4-3 is due to market forces, and is characteristic of the price of any semiconductor chip, for processing and for storage. When a new chip is introduced to the market, the price is relatively high. For the next year or so, it drops slowly. Then the next generation of chip comes out, and the price of the one already well established dramatically drops.

This has happened with the 8086 chip when Intel introduced the 286; it repeated itself with the 286 when the 386 came out, and eventually the price discontinuity hit the 386 due to the 486. The latter suffers the same fate in the hands of the 586 chip.

FIGURE 4-3 Discontinuity can be created due to many factors, particularly so in nonlinear systems. This is an example from microprocessor pricing.

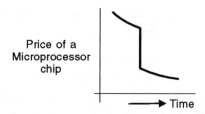

Price of a Microprocessor chip

⟶ Time

Quite similarly every 2 or 3 years the multiplication by 4 of the storage capacity of memory chips sees a drop by so much in the price of the preceding memory chip generation.

6 THE NEED TO RETHINK TIME SERIES AND SOLUTION SPACES

Let us suppose that the financial analyst has been presented with time series data recorded from stock market behavior, and he would like to estimate the critical value at which a catastrophic change might occur. Classical time series, however, offer little help regarding the structure of market behavior.

- In the background of this statement lies the often discussed fact that stock markets, over-the-counter markets, and commodity exchanges are nonlinear.

- By plotting and studying closing prices in a simple linear graph, we basically bias the representation and reduce our own understanding of the forces at work.

Linear presentations of price fluctuation omit the fact that markets are complex, interdependent systems. The price output they produce offers rich possibilities for interpretation, but no easy extrapolations of a linear regression type like the relative strength line plotted in Figure 4-4.

FIGURE 4-4   Time series of market closing price at the stock exchange.

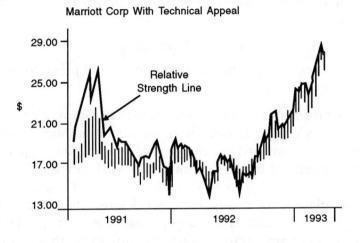

Marriott Corp With Technical Appeal

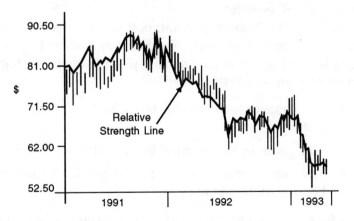

Bristol-Myers Squibb - A Deteriorating Price

Yet regression analysis and the calculation of confidence intervals are not without interest altogether. They are a valid means of *visualization*—turning numbers into graphs, and making feasible visual inspection of data—provided we understand that we are only talking of approximations.

When we do visualize, however, we should keep well in mind that financial market problems typically have no single solution.

- They usually have multiple solutions.
- Therefore, graphics possibilities should permit us to look at these solutions.

As financial analysts who work with nonlinear algorithms know, many chaotic systems have an infinite number of possible solutions contained in a finite space. We will see an example on this statement in subsequent sections when we talk about *fractals*.

Simple graphic presentations work when the attractor has a simple shape, which is well approximated by a straight line or a curve. In more complex systems, however, this graphic approach might not be applicable, though the underlying principle would still be valid.

Looking at a graphic presentation is easy, if we know all the variables coming into play. The assistance offered by classical graph plotting is that we typically place market data together on a cartesian coordinate system:

- The value of each variable is mapped at the same instant in time.
- This gives a phase portrait in a possible solution space.
- The dimensionality of the space depends on the number of variables in the system.

If there are two or three variables, we can easily visualize this information in two dimensions. But if there are more than three dimensions, we should express the data mathematically, stressing the attractor—the region where the solution lies.

Solution spaces, however, do not always look orderly. We have spoken of *strange attractors* based on research in complex systems encountered in physics. As Chapter 1 has suggested, strange attractors have a phase portrait that looks random, but is often limited to a certain range, and periodically may even be orderly.

Typically, chaotic attractors have a fractional dimension. A near incipient catastrophe is close in phase space to some singularity that represents instability. The distance from attractor to singularity can be estimated from the information contained in observable phenomena, having to do with dynamics in the solution space.

Besides the inherent difficulties that exist with dynamic systems, since chaos is nonlinear, conventional linear statistical measures such as autocorrelation are inadequate to describe their behavior. As many financial analysts fail to appreciate,

- Chaotic and random time series have broadband spectra,
- Hence the errors embedded in different predictors.

The mathematical tools we use should be sensitive to nonlinear correlations in time series. For reasons of accuracy, it is necessary to distinguish a nonlinear deterministic system from one that is stochastic and linear.

Such distinction is particularly interesting to forecasting when we would like to know whether a given time series contains the kind of nonlinear structure that might be exploited by a prediction algorithm. At issue is which method could provide significantly better predictions than a linear approach.

As we know from experience with the classical statistical tests, the goal is to accept or reject a hypothesis. In this specific case the issue is rejecting the hypothesis that the original time series is characterized by some form of linearity.

- Rejecting the hypothesis of no difference (null hypothesis) is less ambitious than estimating the solution space dimension,

- But it is also a statistical problem that might be handled in a more reliable way if we use past experience.

Many researchers in economics as well as theoretical statisticians believe that irregular time series have a substantial stochastic component embedded in them. This may be in addition to noise and any nonlinearities. The alternative view is that

- The irregular component can as easily be due to chaos.
- If so, by assuming chaos is of low dimension, the process can be made largely deterministic.

Statisticians who believe that most of the irregular behavior is stochastic tend to use far fewer parameters than would be the case with financial analysts following the alternative point of view:

- That the phenomena which we observe in market behavior are nonlinear; they are chaotic but have a certain orderly structure underpinning them.
- Probabilistic behavior is a valid approach if the irregularity in the time series is predominantly due to stochastic or high-dimensional effects.
- But it can give inaccurate forecasts if the variation in values happens to have only a small stochastic component.

In addition, the question of proper identification of the solution space has not yet been considered in due detail by statisticians. There are also questions relating to the low-noise limit, which have often been bypassed in time series analysis.

7 DYNAMIC EQUATIONS, FOREX TRADING, AND FRACTAL CONCEPTS

The time-dependent quadratic equation we saw earlier in the chapter has the characteristics of a feedback system. What happens at this moment can be described by the following: Z_{t+1} is a function of Z_t, a fact which needs to be further explored.

If because of the reasons we have seen there is an attenuation of Z_{t+1}, then the exchange rate system reaches a new temporary equilibrium. By contrast,

- If differences created by the exchange rate mechanism continue to amplify,

- Change will accelerate until it exceeds a critical level, where more than a single equilibrium exists.

While exchange rate movements can be expressed in time series, bifurcation could happen through government action aiming at damage control by bringing the system into a new, sustainable equilibrium. That is the example with the Belgian franc that we have seen.

But bifurcation can also be initiated by the system that has reached a fractional, or *fractal* state.*

- Fractal is a construct or other object in which *the parts are fractional but still related to the whole.*

- These fractal parts look like clones of one another; that is, they are *self-similar.*

- Even when fractal parts seem to be different quantitatively, like the branches of a tree, they have *a qualitative similarity* to the whole.

The fluctuation in exchange rates can be mapped nicely in a *fractal dimension* that describes how an object fills its space even *if* it has holes and gaps embedded in it. This visualization of fractions contrasts to Euclidean geometry where component parts have integer dimensions. As their name implies, fractals are *fractional* and may also be discontinuous—which is another advantage in using them to map the exchange rate mechanism.

* The fundamental concept of fractals is explained in the following two sections.

In other terms, the important issue behind fractals concerns the means they provide in facing real life situations, whether these concern events in physics, geology, or the financial world:

- A fractal distribution is characterized by a probability that is statistically self-similar.
- Its characteristic is that fractals clone one another in different *increments of time.*
- This distribution is neither normal nor exactly the same in a statistical sense.

The reason why fractal distributions have attracted considerable attention in the type of studies we examine is that self-similar properties can be found in practically all dynamic non-linear systems. They also assist in reflecting feedback processes, as well as behavior of constructs that are far from equilibrium.

Foreign exchange is a good example because it is characterized by critical levels. They are influenced by variations both in space and in time, some of which are due to time windows:

- The opening of the exchange market in Tokyo and in New York is separated by 13 hours;
- Halfway in that time range Zurich, Frankfurt, Paris, then London are active.
- Each of these forex markets has self-similar characteristics to the others,
- Yet in terms of psychology and behavior these markets exhibit differences.

Furthermore, in a spatial sense there is feedback between the forex markets—while during the common time window some of these markets have multiple feedback.

As the different spatial components of the global foreign exchange system operate as a network 24-hours per day, they are subject to a *sensitivity dependence* on one another. Starting from given initial conditions, dollar/yen rates will fluctuate subject to correlations and trends not only among these two currencies but also in connection to other strong currencies in the first world's monetary system.

The fractal structure will show up in every two-by-two currency exchange rate fluctuation, influenced by all the factors we have considered. These include the distributions of the other currencies and the constraints they experience in *their* fluctuation, for instance, the constraints imposed by the European Monetary System (EMS).*

It is not easy to express through linear mathematical models a system as complex as the one described by the foregoing paragraphs, even if it will be most rewarding to forecast future behavior of the forex market from a set of known past values. The way to proceed is to

- Choose a method for solution that permits spatial construction and
- Make feasible the mapping of known values into this solution space.

The goal should be to construct a model for system dynamics by approximating Z_{t+1}, that is, by finding a function that can be used to predict future states. These in turn, can be projected back onto the model to predict future behavior. Such forecasting involves extrapolation in time in the sense that

- We use data from one domain, *the past,*
- To extrapolate behavior in a disjointed domain, *the future.*

This is an inherently difficult problem, but the construction of a nonlinear solution space makes it possible to convert

---

* See also D. N. Chorafas, *Treasury Operations and the Foreign Exchange Challenge* (New York: Wiley, 1992).

---

exchange rate time series into a problem of interpolation in the state space. The trap with current methods in time series forecasting lies in assuming that such behavior is linear.

8 AN INTRODUCTION TO THE THEORY OF FRACTALS

In the mind's eye, a fractal is a way of seeing infinity. Fractional dimensions permit measuring qualities that otherwise have no clear definition, for instance, the degree of roughness or irregularity in an object, and qualitative expressions such as greater, more, roughly equal, less, and smaller. In terms of roughness,

- A twisting coastline has a characteristic degree of roughness.
- Price movements in the stock market have certain similarities to the coastline.*

Neither of the two examples has a linear representation. Both exhibit a degree of brokenness; that is, a *fractal* dimension. Other examples can be taken from qualitative expressions such as:

- The dollar/yen exchange rate holds well.
- The Swedish krona has become weaker than other currencies.
- More stocks advanced than retreated today on the New York Stock exchange.

These are expressions that, while targeting concrete events, contain in themselves fractal dimensions due to vagueness and uncertainty. The changes may be fractional and, therefore, nonsignificant when we say that the dollar holds well against the yen.

The importance of fractal dimensions is that they can be instrumental in showing how the shape of a time series fills its

* See also the example with the weekly plot of stockmarket values in Figure 4-3.

space. This is determined by the forces involved in the series' formation—including the impact of micro- and macroeconomics factors as well as many investors' perceptions of what real value is.

Both fractals theory and fuzzy logic are concerned with *formal principles of approximate reasoning*, which have neither linear nor deterministic expression. Interestingly enough, this is both the general case and a very flexible way of representation. As such, it contrasts to precise reasoning which—as many people do not appreciate—is a *limiting case*.

The ancient Greeks have used both fuzzy and fractal reasoning approaches to find square roots. Their method began with a guess which, small step by small step, lead to a better guess. The process of iteration zooms toward an answer as a dynamic system seeks its steady state. This is a concept of

- Fuzzification and defuzzification
- Working through fractions but aiming at the whole

Such solutions are fast and elegant. In the ancient Greek example, the number of accurate decimal digits generally doubles with each step. A similar approach characterizes Newton's method for higher-degree polynomial equations that cannot be solved directly, as well as other computer algorithms.

- One awkwardness about iteration, however, is that complex equations usually have more than one solution.
- Therefore, which solution the method finds depends on the initial guess.
- Along that track, iteration seeks out whichever of the roots is closer to the initial guess.

A similar process of iterations takes place in the study of complex systems. It is characterized by a transition from *uncertainty* to *near certainty*, a typical example being when we observe the behavior of a long series of events. This is an essential theme in the study of complexity.

The graphs in Figures 4-5 and 4-6 are graphical visualization of polynomial sets. Each starts with a point i represented through complex numbers: i lies in the imaginary and real domains and proceeds through successive iterations. The equation underlying either graph is quite simple:

$$Z = Z^2 - i$$

The visualization acts like a magnifying glass which permits us to see what is in the set. Due to the large number of required iterations, this is an ideal application for a parallel computer.

The parallel software loops compute $Z = Z^2 - i$, where, as stated, i is the initial complex number and Z is a complex variable. The problem can be stated in this form: "Given a location on a plane, perform up to n iterations on that point in order to figure out whether or not the point is in the Mandelbrot Set.* i is in the Mandelbrot Set *if* as n goes to infinity, the values assigned to Z converge.

This type of calculation with Mandelbrot fractals requires a large number of iterations, each iteration contributing to increasing complexity.

- Membership to a Mandelbrot set is defined through testing.
- In essence, iterations show how good the test is.

A relatively small number of iterations, for instance 4,000, produces no sharp picture. The picture in Figures 4-5 and 4-6 required 20,000 iterations on a parallel computer and this number can be significantly increased for greater sharpness. Typically, the deeper the iteration process, the sharper is the picture.

* The contributions by Benoit Mandelbrot are discussed both in this section and in section 9.

FIGURE 4-5   A fractals graph of the equation $Z = Z^2 - 1$, which has been the subject of 20,000 iterations on a parallel computer.

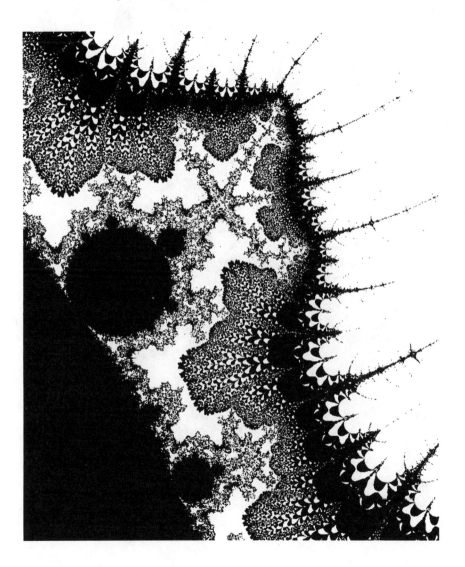

FIGURE 4-6   A closer look at one of the elements in Figure 4-5, clearly
distinguishing the fractal geometry.

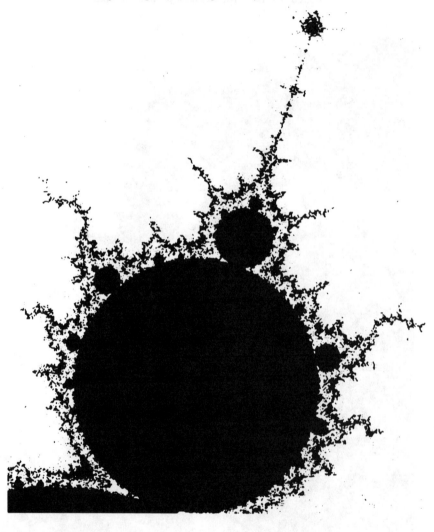

Fractals and fuzzy sets are important in finance because to model chaotic situations we must consider nonlinear functions. Linear modeling techniques are often motivated by the decomposition theorem, which assumes that a random process can be decomposed into the sum of

- An autoregressive process and
- A noise process.

This approach is both complex and inaccurate. By exploiting nonlinearity, we can express the situation we are facing as a purely deterministic system, as we will see through practical examples in this and in the next chapters.

A closer look at fractals brings under perspective the concept and process of patterning. The previous section made reference to the fact that fractals are shapes marked by *self-similarity*.

- *Self-similarity* is symmetry across scale.
- It implies recursion, that is, *a pattern within a pattern*.

Fractal events or measurements have the same traits on a large scale as they do on a small scale. Self-similarity is the trait of objects that look similar at different scales.

This is the reason fractals are used successfully with crystal growth and astronomical data, and they start being carefully examined in finance as many people think of using fractals with the study of time series.

The contribution fractals can make in economics and finance is that analysis proceeds by approximations (as it does in the physical world) because it presupposes taking limits. But this process requires clean data to lock into a fractal dimension, which is not so often the case with economic time series—as we have seen in Chapter 3.

The contribution Benoit Mandelbrot has made through the formalization of fractal analysis is that he specified ways of calculating the fractional dimension of real objects:

- This provides a technique for constructing a shape of a given set of data, allowing geometry to represent irregular patterns.

- The concept is that the degree of irregularity remains constant over different scales, a claim that turns out to be true as many processes display a regular irregularity.

Koch's snowflake is an example. If the process shown in Figure 4-7 in its three initial stages is continued, the fractal dimensions will multiply, leading to a rough but vigorous model resembling a coastline. In this model the length of the boundary is

$$3 \times 4/3 \times 4/3 \times 4/3 \times 4/3 \cdots \text{ to infinity}$$

The area being covered remains smaller than the area of a circle drawn around the original triangle, even if every iteration increases the area defined by the fractals. In a way, an infinitely long fractional line surrounds a finite area.

Benoit Mandelbrot postulated that we can never actually measure the length of a coastline because the latter depends on the length of the ruler we use to measure it. The same is true with financial data as well as with sampling procedures employed in other domains of science.

In conclusion, a fractal dimension is determined by how the object fills its space. A fractal object will fill the space *unevenly* because its parts are correlated not only among themselves but also with the characteristics of the instrument we use and other key variables, some of which often escape our attention.

9 CONCEPTS AND PROCESSES IN FRACTAL GEOMETRY

In ancient Greece, Pythagoras was thought to have developed the now famous theorem about the square of the hypothenuse, a notion that persists today. More recent findings, however, sug-

FIGURE 4-7 Generating a Koch snowflake.

gest that this theorem had been applied 1,200 years earlier, as evidenced through cuneiform texts.

While Pythagoras (570–490 B.C.) most likely learned his famous theorem in Babylon, he is credited with other discoveries that are original. For instance, he assumed the Earth to be spherical in shape (but thought it was placed at the center of cosmos), and he described the motions of the sun, moon, and planets.

Just the same, the development of *fractals geometry* did not happen overnight. Geometry originated in Egypt, Aristotle suggests* because there the priestly class was allowed leisure. But Herodotus (482–429 B.C.) advises that there was a different initial condition. When the Nile flooded a major agricultural track, it became necessary for the purpose of taxation to determine how much land had been lost.

* Metaphysics A 1.

The origin of major discoveries, particularly those dating many centuries ago, is always a matter of guesswork and therefore of dispute. Neither are discoveries coming out of the blue altogether. As a general rule

- They follow, albeit in a discontinuous manner, older notions, which might have been wearing out.

- But they still provide a stepping stone toward new knowledge.

In this sense, the development of fractals geometry is an added value to established geometric tools and concepts, making a new science out of the notion of fractiles. This permits us to describe natural shapes in terms of a few simple rules. Natural shapes as well as time series are best expressed by means of fractional representation.

As long as we look superficially and from a distance at a three-dimensional surface, it appears to be smooth. But when we approach this surface and examine it in detail, it resembles a coast line.

- Not only does it look fractal, but indeed it is fractal, and therefore the new tools are appropriate.

- We can sense the detail, but maybe we cannot handle it because it is mapped into more than three dimensions.

To assist himself in this work, the knowledgeable analyst will look at substructures at the chosen level of reference. He will supplement the old coordinate system with new axes, creating new premises that permit careful study of the chosen point of investigation.

Through fractal geometry we can visualize n-dimensions, while being limited with 3-D in a representation sense. We may swap or rotate around the new dimensions to satisfy, for instance, requirements for twenty different sensitivities that may all change at the same time. The challenge is to map all of them into the model and visualize them at the same time which, in theory, a fractal diagram will permit us to do.

This is the reason why fractal geometry can provide added tools to the theory of complexity. The view from fractal geometry is very different from, but not contradictory to, that of Euclidean geometry. After all, what Euclid did was to create a system of signs and rules that reflected the concepts, knowledge, and tools of his time, which is not necessarily the state of the art today:

- Euclid based his system on a hierarchy of concepts expressed as axioms, theorems, postulates, and proofs.

- He used them to develop plane geometry, which is still very much in use.

But in the meantime Euclidean geometry has been challenged by mathematicians like Gauss and Riemann, who developed new kinds of geometry known as non-Euclidean.

Contrary to what many people may be thinking, Euclid's system rested on *unproved propositions* and included a number of *undefined terms*. Among Euclid's postulates, or self-evident truths, was "Through any given point which is not on a given line, one and only one line can be drawn which is parallel to the given line." Challenged by non-Euclidean mathematicians, this postulate leaves wide gaps in Euclid's theory.

In a manner similar to that of Euclid, Benoit Mandelbrot collected the observations of mathematicians concerned with objects not definable by Euclidean geometry. He combined the work of these mathematicians with his own insight and created a geometry of nature that expresses *asymmetry*, *roughness*, and *fractional structures*.

Fractal dimensions can be a very good yardstick. In essence, this work both complements and contradicts the concepts advanced by Euclidean geometry:

- In Euclidean terms, the closer we look at an object the simpler it becomes.

- A natural object, by contrast, shows more complexity the closer we look at it—as we move from *macroscopic* to *microscopic* views.*

Fractals have this property of complexity; the closer we examine them the more detail we see. Mandelbrot originally defined fractals based on topological dimensions but then rejected that definition. The better way to look at fractional dimensions is as objects in which the parts relate to the whole through some characteristic structural quality:

- A generic quality, for instance, is that fractals are self-referential or self-similar.

- Trees and their roots branch according to a fractal scale self-similar with respect to space.

Along the same frame of reasoning, fractal time series of financial data have statistical self-reference with respect to space. In fact, *fractal time series are random fractals.* Coastlines, too, are examples of random fractals which can be created by using a few continuously repeated fractal rules.

- When flying at high altitude, a coastline looks like a smooth if irregular line.

- But the lower we fly, the more coarse it appears to be.

- A similar observation can be made about exchange rates and stock prices.

There are many ways for generating fractal shapes. The simplest way is to use a given rule, integrating it over and over again. This is the case with Koch snowflakes in Figure 4-7. The process starts with a solid equilateral triangle, then adds an

* See also Chapter 3.

equilateral triangle to the middle of each side, and iterates this process, giving the appearance of a fractal shape.

The opposite procedure will also create a fractal effect, generating the so-called Sierpinski triangle. This starts with a solid equilateral triangle,

- Removes an equilateral triangle from the center,
- Then removes another triangle from the remaining triangles, and
- Repeats for thousands of iterations triangle subtraction within triangles, as shown in Figure 4-8.

This is essentially a process of constructing with holes. It is given life by the technique of removing infinitely many parts, just like the Koch snowflake develops by adding infinitely many parts.

A three-dimensional analog to the Koch and Sierpinski artifacts is the Menger sponge. Its pattern is that of a solid-looking lattice that has an infinite surface area, yet its volume approaches zero.

With an infinite number of triangles or other geometric figures trapped in the finite space of the original triangle, there is

FIGURE 4-8   Developing Sierpinski triangles.

infinite complexity generated in a finite space. However, random fractals, to which exchange and stock prices have been compared, are not symmetrical like the Sierpinski triangle or Koch snowflake.

- Individual branches can vary in shape and size, as
- The scaling of each set of data does not occur by some characteristically consistent measure.

It is precisely this combination of randomness and of a given deterministic generating rule that creates the causality and makes fractals useful to the analysis of financial markets. Another important observation in this connection is that the jagged line of exchange rates or stock prices

- Is not one-dimensional, as often thought, because it is not straight.
- Neither is it two-dimensional, because it does not fill a plane.

Its dimensionality is *more than one*, which is that of a line, and *less than two*, that of a plane. It is a dimension between one and two—therefore, a fractal or fractional reference. Furthermore, fractal shapes and time series are characterized by long-term correlations, and their probability distribution is not a normal bell curve.

PART 2

From Genetic Algorithms to Fuzzy Engineering

5 The Essence of Genetic Algorithms and Their Implementation

1 INTRODUCTION

During World War II an effort was made to quantify military and business-type activities into a formal mathematical language so that they could be manipulated and optimized. This approach came to be known as *Operations Research* (OR), and after the war ended business leaders began looking for ways to apply it—to help themselves manage the resources under their authority more efficiently.

One of the basic tools of operations research has been linear programming (LP). Developed by Dr. George Danzig, LP works by outlining activities and their quantifiers in a matrix form, quite similarly to the Input/Output analysis for macroeconomics developed by Dr. Vassily Leontief.

Linear programming has many variations, one of them being the "traveling salesman" approach, which incorporates an heuristic search. Both LP and traveling salesman can be quite helpful in studying business problems, but both also suffer from the limitations presented by linear models.

Another technique developed since the 1950s for optimizing the use of resources is differential equations as, for instance, promoted by Dr. Richard Bellman in dynamic programming.

- One of the reasons this technique did not catch on in terms of popularity is that few people know differential equations.

- Another reason is that differential equations are blind to the order in which a given set of resources is used.

Other researchers viewed the optimization issue as a combinatorial problem and tried to solve it through exhaustive algorithms. Here again, as the number of possibilities increases, the solution space can grow exponentially, making such techniques impractical for large problems.

With complexity theory, by default if not by choice, *genetic algorithms* are looked at as a possible method for solving combinatorial type optimization problems. Their advantage lies in the ability to

- Hop heuristically, for instance from one schedule to another schedule and

- Allow the solution process to escape from local suboptima in which other algorithms might anchor.

Dr. John Holland originated the genetic algorithm technique, which essentially emulates the process of mutations and crossovers dominating *natural selection*. Hence the name given to this approach.

2 WHAT IS THE SENSE OF USING A GENETIC ALGORITHM?

Genetic algorithms are stochastic systems effectively used for a simulated process of natural selection and for optimization.

Based on the process of biological evolution, they help in deriving solutions to real-life problems by carrying out an emulated evolution on a population of possible choices or outcomes.

The way defined in a biological sense, evolution takes place in organic entities capable of encoding the structure of living organisms. These are the *chromosomes*. A similar process but with the same name—chromosomes—is used by genetic algorithms for encoding reasons.

Within an evolutionary frame of reference, *change* operates on the chromosomes and through them on the organisms (or scheduling issues, transportation problems, financial conditions, and so on) which they encode. As in real life, the simulated biological change occurs through

- Mutations, and
- Crossovers.

Mutations introduce diversity into the population. Crossovers act to combine the better schemata already present.

Genetic algorithms employ trial and error in a direct analogy to how biological evolution works by *mutation*. This process is followed by natural selection:

- Each offspring is tried through some optimization criteria.
- *If* it proves better than the others, *then* it gets to be parent of the next randomly mutated generation.

The *crossover* is a complementary way to the evolutionary process, and it can be as important as mutation. In nature, crossover occurs when two parents exchange parts of their corresponding chromosomes, recombining genetic material. Such a process is fairly easy to simulate and then handle through a large number of iterations.

Genetic algorithms represent a method for optimizing a certain function so that it fits certain observations. In the general sense of optimization, our goal is to find a strategy that consumes the least resources. However, many of the optimization techniques available so far have three difficulties:

- They are sensitive to large or stochastic noise in the data we are using.
- They can be easily misled by local peaks and bumps, that may be unrelated to the overall maxima and minima.
- Their search strategy typically uses the slope of the function to select the next step in the search.

Chapter 3 has explained why noise is most detrimental in the manipulation of financial data, particularly when the data is used for prediction purposes. Local peaks, for instance in a profit function, lead to suboptima and can be misleading in the exploration of the solution space.

The effect of the third constraint is that the slope must be computed at each evaluation. In calculating procedures, however, slopes act as power sponges. Also, for many problems, the local slope does not provide useful information about the location of the maximum; this is particularly true with nonlinear functions.

By contrast, a genetic algorithm relies on a population of solutions to the problem on hand, each possibly being a regression tree. Typically, the concept underlying the genetic algorithm rests on natural systems, most particularly on an ecological approach:

- For each solution we give a *fitness* criterion, for instance how well it classifies the data.
- Then we proceed with reproduction by performance, which amounts to natural selection, and
- We provide for crossover by mutation, taking the better events or factors and making a new population out of them.

This is a highly iterative process and, as it can be proven over time, it is not a bad way to search in a solution space. The difficulty with genetic algorithms is to define *fitness*, a process that can be tricky because to a large extent it is subjective. One of the risks, for instance, is that we can overrate the data.

Proponents of the genetic algorithm suggest that it is strong in the area of optimization and, furthermore, uses only observed values. Hence, slope estimates are not necessary:

- These observed values concern a population of different parameter sets, and
- Each set corresponds to a possible solution.

The process capitalizes on the fact that some of the entities in the natural selection game are more fit to provide a basis for the required optimization than others. Iterations take care of the generation and filtering processes inherent in any natural or human-made system.

The whole procedure capitalizes on the fact that, even in natural selection, species are abstractions not realities. The individual entities or agents in the population are the realities:

- Their behavior is tested against a given criterion, which may be variable or fixed,
- This criterion can be transitional, progressive, or regressive—eventually molding the population.

As in biology and natural science, in the sense of the genetic algorithm applied with artifacts such as financial markets, evolution is the fallback position of advancement or retreat from uniformity, once a simulated life's existence has been admitted. The survival of the fittest is due to the extinction of those forms of life that do not satisfy the set criterion.

Since extinction is a key player, the heart of the genetic algorithm is the generation of new population members based on combining pairs of current chromosomes. Members are selected for reproduction on the basis of their relative fitness. Each parameter for the new member is selected from one parent or the other on a random basis.

Seen from a practical business viewpoint, experience with some applications tends to suggest that two relevant parameters make a strong difference in how quickly an optimum is found:

1. The number of members in the population should be relatively small, but not too small.

Numbers smaller than 10 do not work well; numbers larger than 20 (and some researchers suggest an upper limit of 12) take much longer for the process to optimize, with no visible offsetting advantage.

2. Mutations should be introduced to prevent member cloning from taking the upper hand.

Provided certain rules are observed, the genetic algorithm can help in tuning the hypotheses, which we do so that we can see which issues (or entities) work and which fall by the wayside— and therefore need rethinking. This can be done through a considerable number of iterations necessary to arrive at a useful result.

Typically, through the iterative process—which as we will see in section 3 involves creation, evaluation, elimination, and recreation—the system concentrates most of its search near whichever solution is most fit:

- This checking of nearby solutions is what makes it immune to nonlinear behavior as well as to noise.
- Occasional mutations can lead to far jumps, hence discontinuities, underpinning the ability of the genetic algorithm to find novel, even unsuspected, solutions.

To avoid blind alleys, such as being stuck on a local peak, it is advisable to monitor the new members on whether they have parameter values that are close to the entities being replaced. In such cases, the experimenter can force a mutation by changing one or more parameters by an arbitrary amount.

3 THE MECHANICS OF GENETIC ALGORITHMS

Evolution has created simple natural systems that adapted to the changes taking place in the environment. This has been achieved through a process of mutation and crossover applicable to the lower forms of life. John Holland's artifact has four basic elements:

- Chromosome
- Creator
- Evaluator
- Generator

Under the heading *chromosome** is basically a list of members, entities, or items. These can be bits, characters, or sequences of any type, depending on the problem we are solving.

When we are looking for a numerical solution, a string of digits may be used to represent a number. If we attack an optimization problem, the chromosome may represent a sequential or other ordering of resources, tasks, and so on. In a financial problem involving off-balance sheet products, for example, the chromosomes may be a number of these products, as for instance:

- Different types of options written
- Interest rate caps and floors
- Resource obligations on receivables sold
- Commitments to extend credit
- Standby letters of credit, and so on**

* A better term, which is used in section 6, is *adaptive agent*. In sections 3, 4, and 5, however, John Holland's original term has been retained.

** We will see a more extensive list of off-balance sheet instruments in section 6.

In such a case, the object of optimization may be risk minimization for a given projected profit level or, alternatively, profit maximization at an acceptable level of risk.

The *creator* is characterized by an operation that starts by generating an initial pool of chromosomes. Different procedures may be followed, depending on the outstanding goal:

- In cases where the chromosomes are simple binary numbers, the creator can be fairly *random* in its operations.

- But after the chromosomes begin to make use of more complex structures, such as schedules, they need to fit a *rule pattern*.

Say, for example, that the chromosome consists of a list of tasks, such as options written, with priority values and time constraints in execution. The resources being used are input into a task pool. A creator randomly selects tasks from the task pool and places them in an ordered list until no tasks remain.

In this process, each task may be assigned a one- or two-character name. The chromosome is also given a unique name for reference purposes. This helps in describing the system *as is*, at two levels of detail.

A third major component of the process, the *evaluator*, rates each chromosome by giving the highest rating to those that solve *the most tasks in the least time*.* Hence the criterion of the evaluator is the ability of each chromosome to attack and solve a given problem. In the scheduling example, this is done by

- Subtracting the highest time being scheduled

- From the time scheduled by a given chromosome.

The value derived by this process is returned and placed in a chromosome evaluation list. If a time limit is used, then tasks are

* As, for instance, is the case with scheduling.

only scheduled until the time runs out and the priority is summed up. The values are passed on to a generator for determining the variations of those chromosomes worth propagating.

The *generator* uses mutate and crossover operations to randomly reconfigure the solutions specified by the chromosomes. In other terms, the generator decides which operation it will use to change a chromosome. Among the alternatives are the following:

- Position-based mutation
- Order-based mutation
- Position-based crossover
- Order-based crossover

In one of the implementation strategies, if the generator chooses position-based mutation, it asks the lottery for one winner. But if it chooses a crossover operation, it would ask for two winners.

The goal of an implementation strategy is to emulate the behavior of a natural process where mutations occur in the message transmitted by the process. It is important, however, to take notice that in natural systems the genetic code itself is so basic that it has remained essentially the same in the transition from bacteria to humans. This provides an example of how

- An arbitrary feature can evolve into a truly effective system and
- A dominant process kills off competition and survives by historical evolution standards.

As is the case with nature, through an emulated process of *mutation* and *selection* the members of a population change a great deal through iteration and evolution. The messages transmitted by an entity to its offspring (the next generation) are copied, with a few random errors we refer to as mutations.

The fundamental background that promotes usage of the genetic algorithm is the ability to escape from the constraints and inaccuracies of linear models. As it cannot be repeated too often, linear approaches do not fit the computational requirements when we are moving at the edge of chaos:

- *If* we try to cram our complex business world into the confines of oversimplified structures,
- *Then* the results will not only be suboptimal but also a long way from real life.

This is, briefly, how genetic algorithms work. Specific mechanics depend on the available software, and many implementors have made their own interpretations or improvements of the original genetic algorithm. But in general terms, this is how the system works.

4 SELECTION, MUTATION, AND PERFORMANCE IN THE STOCK MARKET

Fundamental to the implementation of the genetic algorithm is the process of selection, mutation, and generation. The generator mutates the chromosome by randomly picking two positions and switching them:

- It deletes the worst chromosome generated so far and inserts the new chromosome into the living population.
- It also checks to see if the right number of chromosomes have been created. If not, it generates more new chromosomes.

Can this approach be used in connection to stock exchange operations? I posed this query to a mature person who has been working for many years on Wall Street, and his suggestion was that it could be applied in picking stocks within an industry, for instance, airline stocks.

In early 1993 many financial analysts thought that carriers might return to profit after losing more than $10 billion in the 1990–1992 time frame. At the same time, the Clinton administration pledged help for the industry, boosting investor hopes of lower taxes and fresh financing for the airlines—as if the Federal government could afford such promises.

While these out-of-context projections are made (and not every financial analyst agrees with them), the airline industry is becoming increasingly polarized. It bifurcates into two sets:

- Big, high-overhead, slow-growth airlines and
- Smaller, low-cost, high-growth feeder carriers.

The two groups face very different challenges, giving rise to the possibility of experimenting through genetic algorithms. In America, the high-cost, slow-growth airlines include the big three names of commercial aviation: American, United, and Delta. In Europe practically all government-owned or semi-owned carriers belong in this class.

If a model is built within this context, it should reflect the fact that some airlines seek out solutions through mergers. But, as David Ben-Gurion once suggested, two wrongs don't make a right. Swissair, KLM, SAS, and Austrian Airlines planned to merge in the hope of capitalizing on economies of scale. Yet this would have created another behemoth facing increased competition from smaller rivals willing and able to establish local presence.

- Suppose that in the judgment of a financial analyst big-name airlines are due to make a comeback.
- If so, which one do you choose for investment purposes?

The classical way is to examine the time series and try to extrapolate. But, as shown in Figure 5-1 with two U.S. megacarriers, the behavior of big airlines stock has been nearly chaotic.* Can the genetic algorithm be of use?

* April 1992–April 1993.

FIGURE 5-1 There are background reasons for wide fluctuations in stock prices, the bottom line being profit and loss.

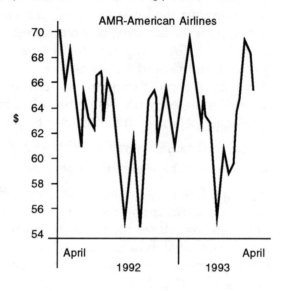

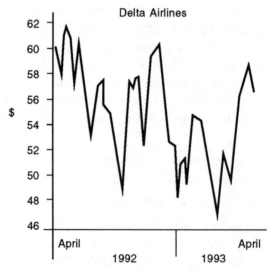

Thinking aloud, the Wall Street expert suggested that it might. The chromosomes will be carriers, and the criteria will be the way management runs the show:

- To save themselves from extinction, all of the megacarriers will make dramatic cost changes.
- The wiser ones will trim down rather than become much larger through ill-consumed mergers.

Companies that are keen to survive have no other choice than restructuring, dividing themselves into independent business units. Otherwise they will become corporate dinosaurs, rejected by the selection and mutation process of the genetic algorithm—because they will be looked down on by the market.

The Wall Street expert also suggested that as far as the selection and mutation process is concerned, the generic algorithm could be tuned to emulate the concept of quality. This process has been tried on a different occasion, where from market research it appeared that investor satisfaction is higher with companies better able than their competition to control costs.

The criterion makes sense. Low-cost airlines currently account for about 20 percent of the industry, but many observers believe that figure could double in the next 5 years as the large carriers' aggressively slim down.

- A lesson should definitely be learned from the failures of PanAm, Eastern, Braniff, and Midway, all of which went out of business in the past few years, battered by huge debts and savage price wars.
- These have been the chromosomes weeded out by the system, precisely the market reaction the genetic algorithm will emulate.

Natural selection works through a large number of iterations, the effects of which we have seen in the discussion in Chapter 4. It is nevertheless appropriate to keep in perspective that, as Dr. Stephen Jay Gould aptly suggests, "Natural selection may act as an executioner, but cannot create the fit."*

Gould uses the Hindu metaphor of the three attributes of the deity of the Hindu triad: The *creator* Brahma, the *sustainer* or preserver Vishnu, and the *destroyer* Shiva. Natural selection acts as a combination of the last two deities of the triad, but without the creative power of the first. This should be kept in mind as we talk of searching solution spaces by means of genetic algorithms.

5 THE PROCESS OF GENERATION IN FOREIGN EXCHANGE OPERATIONS

Selection and mutation in the stock market example we have looked at operates within the broader perspective of a process of generation. In mutating a simple binary number-based chromosome, for instance, the generator might flip a randomly selected position on a chromosome. The simplest crossover technique is to

- Create an initial population of chromosomes within the problem boundaries.
- Do the creating act by mutating and recombining the parent chromosomes.
- Evaluate each chromosome's performance according to stated criteria.
- Generate new chromosomes based on evaluation results regarding behavior in the population.
- Delete the least efficient chromosomes of the population to make room for new members.
- Evaluate newly generated chromosomes, inserting the best fit into the population.
- Iterate through the same loops until it is time to stop.

* *Time's Arrow, Time's Cycle* (Cambridge, MA: Harvard University Press, 1987).

In the course of this lottery system, each chromosome is given one ticket for each evaluation point it has received. The evaluator then randomly picks a chromosome and returns it to the recombiner, eventually cutting chromosomes at a specified spot and crossing over the pieces into new children.

To complete this operation, the program needs to check the population dynamics. If the appropriate number of chromosomes have been created, the generator exits the program and returns the result with the highest value as the winner.

In a real-life application, the chromosome paradigm must evidently be translated into the key variables of the environment we wish to optimize. In a foreign exchange situation, for instance, key resources are those necessary to complete a forex operation. Such resources involve:

- People
- Moneys
- Exchange rates
- Markets

One of the important distinctions to be accounted for is that existing between finite and renewable resources. A finite resource cannot be replenished. Money committed in a transaction is no longer available, but the outcome of this transaction, for instance a swaps contract, may be traded to create liquidity on which to operate.

If the trading desk does not complete all of the tasks it has scheduled before the liquidity runs out or the credit levels of clients and corresponding banks have been reached, the desk manager goes crawling back for more credit. This, too, must be accounted for in shaping the implementation of the genetic algorithm:

- Other resources can be more stringent, constituting system constraints.

- For instance, risk management requirements implied by management, to be observed at all cost.

Up to a point, forex operations resemble a scheduling problem whose goal is to optimize the use of a given set of resources for the attainment of one or more specific objectives. One of the most important elements of any scheduling problem is to decide on the *metric* in which to measure progress toward that goal. Typically, this metric boils down to some relation between *time* and *value*.

How key factors will be used within a specific model is often a function of the experimenter's skill. There may be, for instance, a dual criterion of *time* and *value*. In this context, time may involve

- The time-to-market of an off-balance sheet financial product,
- The window of opportunity in striking a deal with a counterparty, or
- Some other time-dependent criterion for evaluation of success.

Value may directly imply monetary profit and loss. For example, in a variable swaps deal the trader may strive to minimize the risk of running out of liquidity by assigning appropriate value to different deals, with the aim being to maximize the end-of-the-day profit figure.

The criterion has to be realistic and reflect market facts. In many *variable swaps* deals, for instance, every trader may want to sell, and nobody may want to buy. When this happens, there is no liquidity—and this has its impact on the appeal of the financial instrument.

The aim of implementing a genetic algorithm is not to change the specifications of a financial product, no matter how desirable this may be. At least, no projects of that type have been brought to my attention to permit me to make a documented feasibility statement.

The more widely known use of genetic algorithms is essentially optimization—a process applicable in finance as it is in the manufacturing industry. The fact that the method rests on processes known from biology makes its usage plausible. It also permits the reduction of conceptual complexity into a few processes that, however, retain the required characteristic of an inherent diversity.

6 APPLYING THE GENETIC ALGORITHM IN OFF-BALANCE SHEET OPERATIONS

Genetic algorithms can be constructed to solve financial problems in which the resources are assumed to be renewable. Each financial product (and its associated tasks) is represented by a single chromosome. Continuing with the example we started in section 3, off-balance sheet (OBS) deals may belong to either of the following classes:

1. Commitments to extend credit
2. Standby letters of credit
3. Financial guarantees bought and sold
4. Options written (sold)
5. Interest rate caps and floors
6. Interest rate swap agreements
7. Forward contracts
8. Futures contracts
9. Resource obligations on receivables sold (repos)
10. Obligations under foreign currency exchange contracts
11. Interest rate foreign currency swaps

12. Obligations to repurchase securities sold

13. Outstanding commitments to purchase or sell at prede-
termined prices

14. Obligations arising from financial instruments sold short

Each financial instrument involves one or more tasks, and
each task is defined by a commitment, a time period, a value
assignment, and the number of resources it uses to complete
itself. These definitions are clearly set by the rules guiding the
transactions.

Chromosomes are constructed so that they are a legal combination of the chosen financial instrument's tasks, where no
task is redundant. One of the aims is to capture at least a fraction
of the actual diversity that may exist in two-party agreements:

• One approach is to throw all the tasks into a task pool.

The creator randomly picks tasks from the pool, placing
them into a list of tasks and continues operating in this manner
until it has produced a chromosome population of specified
characteristics. When no tasks remain to be manipulated, the
whole list is output as a single chromosome.

• Within this pool the evaluator expands each task across
time.

Adjacent tasks are compared, to determine whether they
can execute concurrently, complementing or contradicting one
another. The *time's arrow* lies in the underlying irreversibility of
a transaction, and the unpredictable uniqueness of each deal in
a sequence of events *linked through time* in logical connection.

It is the job of the evaluator to see to it that each chromosome is judged on the basis of the time sequence its tasks are
scheduled to run. Optimization happens within the window of
opportunity or some other criterion with which the evaluator
will be provided, such as:

- A ceiling on the acceptable *risk* of the OBS transaction.
- Better *equilibration* of futures, options, and derivatives deals among counterparties.
- A *fair value* estimate connected to the deal versus the expected profit level.

Within the so-defined trading environment, once a complete population has been created, the generator produces children. Based on values assigned to the mutation and recombination operators, it randomly decides what type of generating it will further perform.

Lottery selection can be used to choose particular chromosomes for generating offsprings. With this approach, the sum of all chromosome evaluations is taken to be the range across which the lottery chooses.

- Each chromosome is given one chance in the lottery for every evaluation point it has received.
- When the random number returned is within an acceptable chromosome definition, that chromosome is selected for an operation.

This technique can be managed to assure that, as defined by the criteria, chromosomes with better competitive advantages than others are given a greater chance of regenerating.

Constraints are an integral part of the picture. In the typical case, only certain combinations of characters constitute legal solutions to the OBS problem. Hence, it would not be efficient to allow totally random mutations. Instead, either of the following are preferred:

- Position-based mutation
- Order-based mutation

With *position-based mutation*, two tasks are randomly selected, and the second task is placed before the first. In *order-based mutation*, two randomly selected tasks exchange positions. These order- and position-based strategies can be applied to the crossover techniques as well.

In all cases, natural selection plays the vital screening role. Chromosomes with the worst evaluation are deleted from the population to make room for the newly generated ones. The number of those deleted will vary depending on the operation being performed. This is a simplified description on how the genetic algorithm will work with off-balance sheet deals. Purposely, the description has been kept both generic and simple. Each task has been defined as the user of a certain number of resources over a given period of time. However, in real life a more complex model will be needed, one that is able to:

- Account for moves by the counterparty
- Allow for resources to be either shared or depleted
- Assign some tasks to precede others in terms of scheduling and execution
- Make feasible changes in resource use over the course of a given task

Counterparty moves can be reflected in the creation algorithm, and it is also possible that, in the system we aim to optimize, some of the resources can be shared across many tasks. For this reason, it will be desirable to specify the problem in such a way that the algorithm can take advantage of opportunities presented by the concurrent use of resources subject to the constraints that have been established.

7 ADAPTIVE AGENTS AND RESEARCH IN THE CAPITAL MARKETS

Many of the concepts that have been discussed in connection to genetic algorithms are applicable in the domain of microeconomics. One of the projects at Santa Fe Institute (SFI), for instance, uses artificial adaptive agents to study economic strategies evolving over time. This has a practical orientation in the capital markets:

- If we are going to invest in stocks,
- Under which conditions should we do so and
- How should we evaluate buy, hold, sell?

Classical economic theory does not pay much attention to this query; hence, answers cannot be found in a book. We have to develop computer-based models through which a number of alternatives can be tried. Can the genetic algorithm help?

According to the economics research program of SFI, adaptive agents can be profitably used in an environment of bounded rationality that permits experimentation through simulation. Mainly for training purposes, as well as to gain experience, the researchers developed a stock market simulator* able to give buy, hold, sell advice.

In the background of this model are concepts of genetic algorithms enriched with game theory, more specifically cooperative games. The stock market model forecasts stock prices, based on

- Movements in trading volume and
- Prevailing volatility.

The currently available training model uses no adaptive agents, but future, more sophisticated versions may do so. There is, however, a program, ECHO by John Holland, which is examined in section 8.

Restrictive constraints have often been eliminated because they muddy the waters. But while simplifying assumptions allows us to make easier models, they do not adequately represent the problem at hand.

* Under Unix.

An example is the failure to account for market psychology, which significantly influences the behavior of investors, creating the dynamics of buying and selling in the marketplace. Non-traditional financial research, at the Santa Fe Institute and elsewhere, aims to correct this failure.

The difference between the approach that has been chosen at Santa Fe and *program trading* is that the typical program trading construct knows prices, while the model in reference establishes an auction price. Learning algorithms have not been chosen because they were found to perform poorly in auctions. Other projects currently in the works that Dr. John H. Miller was to suggest during our meeting include:

- The use of algorithms to define patterns in DNA sequences, which can be applied in securities trading and

- The implementation of the genetic algorithm in cases where there are discontinuities, noisy data, and/or an enormous data space.

This type of work is appropriate for risk analysis with on-balance sheet and off-balance sheet financial instruments. While learning algorithms have not been chosen for the auction system, they can be instrumental in going through customer data to establish specific business and character patterns.

As Figure 5-2 suggests, a valid solution space may require multiple tools: Genetic algorithms to develop risk categories, classification procedures to group the elements in a homogeneous sense, and a grading system—possibly through fuzzy engineering—to establish customer quality.

With the exception of fuzzy engineering, the other domains are explored at SFI. Genetic algorithmic approaches are also applied in connection to

- Time series of financial data,

FIGURE 5-2   A coordinate system of tools that permits the exercise of more accurate risk management.

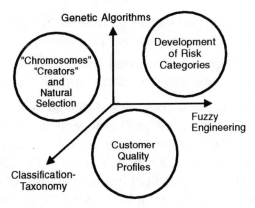

- Large cross-section analyses, and
- Non-parametric statistics.

One of the interests in these projects is building new concepts around tree structures, for instance, tree regression and genetic representation of trees. A major problem in this research is that of representation issues connected to genetic approaches.

All this effort represents non-traditional financial research. It helps us break out of standard procedures. The aim is to improve understanding without oversimplification, a process requiring new concepts and new tools.

8 INCREASED RETURNS AND POSITIVE FEEDBACK

A classification tool under development at SFI will help to create genetic regression trees, to be exploited by the genetic algorithms. This will follow the chromosome, creator, and natural selection structure discussed in sections 3–7.

As this model develops, the output of mutations, generation, and selection processes will be fed into the database with the outcome being a regression tree that provides *risk rating*:

- Risk taking and increasing returns are both complementary and contradictory processes.
- As Protagoras has asserted, there are two sides to every question, and they are exactly opposite to each other.

The model being worked out at the Santa Fe Institute can develop multiple trees, one per homogeneous financial instrument and risk classification. It then takes the outcome of these regression trees and make a new data set to be further exploited.

Though the first practical implementation of the genetic regression tree is as a learning tool with decision steps, further applications are planned with increased hands-on experience. A projected use, for instance, is for currency trading particularly featuring learning *patterns*.

The significant characteristic of this approach is a combination of genetic algorithms and regression tree structures. Another project in economics and finance undertaken by SFI focuses on *increasing return through positive feedback*. Conducted by Dr. Brian Arthur, this is basically a study of *trader behavior*.

As underlined in section 7, investor psychology is one of the fundamental factors that so far has been left out of financial modeling. This is a deficiency on its way to being corrected; it is no surprise that many of the sophisticated projects recently undertaken in economics introduce the human factor—and with it some of the 7 deadly sins like greed and avarice.

In the case of the mathematical model under discussion, the incorporation of *agents* permits us to handle issues connected to adaptability of market forces as well as of investors and traders. From there, extensions are planned to include

- Speculative bubbles and
- Market crashes.

An economic model can be realistic only if we bring into it the way people behave, hence the rising interest in simulators and heuristics constructs where human interactions matter. Brian Arthur's project is using statistical mechanics but also reasoning by analogy. This is applied to cases where information sweeps across the system.

Again at SFI, John Holland is developing a modeling platform known as *ECHO*.* It has a spatial dimension (physical and logical) with each grid point being a distinct entity able to have different properties, as the application requires.

The best way to describe ECHO is as a flexible modeling environment designed to be general purpose. In it, independent agents can interact concurrently at many sites through computer simulation. The model allows researchers to design characteristics of

- Agents,
- Sites, and
- Worlds.

The experimenters are given the means to exercise fine-grained control over the simulations they run. The aim is to provide the widest possible opportunity of gaining insights into a variety of complex systems, including economics and finance.

- The ECHO model is developed within the framework of chaos theory, which states that stems are generally interdependent.
- Relationships between values can have exponents different from classical econometrics, which assumes linear relationships between independent variables.

As this and preceding references help document, the mathematics of complexity offer a greater flexibility than the existing

* Under Unix.

linear paradigms most popular in financial analysis, which essentially become a special case of the new models. Complexity, however, carries with it a loss of certainty in evaluating the problem, as we examine possibilities in a world that can abruptly change when certain critical levels are passed.*

In the agent-oriented environment SFI is now modeling, each agent needs resources in order to exist, for instance, *financing* in the economy, or *metabolism* in a natural system. The simulator makes it possible to specify classes of agents that may evolve and engage in actions such as

- Trading,
- Breeding, and
- Combating.

Other projects focus on nonlinearities embedded in time series for economic and financial purposes. In all these cases, the underlying goal is to look for evidence of chaos—as it has been a common finding among researchers that old techniques miss an enormous amount of relevant structure therefore misleading the investigator.

9 BIOLOGICAL RESEARCH AND GENETIC ALGORITHMS

The implementation of genetic algorithms in foreign exchange operations off-balance sheet, microeconomics, and other domains of financial analysis is still in a research state. By contrast, their use in scheduling problems has been reported, and the same is true of an application of genetic algorithms in the context of biological research.

---

* We will return to this context in Chapter 8, when we speak of possibility theory and fuzzy engineering.

A new approach in molecular biology advocates that *tests of survival* can be done at an accelerated pace in test tubes. Over successive *generations*, which take days or weeks,

- Molecules adaptive to predefined conditions are developed and subjected to evaluation criteria such as screening procedures.
- It would have taken years to synthesize the same results through traditional approaches.

The accelerated test of survival strategy, which is now at an experimental stage, is seen as a new way to make biological products that could become a significant area of *drug discovery*. Use of the genetic algorithm may permit us to create genes that never existed by

- Applying generation principles,
- Rather than relying on gene splicing.

Cognizant scientists believe that the whole process can tie into the *human genome* project. They also think that apart from the theoretical issues it raises, it can also serve in many practical implementations.

Biologists and biochemists look to this genetic test of survival approach as human-directed evolution. The strategy involves survival of the fittest molecules for use in high technology drugs:

- Test-tube evolution starts with a molecule that does a somewhat useful job but doesn't do it well enough for predefined purposes.
- The process sees to it that millions of molecules are created and subjected to a test of survival in the test tube.
- Those molecules that survive by doing the wanted task somewhat better are reproduced by the millions and again put to a survival test.

This straightforward but ingenious procedure is repeated, generation after generation. Within a matter of days or weeks a few molecules evolve that can carry out the desired task with unprecedented efficiency.

To appreciate the impact the new strategy may have, it is proper to recall that drug companies currently screen *half a million compounds*, and they are testing them serially. The new process can generate *a billion compounds* and *test them in parallel*.

- This is in line with technological change, as today a *designer drug* is increasingly done by computer.

- Drug design by computer is *not* necessarily rational, because it lacks a practical infrastructure.

- The use of genetic algorithms and reproduction trees can produce a similar outcome, with the result being survival of the fittest.

In other terms, an able use of the principles of evolution at the molecular level can *speed up* the development of new drugs. It is a whole new way of doing chemical synthesis, including an application of switching theory with genetic material.

- New genes could even be evolved for insertion into cells to turn on wanted genes, or turn off unwanted ones.

- A programmable sort of applied molecular evolution could also lead to powerful new enzymes and catalysts for industrial purposes.

As is the case of the application of genetic algorithms to off-balance sheet operations, foreign exchange and stock market trading, the references being made do not mean that all necessary processes are already in place. *Molecular evolution* is far too new to have yielded any spectacular new medicines yet. Hence,

- Companies working on molecular evolution are reluctant to reveal exactly what drugs they are seeking.

- Even so, some early results start showing up and suggest the method may be practical.

At the macroscopic level, the rapid experimentation the new technique makes feasible is likely to permit testing a number of hypotheses on *co-evolution*. Flowering plants and insects, for example, evolved together. Similar background principles can be tested with financial products and markets, through the genetic algorithm technology we are discussing.

Different approaches can be taken. Instead of DNA, for example, another project is using the genetic molecule RNA, which can also be mutated into an almost limitless number of variants. This is permitting researchers to search for several drugs simultaneously.

One of the significant discoveries is that variations of RNA can be created that bind to almost any one of the hypotheses being made. One of the tentative statements is that this may as well be true of any chemical molecule.*

Still another group of biologists is using test-tube evolution to create fragments of proteins, called *peptides*. These consist of only five amino acid beads.

- The researchers can mine databases of 3.2 million such peptide fragments in a matter of hours or days.

- Such fragments become the starting points toward evolving new peptides that could work better against the target than their predecessors.

Yet another research effort aims to analyze the high volume of data on DNA base sequences flowing from the human

* The query is sometimes posed how a statement differs from a discovery. A tentative statement is part of a hypothesis and remains tentative until this hypothesis is proven or rejected. A discovery usually involves many tentative statements, some of which have been confirmed (leading to the final result) while others were discarded.

genome project. The objective is to find genes that produce proteins of medical importance.

As far as research in the frontiers of science is concerned, one of the major projected benefits from the ongoing efforts lies in the development of a methodology that might lead to a radical reduction in the need for guesswork. As an example, biologists advance the case of animal testing:

- To a large measure, animal testing is done for studies on toxicity and its aftermaths.

- The new process of gene generation and accelerated natural selection can permit to tell in vitro about toxicity.

- The rapid evolution of generations can give clues about whether a molecule is dangerous, say, to the liver, without having to test it on animals.

Reasonably enough, such studies are closely linked to computer-based experimentation. In that regard the necessary technology in now available featuring large database bandwidth and high performance computing. It can be applied equally well in biology, in engineering, and in finance.

6 Predictors, Simulators, and Artificial Life at Santa Fe Institute*

1 INTRODUCTION

The evidence provided in the preceding chapters suggests the need to use technology in order to gain competitive market advantages. This is precisely the reason why we implement intelligence-enriched software artifacts through the use of knowledge engineering and other models.

In the way the term is usually applied, a *model* is a simplified, stylized representation of those aspects of the real world appropriate to a problem we are treating. There is nothing monolithic in the construction of a model, and the process being adopted may take various forms. Typically, these range

- From a set of mathematical equations for computer processing,
- To a purely verbal description of the environment through a scenario, and
- To a set of guidelines and protocols established by procedural definition.

---

* The term *artificial life* is not the best because it gives the impression of something which is non-real, while what essentially is meant is *human-made social patterns*. In terms of terminology, this argument is as true with artificial intelligence.

In this chapter we will look into tools and financial models intended to introduce form and structure that serve primarily as an effective means of experimentation and communication. Particular emphasis will be placed on *community intelligence* as exemplified by SFI's *artificial life project*.

Developed by Dr. Chris Langton, of the Santa Fe Institute and Los Alamos National Laboratory, the concept of *artificial life* rests on the premise that most of the complex systems that occur in nature share a common architecture. The *transition pattern* which is inherent in this architecture has been nicknamed a *Swarm.**

As has been the case with the preceding chapters, the present one presents new tools for economic analysis, focusing .particular attention on the heuristics involved in the new generation of simulation projects. Once the basic concepts underlying *Swarms* have been explained, attention will be focused on other non-traditional economic analysis models.

2 THE CONCEPT OF REASONING BY ANALOGY

Etymologically speaking, the concept of reasoning by analogy has long roots that can be traced back to ancient Egypt as well as to the Greek philosophers of antiquity. What else is geometry but reasoning by analogy? In other branches of mathematics, too, the whole development of algorithmic approaches** rests on analogical thinking.

The modern manifestation of analogical approaches started with scale models, as suggested in Figure 6-1. These were

---

* Webster's defines *Swarm* as a large number or body of insects in motion; a moving crowd or throng. The term fairly well describes the sense of the project at SFI.

** Muhammed ben Musa, called Alkhwarizmi, is credited for developing the concept of algorithms described in the book on Algebra, published some time after the building of Baghdad in A.D. 766.

FIGURE 6-1   Modern analytical reasoning manifested itself with scale
models but transited to digital simulation.

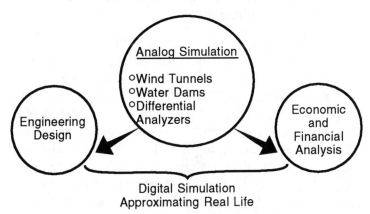

popular from 1927 to 1938. After that time, emphasis switched
toward the use of analog differential analyzers—where the term
simulation was first used—and from there to digital simulators
run on computers.

As seen in Figure 6-1, mathematical models for digital simulation have followed two main avenues of parallel development. One of them characterizes applications in *engineering
design*, and is a direct descendant of analog simulation. Engineering design is also a major contributor to a great deal of
technological progress along the line of analogical reasoning.

The other line in the development of simulators and their
underlying concepts has been *economic and financial analysis*. In
its origins we find the use of game theory, which has come
under different aspects and names, as we will see in the rest of
this section.

- Modeling is not the only aspect financial analysis and
  engineering design have in common.

- The other common aspect is that most simulators
  regard single entities, not agent interactions.

- This simplicity is no more possible with concurrent engineering and the artificial life studies in finance discussed in this chapter.

Precisely because real life requirements imposed in the engineering and in the business domains get more sophisticated, able approaches in both fields rest on the ability to sort out the existing transition patterns. This is a task demanding skill and experience, and Swarms might be a valid means of assisting the designer's hand within a given systems context.

The concepts underlying a mathematical simulator enable the model's users to exercise analytical judgment, supplementing their intuition and observing appropriate priorities. However, with the exception of Markov chains,* most models have so far addressed distinct entities rather than transition processes involving whole communities in spite of the fact that

- The construction and utilization of models addressing community intelligence can be instrumental in clarifying the psychology of financial markets.
- It also permits us to handle factors associated with an increasingly complex economic system that defies classical approaches to economic analysis.

Economic theories centered on the efficient market hypothesis, and linear models for distinct entities are of very limited use. They simply do not give the kind of information the financial industry needs in order to make real time decisions in the face of risk and uncertainty.

This statement is true even if over the years some of the classical-type econometric models have become incredibly elaborate. For instance, a simulator and optimizer developed by a New York money center bank has covered the whole world market.

* See also D. N. Chorafas, *Statistical Processes and Reliability Engineering* (Princeton, NJ: D. Van Nostrand, 1990).

While this econometric model is highly complex, its users don't seem to have a high opinion of the results it gives. The output is produced by means of 4,500 equations and 6,000 variables. Yet, none of its modules really deals with

- Social issues and
- Political factors,

even though both of them, as well as matters relating to market psychology, are often the most important variables of them all. This reference is particularly true of relations characterizing capital markets, money markets, interest rates, and currency exchange rates.

Therefore, it comes as no surprise that financial institutions that have found the limits of classical model approaches are now sponsoring nontraditional research in economics. This does not mean that past experience is thrown out. To the contrary, we capitalize on it by blending sophisticated mathematics and human ingenuity.

As Ross Perot suggested: "I think one thing I might be able to bring to bear at this stage in my life is *a keen sense of the balance between human ingenuity and advanced technology.* When the two fit together, we can avoid the enormous wastes I have seen when relying too much on technology to the exclusion of people."

3 MODELING COMMUNITY INTELLIGENCE

What has been described in the preceding paragraphs in terms of the need to reflect intelligent agent interaction is one of the basic goals SFI's Swarm project aims to accomplish by addressing collective behavior. Among the operating characteristics, for example, is the ability to map the market and its complex structure of independent agents.

The mapping of market interactions, including the social and psychological processes that underpin it, is accomplished by embedding observed transition patterns into the model. For instance, what if all traders are holding back?

- The individual agents that constitute an economy do not necessarily move at the same time or in the same direction. That's why the moves being executed are quite complex.

- Hence, the essential structure of a market model should be a collection of relatively autonomous entities with no central control but a great deal of interaction.

In a Swarm, each of the thousands of dealers and traders makes his or her own behavioral choices, based upon individual evaluation of the local environment, as well as instant and longer-term communication with other nearby or far away markets. In a free economy there is no central authority directing market behavior, and this is what is reflected in the Swarm.

As briefly stated in the Introduction, the concept of a Swarm refers to a large collection of simple independent agents interacting with each other. An example is a swarm of bees, whether in flight or inhabiting a nest. This notion of community togetherness can be extended to other systems, such as:

- *An immune system,* looked at as a swarm of cells

- *A gas,* which is a swarm of molecules

- *Motor traffic,* as a swarm of cars and of the people in these cars

- *A financial market,* whose individual agents are traders

- *A flock of investors,* seen as a swarm whose agents are investors

In terms of financial analysis, what interests us particularly in connection to community behavior is *the ability to emulate an economy as a swarm of economic and financial agents.*

The goal is to bring into the model market psychology and its undercurrents. We can do so by creating a flexible but powerful framework, using a Swarm simulator as a generalized programming tool for studying the complex behavior arising in environments consisting of many interacting components.

In transition pattern studies, simulation is used as a working analogy, which permits us to examine complex systems without actually constructing them. The resulting artifacts make experimentation feasible provided they account for the crucial factors that characterize a real life situation.

SFI's Swarms project adds value to the constructs we have been using so far. Typically, simulators are written by means of algorithms and heuristics, aiming to effectively map the real world. As we have seen in section 2:

- Whenever analogical systems are found to exist, or can be constructed, by experimenting on one of them we help ourselves study the behavior of the others.

- The analogical system on which we choose to work is simplified if we represent in it only the key variables, but this has to be done in a realistic manner.

- To make the model we build able to emulate the complex behavior of independent agents, the way they exist in a financial system, we must account for the transition patterns—hence the interest in Swarms.

Some thirty different projects at SFI and other research institutes have been identified as candidates for a successful implementation of the Swarm programming framework. A pragmatic implementation in finance and economics should proceed through the following:

- Broad as well as deep knowledge of market interactions,

- A mathematical theory making meaningful laboratory experiments feasible,

- The modeling of complex systems and their testing through feedback.

This is a far cry from the linear and not so flexible approaches developed some 50 years ago, which, to a significant degree gave good results in a number of cases. The evolution that has become necessary for competitive reasons is shown in Figure 6-2.

The modeling solutions that business and finance need today are far more sophisticated than the operations research tools we had available following the experience gained in World War II. By including psychological and other factors, our artifacts must go a long way beyond that Input/Output analysis that for more than four decades served the macroeconomic environment.

FIGURE 6-2 From linear, stand-alone models, economic analysts and simulation proceed toward dynamic and flexible artifacts.

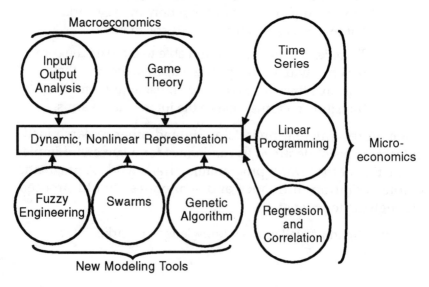

4 CAN WE REFLECT A PATTERN OF GROUP THINKING?

As we have seen through a number of examples in the preceding chapters, what is needed today in financial analysis are the ways and means to effectively serve investment advising and portfolio management services. A similar statement can be made regarding trading in forex, futures, options, swaps, and other derivatives. The tools at our disposition should:

- Help to identify individual investment objectives
- Provide realistic forecasts
- Make feasible that financial services are professionally managed
- Permit experimentation on plans designed to meet a dynamic market response
- Reflect the behavior of a changing, 24-hour economy
- Support ongoing customer management expertise centered on personal services

Meaningful results require both the ability to map the market into the computer and to support personal investment profiles—individual goals, expectations, and other factors necessary to establish a financial policy, from selecting a portfolio to its steady optimization.

The goal of forecasting market behavior through *community intelligence,* as is the case with Swarms, is to provide an analytical infrastructure permitting the maximization of returns while reducing the risk relative to investment objectives. As economic conditions, financial instruments, and most importantly market psychology change, the investment mix has to be managed to reflect not-so-clear goals and evolving market conditions.

The chosen approach must incorporate market dynamics in an effective manner, distinguishing itself from earlier rather static analogies. What makes the issue of *transition patterns* particularly important is that even if individual traders exhibit simple behavior, their collective behavior can be highly complex.

- By illuminating the point at which individual simplicity becomes collective intelligence, Swarm theory makes it possible to focus on the *fundamental roots of complexity*.

- In modeling the concept of *community intelligence*, attention is paid to what constitutes keynote characteristics of markets.

The adopted solution underlines the fact that finance and economics call for deductive, logical analysis and provides a means to reflect upon *group thinking* without resorting to hierarchical modeling. Hierarchical modeling would be unfit for the treatment of free markets.

As the SFI researchers stressed during our meeting, financial markets tend to behave like an ant colony. Thinking by analogy, traders can be seen as agents such as ants or birds in a flock. By simulating Swarm behavior, we bring a flexible sort of *flock coherence* such as that existing in nature, hence the underlying concept of artificial life.

"You cannot have life unless something is cracking up," says an ancient proverb. "Living and dying are phases of the same process and they require a balance." Transition probabilities reflect on market behavior between

- The chaos and order prevailing in the markets
- Making profits and taking the risk of losses.

Such processes can be effectively modeled through a transitional pattern. This is what the mathematics underlying Chris Langton's Swarm algorithms try to do. Such an approach conforms to the fact that an ordinary population of simple agents following equally simple rules of interaction can behave in surprising ways.

We are still a long way from understanding life's behavior and most particularly how societies form and their agents interact. The aim of projects like the one we are discussing is the use of analytical thinking in emulating a population of agents in such a way that their behavioral dynamics are alive in a modeling sense.

Responding to such objectives requires expertise and skill as well as a technology that permits to augment the brain's conceptual capabilities. In a way, artificial life is analogous to artificial intelligence—but there is as well a difference:

- Instead of using models and computers for thought processes,
- We use them to model the basic biological mechanisms of evolution and life itself.

Chris Langton has another idea distilled from the research he is doing, the possibility that life is not "just like a computation." Instead, he suggests, *life literally is a computation*. As in antiquity, it is still difficult to distinguish philosophy and science. In fact, they belong together.

5 USING SUPERCOMPUTER POWER TO FACE PROCESSING REQUIREMENTS

In the sense that has been discussed in sections 3 and 4, the Swarm model resembles what is done with the genetic algorithm as well as with taxonomical classification systems. At the same time, by addressing community intelligence it is more broad-ranging and ambitious, as we will see in this section.

Artificial life is Chris Langton's brainchild. He invented the name and spent most of the past decade trying to articulate the concept. Current and projected applications areas include the following:

- Economics and finance
- Building an artificial cell of the stock market
- Autonomous adaptive robots
- Transportation systems
- Issues of evolution and coevolution
- Studies in geopolitical stability
- Simulating long-term global change
- Self-assembly at the molecular level

The latter project relates to the origins of life, but also extends into domains such as synthesis of drugs, actions of antibodies, and other related studies. These are the domains we discussed in the last section of Chapter 5.

The goal of some of the aforementioned research topics has been to produce a proof of principle that other projects can carry to higher levels of sophistication within a specific applications domain. An example is building Swarms of artificial insects to study autonomous adaptive robots.

Correctly, the SFI researchers design their artifacts to be portable on many different computer architectures, as well as to work over a heterogeneous network of databases and work stations. For speed and performance they can be run on massively parallel computers.

Massively parallel computers make possible the fast execution of a large set of algorithms that can only be handled serially by conventional processors. This means slowly and with great difficulty. But because parallel programming languages are still in evolution, for applications efficiency we must face a number of design and implementation issues.

Within this perspective, SFI's Swarm project is now elaborating working models for evaluating behavior and performance on a parallel computer,* under varying conditions in

* In conjunction with Thinking Machines, the manufacturer of CM-2.

transition patterns. Also planned are formal methods allowing comparisons among different machines.

Since there is no assurance that with the parallel processor version the code will be portable among different machines, a shell has been developed, known as the Swarm Simulation System (SSS). To meet with market success, this shell will have compilers on the parallel computers of different vendors.

From the conceptual aspects of the Swarm transition paradigm to its computational needs, the project must satisfy a number of objectives. From a technical viewpoint, the most important issues are to:

- Obtain the best algorithm with the maximum parallelism, in order to represent the solution space
- Simplify the task of mapping a large number of agents for parallel programming
- Use previous experience to generate the coordination and synchronization tasks for concurrent execution.
- Address a variety of data structures stored in incompatible databases
- Select the best system architecture, tuning it to real-life situations.

Seen from this computer-oriented perspective, parameters such as interconnection topology, number of processors, clustering, mapping, scheduling, and routing strategies must be properly addressed. Such requirements are present in parallel systems but not in serial design approaches, as those followed in the past with the old mainframes.

The message conveyed by the list of prerequisites the foregoing paragraphs have outlined is that with models involving transition probabilities, parallel computation is at a premium, but algorithmic solutions on parallel computers include a number of prerequisites that go beyond the beaten path of processing on mainframes.

The degrees of freedom and the much greater speed gained through parallel computation have as a counterpart greater demands posed in the sense of architectural selection for a given application.

- To approach the associated problems in an able manner,
- An integrated environment for parallel processing must be conceived and implemented.

Attention should be paid to the fact that transitional patterns must have maximum parallelism not only in computing but as well as communications—for input and output problems. Measurements of the ratio between the computing time in a set of processors and their communication time with other processors are needed to establish the granularity of the adopted solution.

Given the computational requirements imposed by a model on transition patterns the best possible implementation of a Swarm system would be through a parallel object-oriented programming language that

- Runs on massively parallel computers and
- Exploits distributed deductive databases.

Computational requirements and objectives speak volumes about the need to properly identify the mathematical and logical issues involved in a Swarm solution. This is particularly true when one of the aims is to develop a shell that can be used in an agile way in modeling swarm conditions.

The general form of the Swarm Simulation System, of which we spoke earlier in this section, is projected to be distributed, concurrent, and object-oriented. Users will be able to specify behaviors of individual agents, for instance, stock traders, making up the Swarm whose dynamic interaction must be described through a programming language able to:

- Specify the properties of the physical environment in which the swarm is embedded

- Define the initial state and distribution of values in that environment

- Proceed with the experimentation and *visualization* of the simulated results.

From data collection to visualization, the aim should be to put all end users in a position to run the simulation interactively, altering the rules, states or arrangements of individual agents. Users should also be able to affect the environment, as the experiment or runtime implementation requires.

6 SWARMS AND SYSTEMS WITH FEEDBACK

A free market is characterized by *feedback*, which means that two channels exist carrying information, such that one channel loops back from the output to the input of the other, or main channel. This can be instrumental in control systems and generally in processes having to do with regulation.

The feedback channel transmits some portion of the signals emitted by the main channel, as is shown in Figure 6-3. These signals come from monitoring the output of the principal, forward channel. Typically, the transmitter is a device with two independent variables:

- The signal to be transmitted forward to the next elements in tandem

- The signal that is fed back, whose mission is to decrease the strain resulting from any error or deviation in the main channel.

Using an established criterion for comparison, the reference signal indicates the state of the output of the main channel,

FIGURE 6-3 A free market is characterized by feedback, which permits a process of regulation to take place.

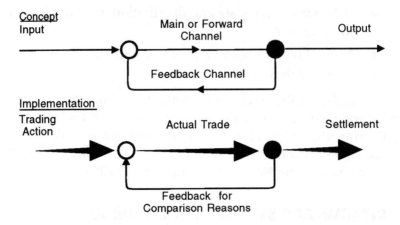

which the system seeks to keep steady or under an established control procedure. This provides monitoring of the output of the main channel on the basis of *actual* rather than expected performance.

In all systems, natural or human-made, forward and feedback signals have a certain probability of *error*. Feedback signals may differ in the time lag they require to affect the system. Such lag is kept minimal so that each feedback signal is fed back to the input of the main channel before the next signal is transmitted.

The word *error*, John von Neumann once suggested, has been used and misused in many cases, with different and often contradictory meanings. In information theory, *error* is viewed not as an extraneous and misdirected event, but as an important, integral part of the process under consideration. In this sense, its importance is fully comparable to the other intended and normal critical factors of an operating system.

Feedback processes have an evident implementation in the financial markets, and their usage can also have a number of aftermaths. If the feedback lag is long, several signals may be transmitted *before* the results of those preceding them arrive to affect trading decisions. In this manner,

- A trader is out of touch with the market.
- Even a whole financial system can get out of control.

Feedback signals differ in their gain or extent of corrective effects. When they are fed back from the output from a steady state, we talk of *positive feedback*. If the signals are reversed, so that they decrease the deviation of the output from a steady state, the operation is characterized by *negative feedback*.

- Positive feedback can alter key variables and destroy the steady state.
- In a systems sense, negative feedback helps in maintaining the steady state.

These concepts are as applicable in finance as they have been in engineering. A negative feedback cancels an initial deviation or error in performance. Hence the importance of the feedback loop as a necessary method for the correction of errors.

Such considerations are part and parcel of *cybernetics*, the study of methods of feedback control, involving interlocking processes with transmission of energy and information. SFI's artificial life project supports a cybernetic feedback system.

Designed to attenuate deviations that can have detrimental effects on the emulated processes, a key element of the Swarm model is the provision of a *feedback loop* between objects and structure. This supports the artificial life pattern that transits between

- Stability,
- Instability, and
- New stability.

The algorithm in the background of this service is expressed in similar terms to those in *ecology*. Indeed, ecology is used as an analog of the emulated industrial and financial systems.

Ecological analogues can be revealing. For instance, between 1950 and 1970 there was a stable ecology of GM-Ford-Chrysler dominating the American automarket. Then Japanese imports came massively into the picture, destabilizing the relatively steady state of the U.S. market for vehicles.

Not only the design of the environment we emulate, and its component parts, should feature feedback in a real-life operational sense, but this concept should also be extended to include feedback from the overall model. This calls for incorporating

- The evaluation of the results of computation and
- The critique of the scenario and its planning factors.

Through feedback, the developer has a chance to revise early judgment and thus to improve upon the state of the artifact. This statement is true for all modeling processes as well as for all financial and industrial studies. Today only the more sophisticated projects observe feedback requirements, Swarms being one example.

7 COMPETITIVE ADVANTAGES OF AN ECOLOGICAL APPROACH

The competitive advantage of the ecological approach we have discussed in section 6 is that it permits building simple models as well as gaining insight about how these models work. However, a number of problems pop up when we put an artifact into practical application:

- Its steady development all the way to implementation requires a great deal of joint work, specifically involving end users.

- Both before and after implementation there should be real-life evaluation of results, and appropriate correction.

- To make the experience really worthy in a dynamic sense, a system must be provided for adaptation of parameters.

"Only when we have a better feeling of the theory that covers the dynamics can we construct the applications areas in a realistic manner," suggested Christian Langton. "Hence the development of theory and the evolution of practical applications go hand-in-hand."

The work Langton has done has benefitted from the transition probabilities developed by the late 19th century Russian mathematician Andrei A. Markov, who invented a method of statistically predicting the sequence of letters as they appeared in Pushkin's verse novel, *Eugene Onegin*.

Markov Modeling, as the method is known, has worked so well in a number of projects that the National Security Agency used it to crack codes. Applied to speech recognition, it offers a crucial shortcut:

- Once the algorithm identifies the first phone in a sequence, it can narrow its search for the next by statistically calculating which sounds are most likely to follow.

- Coping with a large range of possible words still requires millions of calculations for each, a reason why speech-recognition programs originally required large computers.

Similar transition probability concepts can be used with social and cultural transmission. As far as theory is concerned, the leading thinking is that biological and cultural evolution are simply two aspects of the same phenomenon: *The genes of culture are beliefs*, which in turn were recorded in the basic DNA of culture, which we call *language*.

- Along this line of reasoning, current efforts in artificial life are trying to capture *evolution* in the same way that artificial intelligence captures neuropsychology.

- The aim is not to exactly mimic the evolution of the reptiles, but to lead to an abstract model of evolution that can be mapped into the computer.

The assistance such a model can provide is in helping in the performance of experiments regarding a diverse range of systems, from engineering to economics. The SSS shell, which has been introduced in section 5, has this notion in the background.

The motor power behind this concept is the drive for discovering important new ideas that can assist in developing new computational techniques. From one discipline to another, SFI researchers look at this issue in this way:

- There are parallels in the way modeling is done by first-class minds; hence, we can learn a great deal by studying their patterns.

- Another common trait is that in a cooperative world a project can only be successful if it integrates many different skills.

A large number of these skills have to do with advance aspects of information technology—emulation, analogical reasoning, and feedback being among the most fundamental. To a very large degree, life is based on its ability to process information—both in the sense of storage and computation.

Natural systems, for example, usually make complex transformations of available information to produce action. As the English biologist Richard Dawkins once suggested, if we take a rock and toss it into the air, it traces out a nice parabola, obeying the laws of physics.

The rock can only make a simple response to exogenous forces, which can be described in an equation. But emulating a living organism's behavior is much more complex than that.

In addition, the same laws of physics prevail all over the planet Earth. But the laws of humans are different from place to place, and the same is true of the way markets behave. Organizations are made of people and peoples' behavior is not the same from one place to another—or even within the same place.

A paradigm can help explain this concept. The same physical forces that affect a rock are certainly acting on a bird, but the bird also has a lot of internal information processing going on, which makes all the difference in terms of its responses:

- Living organisms simply do not do what inanimate matter does.
- Inanimate matter is just reacting to simple forces, such as gravity.
- By contrast, the dynamics of living organisms are dominated by information processing, and this is influenced by many factors.

In an attempt to reflect on the dynamics, Chris Langton looked at the phenomenology of computation, and he has been able to uncover the existence of many analogies. The challenge is to map these analogies into an emulator of living systems, which the Swarm project tries to do.

In a way, artificial life is the inverse of conventional biology. Instead of being an effort to understand life through analysis—dissecting living communities into species, organisms, organs, tissues, membranes, cells and molecules—the main effort is to understand life by *synthesis*.

That is why so much effort is directed to putting simple pieces together to generate a lifelike behavior in human-made systems. The underlying premise is not a property of matter per se, but *the organization and behavior* of that matter.

- The operating principle is that the laws of life must be laws that can only be expressed in a dynamic form.

- A generic form would be independent of details of a particular carbon-based chemistry that happened to arise on Earth four billion years ago.

By exploring other possible biologies through models and computers, Swarms researchers hope to achieve what space scientists have done by sending probes to other planets, that is, a better understanding of our own world through a wider perspective.

For these reasons, the concept underlying the Swarms project revolves around the goal of delivering access to ideas and tools. Benefitting from this development is the user organization, which, however, has to be active in putting into practical implementation the output of the researchers' brains. The work on tools cannot be proprietary. The proprietary work should be done at the applications level in specific financial models to be built.

8 PROBLEMS AND OPPORTUNITIES IN DEVELOPING PREDICTORS

Prediction Company was incorporated in September of 1991 by Dr. J. Doyne Farmer, Dr. Norman H. Packard,* and Jim McGill. Its goal has been to apply nonlinear mathematical methods of prediction to financial markets. The firm develops advanced algorithms and computer software for use in predicting the future movements of selected financial instruments.

- The mathematical technology is based on relatively new developments in the field of nonlinear analysis, combined with more traditional quantitative techniques for money management.
- The prediction technology currently being elaborated and employed has many potential applications, but a

---

* Both Farmer and Packard are on the faculty of the Santa Fe Institute.

main focus is on the global markets for derivative instruments.

As we have seen in Chapter 5, derivative financial instruments are securities whose value is a function of other values as well as of related underlying variables. Examples are options, futures, swaps, and forward contracts as applied to stocks, bonds, commodities, indexes, and currencies.

One of the projects on which Doyne Farmer and Norman Packard are working is a *liquidity predictor*. The artifact has been developed by means of nonlinear approaches for tracking

- Cash,
- Current assets, and
- Current liabilities.

The mathematical tools being used are generic and, therefore, can be employed in connection to a variety of financial instruments. The chosen methodology works by analogy to the treatment of data in models developed to study fluid turbulence. The reason for this choice rests on the fact that

- The underlying nonlinear equations give a better predictive performance than do purely statistical techniques. Hence,
- Deterministic equations assuring an underlying strange attractor (deterministic chaos) have been used in handling complex cases.

If this implementation of chaos theory has been successful with predictions regarding a trading environment, can it be used with risk management? In evaluating profit and loss? In helping to better focus risk management?

The answer, of course, is nonlinear, so it cannot be given through a simple "yes" or "no." It is influenced by a number of factors that affect the outcome and, therefore, the accuracy of the response. The following are the three top of the list criteria:

- The use of dynamic models in mapping global risk management criteria into market behavior and trader actions.

- The analysis of commitments on-balance sheet and off-balance sheet by counterparty, financial instrument, and trader desk.

- The ability to process market information in real time, including trade feeds and access to distributed databases.

While all three issues are hard to accomplish, the third is the most difficult. The current state of the art in banking technology would not support it—either for global risk management or for the evaluation of profit and loss. "Everyone wants realtime with P+L," Doyne Farmer said. "But none has it. The best they have is the cash position."

Furthermore, each asset type has its own rules. In estimating exposure and P+L, for example, the Chicago Board of Trade has a matrix of market positions that changes in function of the transactions taking place. A change in a given position affects other positions in the matrix. But other exchanges follow different approaches in handling this type of information.

Why are truly real-time solutions the exception? "We are surprised how unsophisticated the accounting of even the most advanced financial companies is," suggested Norman Packard. "Yet every major institution knows that with 24-hour trading it practically does not close its books. It has to maintain them online. Only fictiously the books can be closed offline."

9 THE FINANCIAL INDUSTRY'S ACHILLES HEEL

It may sound ludicrous that after all the billions of dollars spend on computer technology, and the thousands of people who work on systems, computers and communications are a bank's Achilles heel. Yet plenty of evidence helps in documenting that this is exactly what is happening:

- Few of the data processing projects done since the 1950s have been focused.
- Many have rested on old and rusty organizational structures.
- For 40 years, the opportunity to revamp the bank's internal mechanism has been lost.

This amalgam of old programs written for batch processing is what is typically referred to as a *legacy system*. It is still around impeding advanced computer applications in spite of the fact that the dynamic market of the 1990s calls for a great deal of product development and innovation in banking. It is estimated that by the year 2000, product development cycles in the financial industries

- Will be *measured in weeks or months*, not in years.

This has already happened with some financial products such as derivatives, but as it is getting generalized we must create new organizational philosophies to tap the full potential of emerging markets. We must also create new and much more efficient technological solutions.

It is not enough to develop and use models able to operate at the edge of chaos. The whole infrastructure needs revamping. A parallel computer-based infrastructure and the models we construct will become an integral part of

- The new landscape in an era of *customized production* and *online distribution*.

Today, as the majority of financial institutions have found out, effective product variety and relationship banking cannot be maintained because of crumbling structures. Such a situation cannot be permitted to continue. Relationship banking

- Must not only be courteous and friendly,
- But also innovative and accurate.

Understanding the needs of the clients and meeting them in an efficient manner is the job of account executives who have to be supported by sophisticated models, distributed real-time computers, and any-to-any communications.

Many financial institutions are aware of these requirements but few are taking the necessary action. Since many banks today continue being profitable, their management tends to think it does not have to have perfect systems to make a lot of money. Profits are coming anyway.

This definitely is the wrong approach. The strengths and the weaknesses of management, and of the system underpinning the company's functions, are not seen when business goes well and the market bends over to deliver profits. But they become gapping holes when

- Business turns sour,
- Losses mount, and
- Loss exposure gets out of control.

This is the time that separates good from poor management, and where a valid technology can serve as lifesaver to the firm. The interest in developing prediction models that permit insight and foresight in intraday trading through a focused data analysis is closely associated to this requirement.

As Doyne Farmer and Norman Packard were to underline, classical models and statistical tools based on time-honored concepts such as the normal distribution do not help because trading data does not fit these concepts. Clear-eyed analysts have demonstrated that there is

- Noise in the time series
- Delays in data acquisition, or
- Plain unavailability of relevant information.

Not only the Prediction Company but also some of its competitors are working on ways and means to overcome these limitations. A major degree of attention is placed on risk management—not only the daily exposure problems but also the necessary mathematical infrastructure to help avoid catastrophic failures in case of crash.

With derivative financial instruments, the control of risk level is an integral part of prediction models because the contract is stated on risk level, not on account size. That is how it was found in an analytical manner, for example, that holding "running day" deals at the desk level is a real problem.

Running day deals can be handled more effectively through networked independent business units. Hence the concept of *federated organizations* which cutting-edge financial institutions are elaborating, and some have already implemented. As Figure 6-4 demonstrates

- *Federation* should not be confused with *decentralization.*
- In a decentralized scheme the peripheral units work by delegation from central command.
- By contrast, federation is *reverse delegation* with the center playing a coordinating and balancing role.

The mathematics of complexity are powerful tools but do not perform miracles. A financial institution that wants to get ahead has to provide flexible organizational solutions that make rapid response to market forces feasible.

In terms of implementing high technology, federated solutions have the additional advantage of making the underlying mathematics less complex. When the model gets above a small

FIGURE 6-4 Decentralized and federated organizations. Federation provides for flexibility and timeliness.

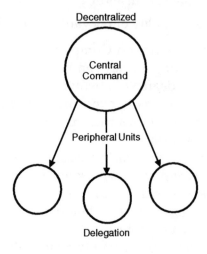

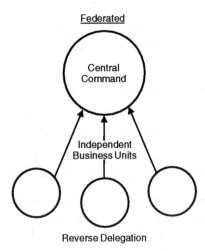

number of variables, the problem becomes immensely more complex. This sees to it that it is not really possible to predict the market, no matter how much we talk about forecasts.

Such a statement is particularly valid in cases where there is no smoking gun—an *evident reason* that created an abrupt change. Such cases are most appropriate for applying chaos theory. The problem with networked financial markets working 24-hours a day is that none knows how many variables there are:

- Millions of people are involved directly or indirectly in transactions.
- The system features hundreds or thousands of variables that change rapidly.

That is why chaos theory is important in economics and finance, but there are also limits. If we have a system of, say, 3 to 6 variables we can still understand it the classical way. When we are faced with hundreds of interacting factors, classical theory is powerless. But besides the new mathematics, we also have to pay full attention to the good quality of the data.

In conclusion, chaos theory and nonlinear mathematics are of assistance but should not be thought of as able to solve all *prediction* and *control* problems. Events such as the crash at the New York stock exchange of October 1987 and the August 1991 invasion of Kuwait happen to be notoriously difficult to predict:

- They are based on psychology rather than logic and
- Strictly mathematical approaches are not going to deliver results.

The difficulty of predicting catastrophes and scouting major breakdowns is not limited to the world of financial markets. In America, the Electrical Power Industries Research Institute (EPRI) is very actively studying prediction problems associated with breakdowns of power grids.

7 Non-Traditional Financial Analysis at MIT

1 INTRODUCTION

Experience from science and engineering documents that abstractions are an important tool for learning as well as for problem solving. Modeling helps not only in thinking by analogy but also in gaining insight into the objects and processes we wish to study:

- Thinking by analogy permits a significant degree of experimentation.

- But a better understanding of background and foreground factors can be just as valuable or even more important.

That much has been explained through the examples in the preceding six chapters. Particular attention has been paid to the mathematics underpinning chaos theory, the use of nonlinear predictors, fractals and the genetic algorithm.

While a good deal of the work presented in Chapters 5 and 6 is carried out by scientists associated with the Santa Fe Institute, this chapter focuses on non-traditional financial analysis at the Massachusetts Institute of Technology and other places. Many of the concepts are similar, but the tools being used are not the same.

Like the models at SFI, MIT also employs simulators but the implementations domain is more oriented toward time series analysis. The aim is to analyze market results in order to establish which factors gave rise to given phenomena in the marketplace.

- Sophisticated users of the MIT model will gain the most because they know what they are after and the order of magnitude of the results they should expect.

- The MIT model targets the means for moving smoothly between levels of complexity, particularly those that allow novice users to become experts as they gain confidence in the method.

But as with all efforts in simulation and experimentation, the key to successful application of the results of the MIT research in finance and economics is understanding the computational model at each level of its complexity.

The user of algorithmic and heuristic approaches such as those we will see in this chapter will experiment with the model of the real world to effectively explore the adaptability inherent in market systems. But the more mature user will focus on models that stand at phase transitions, and will be able to understand how adaptation can drive a system to regions of complexity.

2 MIT RESEARCHERS TURN AWAY FROM MODERN PORTFOLIO THEORY

The premise on which the recent research projects in economics and finance at MIT rest is that markets do not behave according to models implied by the Modern Portfolio Theory. Just as the financial analysts as SFI, MIT researchers believe that the efficient market hypothesis has not proved valid, hence the drive for new models that more accurately characterize the financial markets.

The need for more accurate approaches to the mapping of market behavior is particularly felt in connection to managing risks in terms of global finance. The dynamic nature of global markets requires the effective design of algorithms and heuristics that can do the following:

- Accommodate the fundamental empirical features of price dynamics in financial transactions.

- Facilitate the decomposition of global portfolio risks in a definable and controllable way.

- Forecast risks inherent to transactions, at least within certain ranges.

Along this line of reasoning, MIT has undertaken an exploratory and descriptive statistical analysis project with the objective of establishing the most critical empirical features of price dynamics. Four stock indexes are being used: Standard and Poor's 500, Nikkei Average, Frankfurt Commerzbank, and Paris CAC-40.

Another goal of the project is to address dollar-based foreign exchange rates for the home currencies of these four markets, namely, dollar, yen, deutschmark, and French franc. Returns series are studied individually, through univariate analysis, and together by means of multivariate approaches.

A basic hypothesis of the research effort at MIT is that while expected returns are essentially random, or more precisely consistent with simple random-walk models, return volatilities exhibit other characteristics:

- Nonlinear dependence in univariate series, suggested by significant autocorrelations of squared returns

- Volatility spillovers between markets, more specifically in multivariate series like those currently being studied

Multivariate characteristics are particularly connected to the world market. The MIT researchers have also found that there are cross-market linkages in volatility, which become significant with the degree of dependence increasing during periods of high volatility.

These results parallel those obtained from other projects in non-traditional research, whether done at SFI, other academic institutions, or by the leading banks themselves. If we wish to characterize in a few paragraphs the common ground these different projects establish among themselves, this can best be done by distinguishing between

- The simpler linear models characterizing classical analysis in economics and

- The new approaches aiming to reach at the heart of the complexity of market systems.

One of the key differences between complex and simpler approaches to financial analysis is that the former exhibit interesting characteristics of *adaptability*. A valid definition of adaptability is the ability of a system to respond to a variety of constraints with minimal changes in its structure.

- While it is not entirely clear that adaptable constructs and natural systems are necessarily complex,

- The process of adaptability itself has a number of complex characteristics—if for no other reason that until now has not been so well understood.

Theoretically, the complexity of two systems could be compared by writing two models capable of reproducing the original data streams. This is equally valid with natural and with human-made constructs. It is also true of the data streams such systems produce or represent. Say, for example, that

1. One time series is a daily count of the number of transactions at the New York Stock Exchange during many sessions and

2. The other set is the number of foreign exchange operations by the money center banks in New York.

Can we compare the algorithmic complexity of the data streaming out of these two seemingly unrelated processes? This is one of the objectives the MIT project in non-traditional financial research has taken on. The No. 1 and No. 2 data stream are in no way independent of one another. In reality they are highly interactive—as a great deal of forex transactions are the result of trading financial products.

In fact, if I understand correctly, this closely knit interaction between stock market and foreign exchange processes is one of the prerequisites Bankers Trust has set in financing the MIT effort. Every financial institution should take notice of this reference, which evidently adds to algorithmic complexity but is also a prerequisite to sound financial models.

Many problems stand in the way of measuring algorithmic complexity, and this is even more true in the sense of developing a practical tool for studying complex systems. As we have seen in a number of cases, to face the challenges we need techniques that are much more sensitive to randomness than to order—because this is the way most financial systems typically work.

3 VOLATILITY AND THE ASYNCHRONOUS NATURE OF FINANCIAL DATA

Financial research findings at MIT indicate that effective risk management tools must account for volatility dynamics using continuously updated feedback and associated forecasts. A crucial step is to acknowledge the *asynchronous* nature of financial data and to derive the appropriate consequences from this observation.

- Work on the predictive measures regarding volatility is accomplished with data from Bankers Trust.

- Emphasis is being put on applying modeling techniques to measure daily risk, in a well-defined, focused sense.

Fundamental to this research is the analysis of the behavior of pricing mechanisms, evaluating whether or not existing theories fit the market behavior as reflected in the asynchronous financial data stream. Two significant findings have emerged:

- *Exposure and risk* must be studied over short time periods, such as a couple of hours of holding a deal.

- *Volatility* affects the pricing of interday options as well as their trading.

The approach used in deriving these conclusions was characterized during the meetings as non-traditional, contrasted to the bulk of the work now being done on closing market data. By all indications provided by this advanced research project, closing market data may well be meaningless.

As we saw in Chapter 1, according to Patricia M. McGinnis, the executive director of MIT's International Financial Series, the key question to keep in mind is what you can find out by analyzing transactional data. As the project under her control helps document, the analysis of returns services of individual transactions exhibits volatility clustering, with such clustering being stronger in the equity markets.

During periods of low-to-moderate market volatility, the autocorrelations of both the return series and squared-returns series increased. The implications of these findings is as follows:

- For risk management tools to be most effective, they must account for volatility dynamics with continuously updated forecasts.
- Volatility models for forecasting should exploit structural features of price movements.
- A dynamic approach is yielding forecasts that perform better than methods assuming time-homogenous static features.

Members of this financial analysis team at MIT suggest that multivariate perspectives help to address market linkages, both within and between equity and currency markets.

Contemporaneous cross-correlations have been found to be strongest in the actual returns series of currency markets. Another important finding is that the strength of cross-market linkages increases during periods of high volatility.

Within this frame of reference, the MIT project has addressed money markets and forex operations. It has also examined in significant detail the stochastic models that may be applicable. The analytical results obtained tend to underline three needs:

- Bringing *management's viewpoint* on risk control under a global focus
- Differentiating between strong and poor *reflectors* of risk in a portfolio
- Providing for common *scaling* for the integration of different risks

The researchers working on this project looked for robust, resistant techniques regarding assumptions on the nature of statistical distributions. They approached modeling more flexibly through non-parametric statistics and neural networks, but also underlined the need for a large amount of data—if possible, free of noise—as being a crucial element.

4 TRYING TO VISUALIZE MULTIPLE VARIABLE DATA

The raw data used in the non-traditional financial analysis at MIT consists of daily prices and rates from January 1986 through July 1990. These are the closing prices for the indexes and the nominal spot exchange rates for the currencies, in countries and exchanges mentioned in section 2. There has been no adjustment for dividends in equity indexes.

Emphasis on dynamic volatility evidently calls for addressing the robustness of volatility measures. To fulfill this requirement, the project has explored alternative measures based on percentiles of the distribution of returns. The project focused on

- The dynamics of multivariate volatility/risk and
- Accommodating the significant multivariate and intertemporal stochastic features.

Exploiting their existence was thought to provide enhanced risk-management tools. The study of existing interrelations between market and multivariable volatility led to a covariance matrix of a basket of currencies. The results of this study can be more generally applicable and are thought to be important to

- Money markets,
- Equities, and
- Bonds trading.

Trying to visualize multiple variable data has, however, proved to be a very challenging problem. Therefore, based on the experience they have acquired, the MIT researchers suggest that to obtain results, we should be quite clear on a number of issues, top-most among them:

- What exactly we are looking for
- What we want to measure
- How we are going to measure it
- Which markets we are specifically addressing.

As the MIT project helps document, the degree of correlation among markets varies, depending on their volatility. This provides *a road map for shifting exposure*, if the responsible risk manager has the necessary tools for focusing on the visualization of multiple variable data.

One of the current sponsors of the MIT project has asked the researchers to determine the amount of cushion necessary in liquidating a portfolio and the reserves needed to face risk when one or another investment goes down. A preliminary investigation has indicated that this requires

- The study of market discontinuities and
- The calculation of financial staying power.

Another basic conclusion based on the results of the project is that stochastic nonlinear models are a much better approach than the traditional type of economic analysis. They also provide a much better basis for the effective visualization of the obtained results.

Notice that this statement somewhat contradicts what the projects at the Santa Fe Institute have found, where the conclusion has been that deterministic nonlinear models are preferable to stochastic ones. One of the reasons for the difference might be in the background of the people who are doing the financial analyses:

- Physicists at SFI
- Statisticians at MIT

Where the two research institutes concur, however, in their findings is on *the need for powerful tools to help in coping with vagueness and uncertainty in financial markets*. Both projects point to a different type of data analysis than classically done for financial services, and both suggest:

- Non-traditional methods, including chaos theory
- Algorithms for nonlinear solution space filtering

Early attempts of applying chaos and fractals in finance were not very successful because the physical laws are not in the background, suggested Professor Peter J. Kemptborne and Dr. Alexander Samarov during our meeting. It was further explained that how to define *risk* in the financial market depends on:

- The perspective of the executor—that is trader or senior manager, and
- The level of aggregation being addressed in the calculation of risk.

This research project found that financial returns are typically unimodal and nearly symmetric, regardless of the frequency of observation, for instance, monthly, weekly, or daily. Their distributions are *leptokyrtotic*, which becomes more evident as the frequency increases.

Leptokyrtosis is the condition of a probability distribution that has fatter tails and a higher peak at the mean than the *normal* probability density curve.

- Wealth, for instance, follows a leptokyrtotic distribution because it is self-reinforcing.
- The fat tails of markets imply that the more the trend is in one direction, the more it persists.

One of the reasons for fat tails is that many investors wait until they see a price trending upwards to buy an asset. They therefore tend to reinforce trends.

But leptokyrtotic models also affect the common means of measuring market volatility, because volatility models depend on the standard deviation as a measure of risk.

- The more leptokyrtotic a curve is, the more misleading the notion of a standard deviation.

- The calculation of statistical measures is skewed by the latest price changes.

There are many ways in which a leptokyrtotic feature of the returns distribution can arise. One rather common explanation is that the returns series obeys certain non-normal probability density characteristics. The other possible reason is that the returns process is consistent with time-varying diffusion for price dynamics.

This finding has been interpreted to mean that very high and very low returns are much more frequent than would be expected if the time series arose from a stationary geometric diffusion model for price behavior. The latter model is generally known as the random walks approach.

5 AUTOCORRELATION, CHAOS, AND VOLATILITY

The MIT project developed autocorrelation displays of foreign exchange rates for the four currencies mentioned in section 2. No significant autocorrelations were detected for currency return, which was interpreted to mean that they are linearly unpredictable. The study that has been accomplished so far at MIT further suggests that applying the random walks approach to exchange rates has some negative implications.

- Under random walks, shocks to exchange rates have no tendency to be reversed. Over a given time period the variance would grow without bound with the length of the time frame.

- Since the returns are linearly unpredictable, structural endogenous linear modeling and forecasting of exchange rate fluctuations would not be useful.

Evidence of nonlinear dependence in stock and currency returns has been found by a number of other financial research projects. Nonlinear dependence means that the optimal predictions of future returns is a function of more than linear functions of the past returns—such as weighted averages.

Such nonlinear dependence can be modeled by specifying the functional form of the expectation, variance, or higher-order moments in connection to historical data. The MIT project, for instance, established that, for predictive purposes, the crash of 1987 in the U.S. stock market is best mapped through a squared equity returns series.

For stock indexes, quadratic autocorrelations proved to be highly significant. The evidence that the dependence among squared returns is much stronger than among actual returns should be kept in mind to guide the researcher's hand in similar projects. Let's repeat the sense of that meeting:

- For *stock returns*, the nonlinear dependence is stronger than the linear dependence. This is evidenced through the higher magnitudes of correlation results.

- By contrast, for *exchange rates* the resulting correlations of the squared returns was found to be less significant, hence, not as effective a predictor.

During the working meeting at MIT, an *options* example was also considered. "Typically with investments we take discounted cash flow. But this cannot be applied with options," the researchers suggested. *Options and derivatives need an analytic approach able to measure potential value of holding the asset or liability.*

With options, the model should treat the valuation in a way that reflects the specific nature of the business and of the financial product. This concept comes out of thoroughly analyzing results obtained from evaluating autocorrelations within a single series. It dominates both

- Stock index returns and
- Currency returns.

As a consequence, the hypothesis has been made that some of the significant cross-correlations in the returns series may be due to asynchronous openings and closings of the financial markets around the world.

Correlations in the squared returns series would similarly be affected by staggered market periods. Another result was that the squared returns series exhibited significant cross correlations at higher lags, suggesting that changes in market volatility are persistent rather than spurious.

The project also found that during periods of *higher volatility*, correlations between different markets increase. This can be interpreted as transmission or spillover of volatility across markets, a so-called *contagion effect*.

As a result of these findings, the hypothesis has been advanced that *increases in volatility can be self-reinforcing*, similar to a physical resonance effect. Furthermore, they can persist for longer periods than would otherwise be expected. There is evidence of increased correlations between stock markets during high-volatility periods:

- *If* the distribution of returns is thought to be non-Gaussian,
- *Then* such distribution cannot be simply characterized by first and second moments and the associated time dynamics of those moments.

Such findings call into serious question the current practice of defining volatility in terms of standard deviations and covariances. It also suggests that much more of the information contained in the entire return distribution needs to be captured in order to obtain an effective redefinition of volatility and its behavioral pattern.

6 THE CONCEPT OF RISK AND CUMULATIVE EXPOSURE

As the research by the International Financial Series research project at MIT has demonstrated through the study of price behavior in the financial markets, covariance has much to with risk calculation. This seems to be particularly true in connection to off-balance sheet financial instruments.

Figure 7-1 shows two graphs both centering on off-balance sheet profit and loss. Respectively, they express risk as a function of time and cumulative exposure:

- The upper graph is plotted against *time* and market behavior—and it seems to be chaotic.

- The horizontal axis of the second graph is a compound function of *cumulative exposure* and of time (t).

Cumulative exposure is a factor that gains considerable weight in non-traditional financial research but has never been examined seriously in the past. This speaks volumes to the gaping holes that exist in classical economic theory, particularly to what concerns forecasting.

The MIT researchers suggested that plotting data in terms of *cumulative exposure* rather than time alone can give a curve that is smooth and analytically exploitable, and more likely to forecast within limited bounds, like t_1 in Figure 1. As highlighted in the preceding chapters,

FIGURE 7-1   Risk as a function of time and of cumulative exposure in financial environments.

A. Time Series For P+L With Off-Balance Sheet

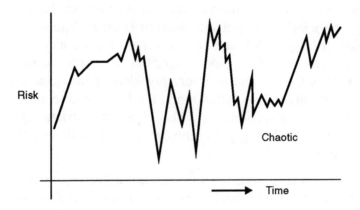

B. Expressing In Function Not Of Time But Of Cumulative Exposure

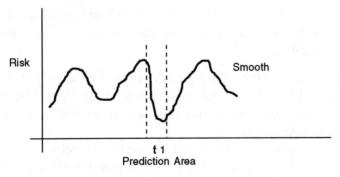

Cumulative Exposure f (t,(x,y))

- With chaotic systems the horizon is not very far.
- Smoothing helps to make the pattern more predictable.

Academic research not only at MIT but also at Princeton and other universities has found major weaknesses in the idea that only financially relevant information is taken into account in market pricing. As we have seen, this has been a major argument both with the use of the genetic algorithm and with Swarms.

One of the interesting issues revealed by financial research at leading universities is that market indexes tend to avoid closing exactly on levels ending with two zeros. Markets fight shy of, say, a 1,500 closing price; they retreat a few times and then leap over it:

- This is evidence favoring an inductive argument that there really is such a thing as a *psychological barrier* for a market.

- Like the psychological barrier, *seasonality* is also a piece of formerly unscientific market thinking that keeps making its presence felt.

- The same can be said of a number of market *sensitivities* the foremost financial institutions are now keen to explore.

Another result of the MIT research project has been that the serial correlation between returns changes with volatility, but in the opposite way. The autocorrelation of returns is quite high when the volatility is low.

This finding is interpreted to imply that returns are more predictable during periods of low volatility, though a difference between the financial markets has also been found—that is, from one stock exchange to another:

- Tokyo was found to be most sensitive to volatility spillovers.

- New York and the European exchanges were only moderately sensitive.

- In particular, New York is less sensitive to volatility spillovers than the other markets.

These and similar results provide evidence that new modeling and estimation techniques are needed to adequately describe and forecast volatility in multinational currency and equity markets. Such outcomes makes a compelling case for a new definition of volatility, as well as for more powerful volatility modeling paradigms.

Among the modeling paradigms suggested by the MIT researchers are heavy-tailed marginal return distributions, volatility dependent autocorrelation, and cross-correlation of actual returns, as well as tools exhibiting dependence on volatility as reflected in squared returns and the ability to model shocks—that is *outliers.*

These findings further underline the need for building nonlinear models for the exploitation of financial time series, which tend to have non-linear dependencies. The following are some of the tentative conclusions of the project in reference:

- The *variance can be more predictable than the mean,*

- Benefitting from *chaos theory,* nonlinear models offer more dependable results.

- Further research should examine financial time series through *fractals.*

The MIT researchers, however, have some reservations about how much current tools from complexity theory are ready to contribute to the process of financial analysis. They underlined the need for theoretical breakthroughs in finance and economics before algorithms and heuristics from the natural sciences can be used effectively.

Chaos has been successful in physics because it is a science that deals with non-noisy data, which is not the case in finance. Where chaos theory has relevance in finance, it was suggested during the MIT meeting, is its ability to examine the influence of

- Initial conditions and
- Butterfly effects.

Similarly, with long-memory time series there may be advantages with fractional differencing, hence, the likely applicability of Mandelbrot's fractals theory.

Dozens of projects are now running in America in this domain, but the results have not been widely communicated. Those that do not appear particularly successful have found difficulties with the noisy data existing in finance.

Therefore, one of the leading hypotheses concerns the ability to filter noise through heuristic models and high performance computers such as MasPar, Connection Machine, and Intel's parallel supercomputer. The MIT researchers consider this to be one of the most important projects of financial research during the coming years.

7 WHY LOGISTICS EQUATIONS NEED MEMORY SYSTEMS

As we have seen on several occasions, from the Santa Fe Institute to MIT and other universities, researchers in economics and finance reject the Modern Portfolio Theory and the hypothesis of efficient markets. They think that both concepts are misleading, and just as ill-advised as the use of linear models to express the dynamic reaction of the world's financial markets.

If this line of thinking is valid, and current evidence suggests it is, then which algorithms can help in identifying profit opportunities over a period of time? Some financial analysts suggest genetic algorithms, others fuzzy engineering, still others the logistics equation we will examine in this section—after a brief reminder of the weaknesses inherent in the efficient market theory.

By *efficient markets*, few economists mean that the price of a stock or of a currency—that is, its exchange rate—actually reflects true value. Most economists use the word *efficient* to describe a market in which the price reflects all known information. This is the basic concept now being challenged.

- If the efficient market hypothesis were valid, there would have been no opportunities to profit from real time availability of market information and the use of sophisticated models.

- In an efficient market, future prices will change only as the market discovers entirely new opportunities.

This is not, however, the case. As the *inefficient market* hypothesis suggests, which is currently spoused by most advanced financial research projects in America, there are profits to be made by exploiting the many market inefficiencies. Therefore,

- Attention is now paid to the development of algorithms that are able to unearth such inefficiencies, suggesting ways to capitalize on them.

- Emphasis is placed on online real time exploitation of databases, with database mining for discovery purposes and capitalization on market opportunities.

Both issues are judged to be vital to a bank's future competitiveness in financial markets, which are more demanding than ever. Starting with the algorithms, one of the models used for this purpose is the *logistics equation*—which is sensitive to *time variance* as well as *nonlinear effects*.

The concept of *logistics equations* has been introduced through a relatively simple model in Chapter 1, though the equations we have used were not named in that way. From the simple example we have considered with reference to foreign exchange rates, we have seen a number of important characteristics that affect nonlinear dynamic systems.

The power of the logistics equation lies in the fact that, while it is a relatively simple and understandable model, it can exhibit a wealth of behavior on the edge of chaos. This includes a transition from orderly to chaotic patterns, as exemplified through the following example. In the algorithm

$$Z_{(t+1)} = f \cdot Z_t \tag{1}$$

the factor "f" varies as a function of the distribution that prevails in the system. Depending on its value, the outcome is disturbance characterizing conditions encountered in financial markets that move at the edge of chaos.

What is different from the approach presented in Chapter 1 is the notion that the value of "f" can also be conditioned by *memory*, in the sense of influence of past events. This introduces the concept of the influence *a memory system* can have in finance:

- Though presently there is no reason to believe that nature has memory, such a tentative statement has meaning with natural not with human-made constructs.

- Organizations are made of people, and people have memory—if nothing else, the most ingenious capitalize on past experience.

- Other human-made artifacts, in fact including organizations, have computer-based memory to which we usually refer as a *database(s)*.

Figure 7-2 shows an organizational structure with components that help provide fast response to market challenges. Such a structure must reflect the growing need for powerful algorithms, heuristics, and databases in a coexistence scheme with legacy applications. If the latter are the only support, then the solution is one-side, ossified, and inefficient.

FIGURE 7-2 Efficient answer to market requirements has many sides that should integrate into an aggregate.

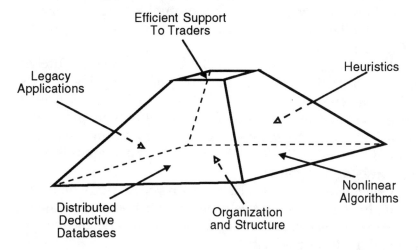

Notice the key role played in Figure 7-2 by distributed deductive databases. As a memory system, they are a logical and physical construct whose state can currently provide information concerning:

- What happens and has happened in the world that is external to this memory system (reflected in *hard data*)

- Prediction algorithms aiming to extend this information toward a time different than the present (*soft data*).

Based on these two references, a valid definition of the memory system is a means of *ferrying information from one moment in time to another*, coupled with the possibility to exploit the differences:

- In its current state, t_0, the pattern in the database provides information concerning the state of the world.

- This includes the value Z_t as well as much of the information we need to compute "f", which subsequently helps in the projection.

A hypothesis regarding the future will be so much more valid if "f" has been properly defined and expressed in mathematical form. This is why a number of studies have investigated the relation between the various aspects that characterize the different arrows of time.

In areas that interest financial markets, such as foreign exchange operations, for example, many of the ongoing projects in financial engineering assume that *the psychological arrows of time* derive from the thermodynamic arrow of time, practically the second law of thermodynamics.* No rigorous mathematical proof of this connection has yet been offered, though it is gaining increasing acceptance.

One interesting issue a Harvard University study on financial analyses suggests in this connection is that market inefficiency may persist because traders and investors devote too few resources to dealing with it:

- Though huge amounts of money move to and from the forex market, most trades are quickly unwound.

- By contrast, the profit opportunities identified by Harvard arise over long periods of time.

To make money by capitalizing on these findings, the investor needs a memory system and the appropriate algorithms. Short of an exploitation of market opportunities through high-performance computers, traders and investors will have to tie up money for months or even years—an eternity for forex dealers.

8 CAPITALIZING ON COMPUTER STORAGE AND AGILE ALGORITHMS

There is virtually no subject in finance that cannot be viewed under the magnifying glass of algorithms, heuristics, and com-

* See Chapter 2 on entropy.

puters. Though there is still much to be done, such as accounting for the psychological factors often dominating the markets, the concepts and tools we have today can offer impressive results—but few financial institutions effectively exploit them.*

A study published by the Santa Fe Institute** postulates that *without* reducing the psychological arrow of time to a mathematically well-defined phenomenon,

- There is no way to rigorously prove or disprove a relation between the psychological arrow of time and the thermodynamic arrow of time.

- We need mathematically defined connections able to map the human ability to remember the past.

It is presumed that there is really no aspect of the psychological arrow of time that cannot be explained by the asymmetry of human memory. The SFI study further shows that the asymmetry of human memory is a direct reflection of the asymmetry of the second law of thermodynamics. If this hypothesis is retained, it helps explain why the future is both

- The temporal direction into which information is dissipated (which is to be expected due to the second law) and

- The direction into which information is preserved through our ability to remember the past.

The implication of this analysis is that if the second law went the other way, then the psychological arrow would point toward the past, not the future, as far as human response is concerned. In contrast to natural systems, however, the study in reference demonstrates that

---

* As will be demonstrated in section 9.

** David H. Wolpert, *The Second Law, Computation and the Temporal Asymmetry of Memory* (Santa Fe, NM: Santa Fe Institute, 1992).

- Computer memory need not be directly affected by the second law of thermodynamics and

- Databases can be used with proper artifacts to infer the future as readily as they reflect the past.

This is an important finding because it indirectly postulates that databases, and therefore human-made constructs, do not necessarily need to abide by the laws characterizing natural systems, even if they emulate, complement, or replace them. Such emulation, for instance, happens in the case of databases.

The SFI study postulates that, in principle, databases possess no psychological arrow of time. This is, however, a weak statement because computer memory can be enriched with *sensitivity factors* to emulate a psychological arrow.

If we look back at equation (1) in section 7 and expand it into a more complex, nonlinear logistics equations such as the quadratic (which we have studied in Chapter 1), we can put to profitable use the arrow of time:

$$Z_{(t+1)} = f \cdot Z_t \cdot (1 + Z_t) \tag{2}$$

The function "f" can be calculated through memory-stored values. For instance, it can be extrapolated but also interpolated; inducted, deducted, or abducted (Bayesian hypothesis: If A then B).

By massaging the time series, the values taken by "f" can lead to a stable or unstable system. The former will be characterized by attenuations; the latter will be subject to amplification as a function of time. But the values "f" takes can also represent a process of bifurcation eventually leading to chaos.

- Figure 7-3A has been plotted on the basis of a logistics equation with a fluctuation between two values acting as limiting conditions.

- Figure 7-3B illustrates a large number of possible values eventually leading to a chaotic situation.

FIGURE 7-3 Bifurcation in a logistics equation with two and many possible final values.

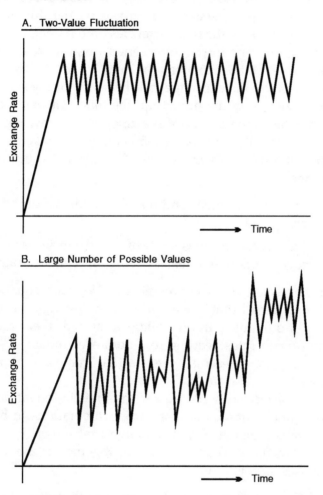

A. Two-Value Fluctuation

B. Large Number of Possible Values

Exchange rate fluctuations within the former Exchange Rate Mechanism (ERM) of the European Union are an example of the graph in Figure 7-3A. In general, exchange rates tend to fluctuate more widely, but sometimes international agreements keep them within preestablished margins.

Since the countries to which they belong were members of the ERM until July 1993, the exchange rate of the Deutschmark and the French franc was characterized by the fluctuation in Figure 7-3A. If one of the two currencies hit the floor, the reserve banks of the two countries intervened to support it; and the same was true if it tried to break the cap.

By contrast, the exchange rate behavior of the dollar and the yen—like that of the dollar and the mark—is better characterized by the large number of possible values shown in Figure 7-3B. Notice that if small enough time ranges are taken, the fluctuation will tend to resemble that of Figure 7-3A, but outside these ranges,

- Foreign exchange conditions approximate the edge of chaos and

- Can switch to chaos if one of the currencies is hit by severe inflation or features very high interest rates.

To appreciate the uses to which the logistics equation can be put, let's recall that it was originally developed to model population dynamics. In an ecological system there are birth rates and death rates, leading to a nonlinear model of growth and decay. This represents a system that may have more than one possible steady state.

This is precisely what makes the logistics equation valuable in financial market studies, from fluctuations to bifurcations. Mitchel Feigenbaum has shown that the critical points where bifurcations occur come closer together as the value of "f" increases. In this way

- The system proceeds from order to disorder,

- But it does so in a way which, in the background, reflects some regulation.

The research Feigenbaum conducted led to the proposition that this rate of drift toward disorder is constant and is universal for all parabolic nonlinear systems. The value of "f" that causes bifurcation tends toward 4.6692—called Feigenbaum's number F. It allows us to predict when the next critical level of "f" may arrive.

9 BANKERS TRUST POSITIONS ITSELF FOR GREATER COMPETITIVENESS IN THE MARKET

A well-chosen and properly implemented information systems strategy must support powerful algorithms and heuristics but must also support distributed, diversified, heterogeneous databases. This is the lesson to be retained from the discussion on research results presented in this chapter.

An effective solution will integrate all of the facilities offered by the most advanced segments of the computer industry with financial analysis and economics research centers. The architecture chosen for the 1990s should provide well beyond the old legacy chores—which are no longer competitive in the context of banking automation. Instead, the two focal points should be:

1. Networked distributed real-time systems able to create fully interactive databases beyond weeding out paperwork

Database mining, data stream filtering, and non-crisp queries seem to be three of the priority issues to which current research interests are addressed. The necessary infrastructure is expressed through the block diagrams of Figure 7-4, which emphasize some of the important input and output characteristics.

2. Nonlinear mathematics and fuzzy engineering research tuned to make a steady extension of the frontiers of financial analysis feasible.

Based on this principle, Bankers Trust has not only engaged in its own premises projects, focusing on the development of nonlinear models for financial analysis—particularly in the trading area—but also sponsors prediction projects at leading universities.* But unlike other financial institutions, it takes an active role in the research it sponsors, all the way

- From planning
- To evaluation, and
- To technology transfer.

Planning, evaluation, and technology transfer are three processes that converge in terms of the solutions being sought after. An example is what Bankers Trust calls *straight-through automation*, executed in an input/output sense by the end user, without the computer specialists' intervention.

- The results of this drive co-involving the end user, are impressive.
- Today 85 percent of transactions at Bankers Trust are processed without manual intervention, and the share is increasing.

The coinvolvement of end users is not limited to the bank's own personnel. It also involves the bank's customers in integrative applications. Such wise strategy rests both on agile software and the online use of workstations through *intensive customization*.

"Through the use of technology we can produce customized solutions at the cost of mass production," suggested Dr. Carmine Vona, executive vice president for Worldwide Technology. The goal is to drive down costs of incremental processing, and this is done through knowledge engineering.

The principle underlies this strategy can be expressed in two short sentences, which as a management policy constitute a very good advice:

---

* For instance, the MIT project on non-traditional economic and financial analysis, which we have seen in this chapter.

FIGURE 7-4 Non-traditional approaches to input and output requirements connected to computer systems.

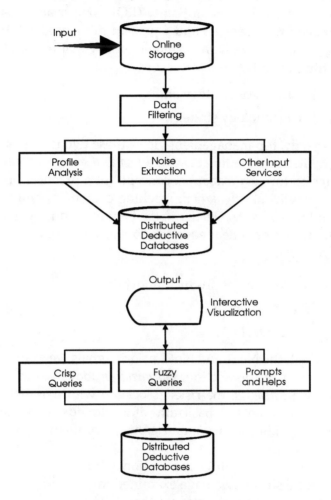

- If you do not have capital but have good people, good people will create capital.
- If you have clients and capital, but no good people, you are on your way to losing both.

The emphasis on human capital and its steady development in no way diminishes the profitability criteria Bankers Trust uses. Today, Return on Equity (ROE) stands at 25 percent, as contrasted to between 5 and 6 percent in the mid-1970s. The turning point was a new management policy that required careful resetting of both

- The business strategy and
- The technology strategy.

Correctly, top management views these two issues as highly interrelated and leading toward a *financial services architecture*. Such architecture is no abstract concept but a practical proposition that begins at *origination*: reaching customers online anywhere in the world. The leader in the banking industry not only needs to master nonlinear equations but also the following:

- Globalization
- Acceleration of product innovation
- Risk management
- Cost control

Through the No. 1 and No. 2 priority goals we examined in the beginning of this section, *globalization* looks worldwide to get money and hedge the risks associated with currencies and financial instruments. A basic aim of worldwide networking is to provide global positions, and enhance profitability through hedging power.

Accelerating product innovation requires the advanced mathematical studies we have examined in this and the preceding chapters. A wise product strategy is to package risk management expertise, then sell it to other institutions. Helping other banks diversify the risks they are taking in their wholesale and retail dealings creates an income stream.

8 Using Fuzzy Engineering in Financial Environments

1 INTRODUCTION

The goal of prediction theory is to generalize from the information elements we know and apply that generalization to those whose pattern we are trying to learn. This is the general problem of *induction*. The challenge is how to put the known procedures into effect when financial systems are dynamic and their output presents discontinuities as well as uncertainties:

- *Uncertainties** occur when we are not absolutely clear about the information elements at our disposition.

- The degree of certainty is usually represented by a *quantitative* value,

- By construct, most problems encountered in finance are *qualitative*.

The background reason for *fuzziness*** is that the boundary of a piece of information is not clear-cut. Expressions such as

---

* Webster's defines uncertainty as the quality or state of being uncertain. An uncertain issue is something not exactly known; not determined, certain, or established; a contingency.

** Fuzzy is something not clear or blurred; involving vagueness and uncertainty.

"more or less," "roughly equal to," "somewhat greater than average" are examples.

In some situations *uncertainty and vagueness* may occur simultaneously. Such situations have in the background inexact knowledge, unreliable information, differing opinions, and/or the inability to express a given concept or piece of data in quantifiable terms.

Precisely because of vagueness and uncertainty embedded in financial problems, not every mathematical tool can serve prediction purposes—nor can even the most sophisticated analytics be applied in every situation:

- A polynomial fit that oscillates wildly between data points that appear to lie on a smooth curve will be a bad choice for predictive reasons.

- A tool that presupposes crisp* data or situations will not answer the challenges posed by vague conditions involving a significant measure of uncertainty.

The basic idea underpinning *fuzzy engineering* is that the entire domain of possible observation and associated values can be characterized by both fuzzy and crisp characteristics. Figure 8-1A shows three crisp measures for expressing a given dimension. For instance, the metric 2 stands for small, 4 for medium, and 6 for large. By contrast, as seen in Figure 8-1B, with fuzzy dimensions

- *Small* varies from 1.0 to 3.5; the closer to 3.5, the less possibility the side is small.

- *Medium* varies from 2 to 6, but the highest possibility is at dimension 4.

- *Large* starts at dimension 5, and the possibility is equal to one at dimension 6 or greater.

* 0 or 1 type.

FIGURE 8-1   Crisp and fuzzy functions in expressing size, from small to medium and large.

A. Crisp Measures

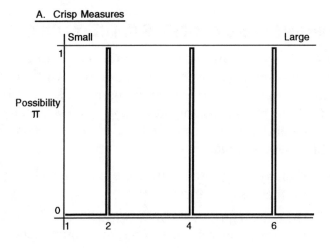

B. Fuzzy Measures

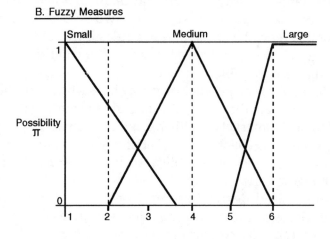

As this example demonstrates, a given domain such as dimensions or measurements can be subdivided into a number of subsets that usually overlap—hence the fuzziness characteristics. The importance of such functions is that they are very close to real-life data in financial markets and, therefore, in capturing the market's pulse.

2 IMPLEMENTING CONCEPTS IN FUZZY LOGIC

Fuzzy logic is working with uncertainties. Though we can always use some certainty factors in an artifact, there are no crisp boundaries, as we have seen in Figure 8-1B. The model we make is characterized by the amount of *impression* into which uncertainty and vagueness are embedded. This is very close to a real-life financial situation:

- There is a degree of truth in the statements being made, but there is also uncertainty.

- The reason for possibilistic expressions is due to inability to calculate crisp measures, or incompleteness.

The large majority of mathematical models available today in the financial industry are based on two-valued logic. In systems of this type, the action part of a rule either holds completely or not at all, depending on whether the conditional part is fulfilled or is not fulfilled.

No matter how popular they may be, such approaches cannot accommodate the concept of diagnosis regarding the behavior of financial markets. Neither can they express prescriptions to be provided to client and market problems. What is needed is multivalued degrees of possibility, such as the example we have seen in Figure 8-1B.

Multivaried degrees are most important not only in the case fuzziness but also in responding to unforeseen situations, which are typically complex and cannot be handled by means of probability theory. What is the difference between *probability* and *possibility*?

- Probability theory synthesizes a body of *precise* and *differentiated* knowledge.

- Possibility theory reflects *imprecise* but *coherent* elements, which mutually confirm themselves.

This is quite similar to the fundamental notions we have examined with chaos theory.* As you will remember, chaos has in the background an orderly process, though when we move at the edge of chaos events are practically unpredictable.

Probabilities are better suited to *physical processes*, such as those we examine in engineering, in chemistry, and in physics. Possibilities serve in a more accurate (but imprecise) manner in the treatment of *logical processes*—encountered in finance and generally in management—which, however, must be characterized by coherence.

A treatment of conditions at the edge of chaos, and therefore containing unforeseen situations and incomplete information, calls for representation and processing based on multivalued logic. In such a domain, actions can hold with many different even fuzzy degrees of possibility.

- This brings into the picture the so-called *certainty factors*,

- Though *uncertainty factors* would have been a better term.

Drawn to answer a query posed by tourists, Figure 8-2 expresses degrees of water temperature in the French Riviera during the month of May. Notice that the *certainty factor*** increases from 15°C to 17°C. In fact, it goes from *zero* certainty to *one*, but it does so with a slope.

Based on past experience, the flat curve prior to 15°C indicates that there is no likelihood the water temperature is less than 15°C. Other significant observations are that

- A water temperature of 17°C or 18°C (or any value in between) has the same possibility equal to 1 and

* See also the last section on fuzzy functions, genetic algorithms, and fractals.
** Which in Figure 8-1 we called *possibility*.

FIGURE 8-2   Expressing the variation in water temperature through possibility theory.

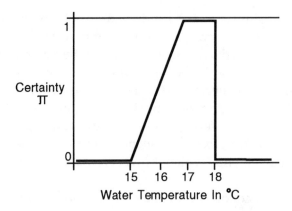

Water Temperature In °C

• There is no evidence the water temperature in that region can be more than 18°C.

It important to observe that 18°C is a limiting condition and can happen with a possibility of 1, 0 or any fraction in between. In other terms, 18°C is true and false at the same time.

One of President Truman's biographers writes that having made the statement: "I am looking for a one-armed economist," Truman was asked what he meant. "I want a consultant," Truman answered, "who would not give me an advice and immediately thereafter add: 'On the other hand . . .' "

That is precisely how experts in economics and finance evaluate the market's behavior. Both a given event and its antithesis may be just as likely to occur, depending on initial conditions and other factors. This is similar to our example where the possibilities that the 18°C water temperature happens and does not happen may be equal.

Fuzzy logic can be three-valued, multivalued, and infinite valued. Using the models this approach makes possible, many more financial observations can be considered as evidence for a given diagnosis than is ever the case with two-valued crisp approaches:

- In the case of a crisp answer, only conclusive evidence can be accepted, in the form of a *yes* or *no* response.

- Among other shortcomings, this results in reducing the amount of evidence on which a market diagnosis can be based.

Many examples exist where fuzzy logic can be valuable in handling unforeseen situations in the financial markets. One example is in the concurrence of anomalies. The superposition of any degradation in data streams recorded within a given market system leads to what in the preceding chapters we have called *noise*:

- Many financial analysts fail to appreciate that noisy financial data can be handled better through fuzzy sets due to the multivaried logic's ability to recognize concurrent anomalies.

- In turn, this permits significant contributions to diagnosis, and therefore helps in avoiding a breakdown of the prediction system, by reducing its certainty.

Such estimations of possible anomaly superpositions can be an invaluable asset to the definition of test runs on financial time series as well as to research done through simulators to conclusively identify the system's state. They could also provide the basis of deeper reasoning in conjunction with the heuristics driving sophisticated *quantitative models*.

3 FINANCIAL ANALYSIS THROUGH FUZZY SETS

The typical computer programs today written for purposes of financial analysis are useful in applications that require or presuppose precise data. Fuzzy engineering artifacts are designed to deal with a more realistic world in the financial markets—where there is noise in the time series, information cannot be manipulated so precisely, and judgment or evaluation can be only approximate.

By employing fuzzy logic, a financial analysis program has a much greater chance of *accurately* following a perception of the situation prevailing in the real world. This has been properly exploited by Japanese researchers in the banking and investment industries, for instance, Nikko Securities and Yamaichi Securities in collaboration with the Laboratory for International Fuzzy Engineering (LIFE).*

The concepts underlying the implementation of fuzzy engineering are not altogether new. At least in terms of methodology since the work on analogical reasoning done during World War II, we have a sound theory based on mathematical statistics but supporting a three-valued logic:

- Accept
- Continue testing
- Reject

Such a theory can nicely be used by iterative search process. As we have seen in section 2, fuzzy logic can be three-valued or multivalued, in contrast to the binary computer and the way programs have been classically constructed.

Bankers Trust, for example, has very successfully used the three-valued "Accept, Continue Testing, Reject" model in connection to loans. Known as Risk Adjusted Return on Capital (RAROC), this important piece of software permits reflection on the uncertainty present in any loan, subsequently monetizing them through a higher interest rate—rather than following the dry process of accept/reject.

* Of Yokohama, Japan. LIFE is partly financed by MITI and partly by investment banks, commercial banks, and manufacturing industries.

Multivalued approaches permit us to amplify the boundaries of hypothetical reasoning, a process that is very important in financial analysis. They do so by introducing tools for handling knowledge that is

- Uncertain
- Incomplete
- Nonlinear, and
- Works by default.

Typically, any reasoning mechanism oriented to the analysis of market data and associated predictions will incorporate an amount of *uncertain knowledge*. Because we are not able to handle non-monotonic logic and default logic through classical tools, we have often resorted to oversimplifications by weeding uncertain knowledge out of the system altogether.

By contrast, fuzzy engineering provides a multivaried logical framework for hypothetical reasoning. This permits developing *unifying concepts*, which leads to better constraint satisfaction. It also makes using search algorithm for *multiple contexts* in databases feasible.

Along this frame of reference, Japanese researchers are carefully considering the practical use of fuzzy engineering in conjunction with financial problem solving, from diagnosis to prediction and optimization. Typically, these projects are non-traditional research and utilize domain-dependent knowledge, including:

- *Deep knowledge*, such as description of structure and functionality,
- *Common sense* knowledge, as exemplified by physical laws, and
- *Constraints* connected to the conception, generation, and testing of hypotheses.

Figure 8-3 gives an appreciation of the procedural approach being followed in this work. Fuzzy engineering permits the maintenance of multiple contexts, including inference control, effective search techniques, and interfacing between the truth maintenance and the problem solver—adapting to the financial domain being investigated.

Within the procedural perspectives that have been outlined, fuzzy functions can be used to emulate both logical and physical phenomena. Say, for instance, we are devising a trading strategy for buying bonds for an investment portfolio:

- We make the hypothesis that the strategy should depend on whether it is a low- or high-volume day.

FIGURE 8-3 Using knowledge engineering to conceive, generate, and verify hypotheses in financial analysis.

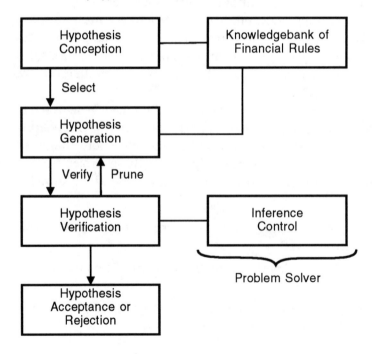

- For this case, we can define fuzzy subsets corresponding to the vague notions of *low* and *high*, expressing these subsets in terms of fuzzy volume figures.

This can be effectively done in the way in which it has been done in Figure 8-2, using water temperature as an example. Subsequently, we can plot these configurations using a belief function, as will be explained through specific examples.

4 ADVANTAGES FROM THE IMPLEMENTATION OF FUZZY ENGINEERING

One of the advantages of using fuzzy functions as an abstraction for real-life data is that all aspects are expressed as parameters with a meaning which can be intuitively obvious. This gives significant power to the structure of the model into which these fuzzy functions are being mapped.

A second advantage from the implementation of fuzzy engineering in a financial analysis context is that *possibilistic mathematics* make additive functions feasible, a process not doable with probability theory. A third advantage, is that solutions can be formulated with graphical representation, all the way to visual programming:

- This helps us visualize both the behavior and the trade-offs necessary in connection to a given problem.

- Graphical presentation is a highly individual matter, but it is also a powerful tool.

The fuzzy diagram with the overlapping "small," "medium," and "large" conceptual boundaries explains the meaning of this reference. In the majority of business operations, both the data included in the larger set are fuzzy and the boundaries of the subsets are not sharp. Hence, classical probabilistic or deterministic tools will be suitable neither for representation nor for calculation. What is needed is

1. A tool able to represent non-crisp values, and to map the vagueness and uncertainty involved in a given situation.

2. A function that transforms points in the wider domain set we are studying into points in a more limited, manageable range set.

The role of the second function is to *defuzzify* the fuzzy set by means of appropriate fuzzy engineering tools. We will see specific examples with the valuation of securities. Defuzzification is crucial in obtaining the functional values with which the financial analyst is able to work.

What the foregoing paragraphs express in terms of financial analysis is no different from what happens in other scientific fields. Classical science was born in the 17th century based on the laws and the discoveries of Galileo Galilei, Descartes, and Newton.

- It grew through the great scientists of the 18th and 19th centuries, who interpreted in their own way the canons of antiquity, particularly those of Aristotle.

- In the process of its evolution, classical science has been to a very large extent finite and deterministic. Hence, it is no wonder that this is the case with traditional financial analysis.

But is this suitable to the handling of situations characterized by complexity in a market more competitive and more demanding than ever? Present-day markets require sophisticated assumptions as well as fuzzy valuation models. An example is the expected prepayments on a portfolio of loans assuming various future levels of interest rates.

While simplified assumptions may sometimes be used by a bank to give a reliable estimate of fair value of its portfolio at a reasonable cost, this often proves to be inadequate when large

sums of money, cross-border deals, and multicurrency investments are involved. We have to account for fuzziness in estimating market value, a process that must reflect

- Changes in market value due to changes in overall
  general interest rates and
- Changes in market value due to cash flows affected by
  market premiums for credit risk and market risk.

In the United States, for instance, the Financial Accounting
Standards Board (FASB), keeping ahead with technology, is currently working on extending the contingent chains theory
through fuzziness. The top investment bankers are on the same
wavelength. At Goldman Sachs, Dr. Fischer Black* works with
fuzzy engineering in modeling customers' options.

- Other institutions are analyzing stock options given to
  company executives.
- Similar fuzzy engineering models can be applied for
  other types of options and claims.

During the FASB meeting reference was also made to U.S.
insurance companies using high technology to study insurance
claims and warranties. Here again, fuzzy engineering is effectively used in connection to contingent claims analysis.

5 THE CYCLICAL NATURE OF FINANCIAL BUSINESS

Progress is cumulative in science and engineering but cyclical in
finance. Whatever might go wrong with the credit market in the
1990s will not be due to a lack of knowledge about loans but to
the fast growing amount of risk embedded, for instance, in settlements and netting facilities made feasible through electronic
payments.

* Father of the Black-Scholes model, which he developed in 1970 when at the
University of Chicago.

Settlements are speeding over New York's Clearing House Interbank Payments System (CHIPS) as well as London's CHAPS and the other exchanges.

- Between 1988 and 1989, an average of $800 million was exchanged per day over CHIPS.

- Four years later, in 1992/93 this average has reached and broken the $2 billion level, a 250 percent increase.

Has the financial industry positioned itself to face the challenges resulting from these large numbers and the risks embedded into them? While in terms of technology banking has almost never looked back, progress has paid scant dividends in risk management. The immediate prosaic truth is that

- A lot of counterparties outstretch their hand.

- Therefore, these counterparties may not be able to face up to their financial responsibilities.

This is particularly true in the case of *panic*. A panic exposes the essence of banking as no lecture or literature can do: Many formerly good debts suddenly turn bad, greatly increasing the size of the exposure.

No bank is a safe-deposit box. Its assets might have been committed in investments that have failed to balance the risks involved with the rewards of profits. It is very difficult to strike a policy that is both imaginative and conservative.

- This simply cannot be done through deterministic or even probabilistic models for decision-making.

- *More* is necessary, and this more comes from the ability to express fuzzy notions in *a comprehensive manner*.

This is precisely the contribution fuzzy engineering can offer to the financial business, and it is wise to discard the notion that past experience, taught by our grandfathers, will help to face the coming challenges.

The past may be a prelude, but financial events will never really duplicate themselves. As George F. Baker, the legendary New York banker, once remarked: "Every time is different."* Only by carefully studying what has taken place we can learn certain instructive rules which we better express in a way that permits to industrialize knowledge, spreading it through the enterprise.

Reading between the lines of past financial events, we can see the germ of *a theory of the credit cycle,* which involves a fair amount of vagueness and uncertainty. It tells that bankers and investors in crowds have an impact on one-another, hence bringing the Swarms concept into the picture:

- What they *do* or *do not do* is influenced by the behavior of other bankers and investors.

- The resulting moves are conditioned by circumstances as much as by any calculus of risk and reward.

Under the pressure of competition, investment bankers will cut corners. Eager to participate, investors will pay no attention to the underlying factors. As a result, the creditworthiness of securities being traded deteriorates.

Booms produce complacency in almost equal measure to wealth. The longer the good times last, the deeper the conviction grows that they will go on. As a result, the financial world gets inclined to take the good years on faith—yet these are largely *fuzzy news.*

The *boom* creates many business geniuses, but few retain their gifts in the slump. Another lesson from boom years is that lenders and borrowers periodically *suspend their judgment.* They become more speculative as the financial market gets more bullish. This is precisely the time to apply the controls.

Like the democratization of lending through such instruments as mortgage-backed financing (MBF), *the securitization of*

* James Grant, *Money of the Mind* (New York: Farrar Straus Giroux, 1992).

risk presents significant business opportunities, but also seeds the next panic. Is there a lesson to be learned from experience?

The lesson is that we cannot effectively manage complex situations without the appropriate tools. Whether we prefer the use of nonlinear models, genetic algorithms, fuzzy engineering, neural networks, or other tools of the new generation of intelligent artifacts is not so terribly important. What is vital is that

- We *understand* the problem and
- We are able to express it in both *qualitative* and *quantitative* terms.

Risk management is inseparable from the existence and usage of financial instruments. Even if fully secured, every loan is a kind of speculation. The degree of risk varies according to

1. The character and strength of the counterparty,
2. The quality and spread of the collateral.

Because the market for derivative financial instruments is so new, the quality of off-balance sheet issues has to be considered, both in an accurate way and in very conservative terms—not as an average.

The *character* of the counterparty, and therefore credit risk, cannot be expressed in quantitative terms. The use of fuzzy sets permits qualification, as the examples of "small, medium, large size" and on "water temperatures" have shown (respectively in Figure 8-1 and Figure 8-2).

As advice, what the preceding paragraph stated is no different than what J.P. Morgan said when he stressed that *the basis of credit is character.*

"Is it not commercial credit based primarily upon money or property?" Samuel Untermyer asked.*

---

* During the 1912 investigation on the Money Trust, by the U.S. House Banking and Currency Committee, whose special legal counsel was Untermyer.

"No sir. The first thing is character," Morgan replied, "Because a man I do not trust could not get money from me on all the bonds of Christendom."

J.P. Morgan was renowned for his ability to know each major client personally, thus judging character and performance. This can only be done with great difficulty, if at all, in the present world of networks and electronic banking. Hence the wisdom of developing *quality databases* and fuzzy engineering models not only on trading partners at the institution level, but also on their executives and dealers.

6 BENEFITS FROM A FUZZY COGNITIVE MODEL FOR FINANCIAL OPERATIONS

Causal concepts can be expressed through a fuzzy cognitive model, which is helpful in representing the operations of a stock exchange or other financial market. As in the example we examined in the preceding sections, the sequence of events can be qualitatively expressed by a fuzzy associative memory system such as FAMOUS by LIFE.

This is a real-life application that can serve as a first-class example. The modeling method Dr. Toshiro Terano* and his co-workers have followed features

- Unsupervised learning with fuzzy knowledge representation and

- Causal inference with feedback through associative memory.

The Laboratory for International Fuzzy Engineering suggests that such a modeling approach can be useful for abstracting trading concepts and for refining fuzzy causal relations as

---

* General manager of the Laboratory for International Fuzzy Engineering (LIFE).

outline knowledge. It is also helpful for the expression of subjective information.

The model developed for implementation in a financial environment is able to represent the dynamic characteristics of objects, both trading decisions and the transactions themselves. The model maps qualitative and quantitative information in a flexible way:

- As the scale of financial operations increases towards global banking,
- The transactions being executed involve a growing number of financial products.

These two events have a compound effect, the result being that the aggregation of several detailed quantitative characteristics and associated information becomes more difficult to synthesize. Traders, investment advisors, and managers do not recognize objective phenomena in quantitative detail.

The premise underlying the LIFE project lies in the model's ability to conceptually recognize the sequence of events; similar objects can be classified using the criteria for superordinate concepts, which facilitates generalization. A modeling method using the notions underpinning FAMOUS can help financial experts

- Define the interaction of financial events using abstract concepts and
- Describe such interaction by employing network knowledge representation of causality.

The causality of network knowledge can be defined by using a learning rule and inference by associative memories, as explained in the opening paragraphs of this section. The financial implementation can be realized in two stages, both addressing *qualitative* modeling aspects:

- By abstraction of concepts and
- Through similarity of chosen objects—hence by analogical reasoning.

Modeling by the abstraction of concepts is based on the premise that financial experts can predict future situations and define the appropriate action to cope with them. In so doing, they are not pursuing perfect conformity but understand the *casual relationships* of the temporal sequence of events and, most importantly, can *conceptualize market behavior*.

Traders and investment experts carry out their decisions and actions, which constitute the operation of a market system. Typically, they do so using causal—hence qualitative—knowledge that summarizes instances:

- This is done by association or intuition,
- Not only through logical approaches.

In the case of causal knowledge, the certainty of the correlation between cause and effect is rarely clear. Furthermore, the degree of influence that a cause exerts on effect is a fuzzy relationship:

- Experts recognize the degree of correlation between cause and effect subjectively.
- Hence the concept itself is a fuzzy set, whether this happens in the financial domain or elsewhere.

Modeling of similar objects follows a procedure that shows other objects with the same or analogous dynamic characteristics. This, too, requires appropriate representation.

If, for example, similar financial markets are modeled individually, the adjustment of these individual parameters requires great effort. But if similar objects can be defined for processing by abstraction of concepts, the modeling of similar objects can be easier. It can be done by changing the criteria for judgment.

Modeling by the abstraction of concepts, however, requires setting individual criteria for judgment within the superordinate concept. That is why object-oriented approaches can be very helpful in this task.

Modeling using object-oriented, therefore ephemeral, hierarchical structures has been found to be a useful means for the generalization of algorithms addressing similar entities. Furthermore, initial knowledge obtained by this method can be generalized by abstracting different aspects of situations that impact on a given object.

7 PAYING ATTENTION TO THE INFERENCE METHOD

One of the imaginative projects LIFE has done is a fuzzy engineering model for diagnostic reasons, oriented to manufacturing operations. Its infrastructure, however, is so generic that without any significant change it can be applied to finance.

As shown in Figure 8-4, which is a modified version of the block diagram corresponding to the original project—to conform to financial conditions—there are four key elements in this infrastructure:

- Precursor
- Accident
- Action
- Result

In a financial industry application, they can be kept in the same order in which they have been applied in manufacturing, changing only the element *accident* into the *difference* between

- A financial prediction and
- Actual market values.

This approach permits to keep intact the concept and procedures associated to the knowledge bank of known cases. In

FIGURE 8-4   Overview of a diagnostic system for operational support.

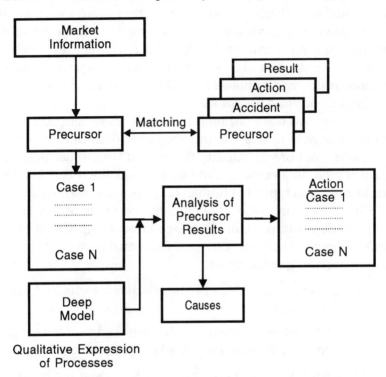

this manner the prevailing structure for analogical reasoning does not need to be altered; only the focus and content of these cases must change.

Both in manufacturing and in the financial markets, fuzzy sets help in handling an idealized abstraction in an environment with vagueness and uncertainty in the background. The so developed inference engine permits effective handling of *fuzzy data*, that is,

- Time Series that involve noise

- Information that is essentially subjective, and

- Cases that are ill-defined or ambiguous.

In describing the process of weighted decisions, fuzzy sets act as *qualifiers*. Their proper place is that of an intermediate layer between known modeling solutions and the system's architecture. As it cannot be repeated too often, few real-life business decisions can be described in yes/no answers. Hence, multivariable logic provides a flexible alternative on which we will be well-advised to capitalize.

If a process does not reflect random characteristics, and if we are not able to express our thoughts quantitatively, then we'd better not use probability theory. But we can use possibility theory, helping ourselves to express ill-defined and ambiguous information typical of human cognition and reasoning.

In connection to the development and usage of this model, LIFE made an important reference concerning the *inference method*. Since a fuzzy cognitive model uses a network structure of corresponding connections,

- Causal relationships can be effectively expressed in a matrix form.

- The inference arises from the causal edge of the model and the activation (or grade) of the nonlinear function.

This nonlinear function represents the nodes (or concepts) embedded in the model. Hence, the prerequisites of nonlinearity so much underlined by the MIT and SFI researchers is being observed.

In the case of LIFE, inference is carried out by matrix calculation of the state vector of the node's grade at a discrete time step. The weight of causality is used, along with threshold value conversion. This gives a sort of associative memory *neural network* with feedback, where inference is the process of recollection by association.

- Most feedback neural networks minimize the fuzzy entropy of the network state.

- Hence, the recollection through associative inference decreases the fuzzy entropy.

The strength of the causal relationships of the model lies in the fact that they are refined by using the change of the activation of each node over time. This makes feasible unsupervised learning using only input data, a process known as differential learning.

As the implementation of the artifact that LIFE developed helps demonstrate, this type of fuzzy cognitive model can recognize real-world situations and be used to integrate knowledge obtained empirically:

- The nodes represent abstract concepts that expert traders grasp intuitively from events.

- Nodes do not generally show values but express the degree, or truth-value grade, for each event or concept.

A fuzzy cognitive model can be seen as fulfilling the goal of refining causal knowledge. This is effectively executed by representing the causal relationships that experts use to predict a market situation or financial data flow based on a variety of conditions:

- Differential learning can inductively refine an initial knowledge given as an outline from input data.

- Inference by means of feedback associative memories in the fuzzy cognitive model can help obtain predictions close to the intuition of experts.

The adopted integrative solution permits the expression of information easily understood by human users. Similar models can therefore be built that qualitatively represent the interaction of events and can be applied in the modeling of interactive financial markets. This is particularly important in situations with dynamic characteristics.

8 INTEGRATING FUZZY ENGINEERING AND NEURAL NETWORKS

Fuzzy engineering artifacts assist in devising ways and means to match loosely defined patterns and create paths to deal with novel situations. As we have seen through practical examples, the vagueness and uncertainty embedded in a fuzzy construct typically reflects the thinking styles of the human brain.

In Japan, a fuzzy engineering expert system helps investment banks in the design of their new financial products. It does so by using a combination of the following:

- Fuzzy modeling
- Neural networking
- Case-based reasoning
- Rule-based reasoning
- Hypothetical reasoning

It also employs a learning subsystem. The usage of such an artifact, one of the Japanese brokers suggested, has resulted in an 85 percent drop in financial product design cycle time and a 30 percent increase in design accuracy.

The important background reference in this example is the compound effect obtained through the joint usage of fuzzy engineering and neural networks. Each is associated to specific functions within the chosen implementation domain. As Toshiro Terano suggests:

- Fuzzy engineering is the strongest when addressing conceptual functions.
- Neural networks perform best when designed to emulate the lower brain functions of the cerebellum.

Taken together, fuzzy sets and neural networks permit effective handling of compound conditions that present themselves in the financial markets. They make feasible representation of multidimensional rules leading to the analysis of the meaning of the relationship between the antecedents of these rules.

One of the research projects in the domain of fuzzy models for financial analysis distinguishes two kinds of fuzzy rules based on the variables and the premises characterizing these variables. The premises may be

- Interactive or
- Non-interactive.

What is meant by *interaction*? Intuitively, two variables X and Y are non-interactive if the restriction of X does not involve increases in Y. If it exists, such an interaction may be

- More or less strong, or
- Weak and local in a subset

To develop a valid model that integrates different methods such as fuzzy sets and neural networks, we have to properly determine the existence of interactions, localize each one of them, and establish the intensity of these interactions. This must be done both within each module and between the modules of fuzzy sets and neural networks.

How can we represent the established interactions? Among possible approaches two have proven to be the more rewarding and are therefore suggested by financial analysts with experience in this domain:

- The use of multi-variable functions
- The employment of fuzzy rules

A fuzzy rule will partially represent an interaction between the variables of the premises and the variable(s) of the conclusion. This is practically what the LIFE fuzzy model we saw in Figure 8-4 has done.

Based on practical results with financial modeling obtained in Japan and elsewhere, the message this discussion conveys is that approximate reasoning seems to be suitable to solve problems with uncertainty and a good amount of interactivity. At least this is the conclusion reached by learned researchers:

- The handling of interactivity through possibility theory is less restrictive than the notion of dependence between random variables in probability theory.

- When we use possibilities functions, we can consider that variables are non-interactive even if they are not absolutely independent.

The able handling of interactivity of variables is a very important notion in financial analysis. Not only do we have to take account of it, but we also have to provide tools that effectively map it into the processes we model.

All this is very relevant in connection to studying the behavior of financial markets because what we are essentially saying is that approximate reasoning permits a greater adaptability for

- Knowledge representation
- And, therefore, for decision-making in trading and investments.

Whether alone or in conjunction with fuzzy engineering, neural networks are currently becoming popular in financial circles, but some people suggest that it is often difficult to say precisely what a neural network is and what may be a nonlinear function approximator:

- A function representation uses as parameters weights and thresholds,
- The parameter-fitting equation is often a learning algorithm.

Neural nets have been used in time series forecasting in connection to problems involving chaotic processes. However, when compared to some other methods of function approximation, they have the disadvantage that for most algorithms parameter fitting is slow, unless we use massively parallel computers.

In conclusion, possibility theory and therefore fuzzy logic provide the tools for the conceptual representation and reasoning of knowledge. For their part, neural networks focus on specific, well-defined domains that require execution of repetitive functions.

Interestingly enough, such synergy also prevails between fuzzy engineering and the other tools we have examined in the preceding chapters. Section 9 brings this issue into perspective by looking into how fuzzy functions, genetic algorithms, and fractals can work together.

9 FUZZY FUNCTIONS, GENETIC ALGORITHMS, AND FRACTALS

Fuzzy engineering functions constitute a simple but powerful method for the analysis of financial problems. Their competitive advantage is the result of their elegance, their ability to emulate processes involving vagueness and uncertainty, as well as their ease of adaptation to complex problems.

Fuzzy engineering can easily be integrated into other tools. For instance, it can be used for simulation purposes, feeding data into a genetic algorithm to be used for optimizing functional representations:

- What fuzzy functions can emulate, the genetic algorithm can optimize.

- The combination of the two technologies provides value-added means for financial analysis.

Taken together, fuzzy sets and genetic algorithms offer a better alternative to the traditional experimental approaches, making nonlinear handling of statistical data feasible.

After all, what are the alternatives? One is the use of polynomials of quadratic or higher order equations. We master the use of higher than quadratic functions in physics but know precious little about how to put them in realistic and profitable use in economics.

A similar argument can be made with a number of tools, but from the viewpoint of their shortcomings. This does not mean that linear equations, regression analyses, polynomials, orthogonal function sets, finite difference grids, logical relationships, and other constructs have not successfully solved problems in economics—they have. But

- As the problems in economics and finance become more complex,

- The limitations of existing mathematical tools are increasingly visible.

Local fitting is a time-honored approach done with many representations by fitting the parameters based on points within a given region. The basic idea is to allow for considerable flexibility in building a globally nonlinear model while fitting only a few parameters in each local patch which, newer approaches suggest, may emulate a fractals structure.

As we know from more classical graphical analysis, for any functional representation that forms a complete set, it is always possible to fit the data perfectly by using a sufficient number of parameters. But for the purposes of making predictions, this may be a very poor choice as, for instance, when the data consists of a finite number of samples from a smooth function whose derivatives are all small.

A polynomial whose order is equal to the number of data points will always fit perfectly, but will typically oscillate wildly between samples, as Doyne Farmer suggests. It is important to appreciate that here we are not speaking of situations that are decisively black or white, but rather of real-life cases with many shades of gray.

Another approach to the solution of financial problems and their prediction requirements is fractals, which we considered in Chapter 4, stating that we can use them to exploit a one-and-a half dimensional solution space. However, what was not yet said is that

- The fractal form we obtain can be quite complex even with a limited amount of data
- In some cases, a fractal functional form might result in a larger estimation error than we are bargaining for.

The message is not that fractals theory is not applicable in finance but, rather, that we are still learning how to use it. Therefore, our knowledge bank still has a limited set of rules. Can we develop systems rules that provide a better solution? One approach is to

- Work out a fuzzy function for each element that influences the outcome, which may approximate a fractal presentation.
- Then use fuzzy engineering to integrate the different elements into a composite structure.

An applications-oriented example is using fuzzy engineering to develop a compound budgetary estimate composed of many partial budgets, each involving uncertainties as to the forthcoming final appropriations. A similar example is integrating sales estimates from different sales offices and markets to generate cumulative production schedules.

Whether in finance or in manufacturing, the mathematical tools we are discussing do not radically alter the experimental methodology. Whether we use fuzzy engineering, genetic algorithms, or neural networks, when we perform an optimization we must select the form of the system within which we will work. This is done through the needed abstraction that provides the means to derive knowledge from information elements.

The underlying concept is to transform observed data, through calculations, into a trend, pattern, or conclusion. What changes in the experimental methodology is the form defining the nature of the calculations, which can have a strong effect on the visualization of the results.

All forms of mathematical abstraction share common traits. They specify a transformation of a set of observations into a set of conclusions, which is the aim of analysis. But they can also promote or inhibit the outcome we are after, namely obtaining usable experimental results.

PART 3

Implementing Advanced Financial Analysis

9 Dealing with Uncertainty in the Financial Markets

1 INTRODUCTION

In Chapter 8 we have seen how possibilistic logic extends the concepts and rules of qualitative expressions to real numbers. We have also seen several examples that demonstrate that not only can we manipulate shades of grey in trading and investment decisions rather than only expressing true (1) and false (0) statements, but we can in addition express *qualitative* opinions in a way to be manipulated by computer.

The strength of fuzzy engineering lies in its ability to handle subjective judgments. As contrasted to *probability* theory, *possibility* theory* makes it possible to employ all fractions between 0 and 1 to express partial truth and fuzzy concepts such as

- Smaller or greater,
- More or less,
- Higher or lower,
- Better or worse.

* Which underpins the processes of fuzzy engineering.

The result of being able to deal with vagueness and uncertainty is that we can address facts, events, and objects that, because of their nature, can never be crisp. Evidences and hypotheses can be combined in a consistent manner.

With possibility theory, the mathematical foundations are rigorous enough and are improving. We also have the alternative of using Bayesian solutions* and, as a limiting case, probability theory, which has well-established foundations because of centuries of scientific work in this domain.

Through the examples we will see in this chapter, it will become evident that the result of implementing possibility theory is the ability to handle complex functions rather easily. Its usage permits us to discover experimentally the outcome of hypotheses we test through *our own qualitative reasoning*. This serves the role of the *financial engineer* well, whose mission typically includes

- Delivering new products at a fast pace,
- Significantly enhancing existing products, and
- Dealing with market developments practically in real-time.

Since the early 1980s a lot of screening and massaging of financial information has been based on spreadsheets, but this approach is no longer competitive enough because everyone is using it. To keep ahead of competition we need the following:

- Powerful algorithms and heuristics for financial analysis.
- The ability to handle fuzzy data as received from the market.
- The tools to deliver very fast solutions, ahead of other banks.

* See D. N. Chorafas, *The New Information Technologies—A Practitioner's Guide* (New York: Van Nostrand Reinhold, 1992).

These requirements are particularly pronounced in the areas of forex, securities, and treasury. During the research that led to this text, financial institutions frequently stressed that what the central computer operation typically produce is too little, too late.

The present chapter demonstrates how and why handling fuzzy financial information is a challenging but doable job. It first introduces the meaning of uncertainty as seen from the fuzzy engineering perspective. Then it suggests ways to defuzzify vague or uncertain information, using practical examples.

2 INITIAL CONDITIONS AND POSSIBILITY THEORY

In the beginning of the 1930s, under the influence of quantum mechanics, the idea of discontinuity of space and time took a new form. The impact of the notion of *uncertainty* created the base of several new concepts, including the proposition that in the minimal regions of space/time a given particle will not have a precise location.

Some of these ideas have excited the imagination of scientists for centuries, but they have rather recently been concretized by Dr. Werner Heisenberg. His S matrix is an operator that permits us to

- Describe the state of a system after diffusion and
- Do so effectively, provided we know the system's state before diffusion.

This places emphasis on initial conditions, a concept that has been explored since the beginning of the book. As you will recall, reference to initial conditions has underpinned all discussions, from nonlinear equations to the butterfly effect.

The *initial conditions* provide a starting point for a transient process, with subsequent modeling leading toward some sort of algorithmic solution. For instance, initial conditions may consist of

- A starting velocity field within the system's boundaries and
- Linkages permitting the system and its components to respond quickly to transients.

Typically, in mechanics and in fluid dynamics, initial conditions are prescribed at one instant for each point in the solution space. Generally, these initial conditions are critical, though they are rarely treated in that way.

The criticality to which reference is being made rests on the fact that an initial condition is actually a part of the final solution, the state of which is often a guess. Yet any problem has initial conditions that can be instrumental in defying the solution space.

Another critical issue in the path toward a solution is *iterations*, on whose wisdom we have also paid considerable attention. The importance of iterations rests on the fact that since the initial conditions are guessed at, the final conditions will be different and hopefully closer to what might have been an initial *correct* guess. Refined guesses are fed back into the simulator as a new initial condition, and the process continues until we are satisfied with the results:

- The general procedure for building any working model involves iteration.
- First a fundamental grid that most simply represents the system under investigation is built.
- This is then used for simulation runs, and improvements are made.

For instance, the areas that show discontinuities and/or extreme divergence are singled out for refinement. The mesh may be divided into smaller elements in problem areas, their density being made to match the areas of high gradients. The new model is then resubmitted for solution, and the process continues.

Under the concepts of possibility theory, for instance, we may be guessing the correct grading of corporate bonds received as collateral, but we are not sure about it. Every investment advisor does so, and any guess is fallible, but if through iteration we can refine our initial estimate, chances are that we are moving closer to correct results.

Guesses made by securities analysts and investment advisors represent fuzzy estimates we aim to distill. This can be done through *defuzzification*, as we will see in this and the next chapter. Taking an analogy from physics, what defuzzification essentially does is to establish boundary conditions.

The concept is known from mechanics, fluid dynamics, and probability theory. With probability theory, this is the case with *confidence intervals*, which we compute at a given level of significance, for instance a = 0.05. With this we know that

- The regression line represents an expected value, and the majority of points of the distribution will fall within the confidence intervals.

- With a = 0.05, statistically we have a 95 percent assurance that this will be the case—in other words the error margin is 5 percent.

With fluid dynamics, boundary conditions are used where the velocity is specified on a boundary. For instance, essential boundaries can be the characteristics of the incoming flow and the wall of a pipeline. A similar model occurs at the outflow zone.

Boundary conditions established by means of defuzzification is an essentially subjective process but also very important because it permits us to better define the area within which we make our guesses. A better focused approach also briefs attention to the need to make available to ourselves the tools and measures that make understanding and mastering the concept of uncertainty feasible.

It is quite vital to underline that *uncertainty* and *randomness* should not be confused. Whether in science or in the arcane arts of financial and economic analysis,

- A *probability* measure addresses the randomness in the system.

- A *possibility* measure is a means for handling uncertainty, therefore fuzziness.*

Uncertainty has always been present in the human mind, but, as Dr. Tibor Vamos aptly suggests, its existence was more recognizable in the experience of earlier people than has been the case in our times. Yet uncertain outcomes are regularly present in everyday life, a fact that, on and off, stimulated a process of generalization toward a unified view.

3 THE MEANING OF UNCERTAINTY IN FINANCIAL DATA

Uncertainty is not really detached from *certainty*, and the Epicurean philosophers of ancient Greece paid significant attention to this fact. Socrates and Plato ridiculed the Epicureans and bypassed this problem of uncertainty, but in the syllogisms of Aristotle are two modalities beyond the certain or necessary (anangaion):

- The possible (dynaton)

- The contingent (endechomenon)

Both express uncertainty. There are also concepts of uncertainty that can be easily put into mythological and religious

* In essence, the probability measure is the limiting case of the possibility measure.

frameworks. The easiest answer to the uncertainty people feel is that of espousing the divine hypothesis. But this is not the solution in the context of financial analysis and the prediction of market behavior.

By contrast, the main goal of any mathematical technique we use in connection to finance and economics is the employment of multidisciplinary know-how able to promote computer simulation comparing real-life and numerical results. The practical implementation of whatever is said in this and the preceding chapters rests on our ability to do the following:

- Identify the key factors that come into play
- Analyze the suitability of various methods
- Determine which should be used and how they should be refined

The broader purpose of any tool, and fuzzy engineering is a tool, is to provide assistance with problem solution. Therefore, it must have applications in the financial field and help increase our knowledge of diagnosis of market events, identifying critical areas, and permit documented solutions.

As it cannot be too often stated, however, the building of simulators only addresses part of the problem. The even greater challenge is that of data flows and databases. Financial data are often characterized as *noisy*. In reality, in the majority of cases they are fuzzy, and such fuzziness may have different causes. The three more pronounced are:

- Uncertainty
- Vagueness
- Imprecision

Imprecision refers to lack of specifity of contents of an information element. For instance, "The dollar inflation rate this year will be between 3 percent and 5 percent" or "It may be 4 percent give and take 100 base points." Figure 9-1 presents this statement in graphic form but also makes it somewhat more crisp:

- The certainty is equal to 1 that inflation this year will be equal to 4.0 percent.

- The certainty that inflation will be 3.5 *or* 4.5 is 50–50 for each guesstimate.

FIGURE 9-1   Imprecision in the expression of projected dollar inflation.

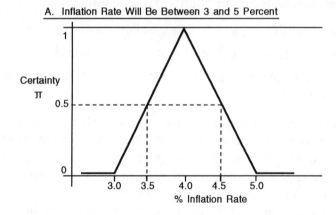

A. Inflation Rate Will Be Between 3 and 5 Percent

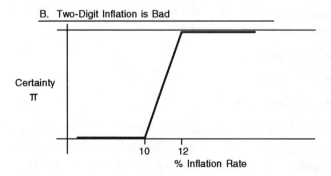

B. Two-Digit Inflation is Bad

- It is not expected that the annual inflation will be either less than 3 percent or more than 5 percent.

The curve in Figure 9-1A defines the possibility distribution function. Any resemblance to the normal distribution curve of probability theory is illusory. In fact the curve in Figure 9-1B is also possibilistic and represents the predicate: "Two-digit inflation is bad for the economy."

Vagueness is the effect of lack of sharp boundaries—hence of confidence intervals—whether this is denoted by approximate numbers or by words, for example: "A low inflation rate is good." In this case, the term "inflation rate"

- Is expressed in a context dependent form but
- Is ill-defined even in a single context.

As the opening paragraphs of this section suggested, *uncertainty* refers to our partial ignorance of the specificity of a certain information element and its description. For instance, the probability of getting a "4" by throwing a fair dice is 1/6. There is no certainty the "4" will show up.

All three conditions seem to be unwanted, but this is not necessarily true. The point often missed is that within a given state of knowledge and of information flow, imprecise, vague, and/or uncertain statements can be more *precise* than supposedly "sure" statements or patterns.

In order to function properly in the context of the world's financial markets, we have to live with the uncertainty financial situations exhibit—but we can improve upon the knowledge and information at our disposition by

- Having access to rich databases,
- Developing the right models, and
- Using filters that weed out noise.

The justification for using fuzzy engineering models is that we are producing cleaner data as well as knowledge that is part of the basic intellectual capital of traders, investors, and other professionals.

4 CAN WE LEARN FROM OTHER IMPLEMENTATION DOMAINS?

In engineering, and most particularly among Japanese technology firms, fuzzy adaptive control has become a successful application of fuzzy theory, and is used in many practical solutions. Fuzzy rules have a higher ability for knowledge representation because they permit encoding knowledge by means of representing pairs of a reference model for a process and its controller. In order to realize a robust control, this approach does the following:

- Adapts control gains using reference models given in fuzzy rules, hence exploiting the feedback

- Employs object-oriented solutions for databasing and programming, producing mode agile codes for computers

This dual approach helps to directly evaluate a process output and connect it with some suitable reference model. In Chapter 8, we have seen as an example Japan's Fuzzy Associative Memory Organizing Units Systems (FAMOUS). As it will be recalled, the fuzzy associative memory can automatically create membership functions.

Fuzzy engineering models for financial analysis can be developed and employed in a quite similar manner to FAMOUS. One application along this line of reference has three features:

- A fuzzy knowledge representation through causal relations

- Object-oriented knowledge management by means of associative memories
- Fuzzy inference implemented in an associative memory manner

This fuzzy engineering approach to financial data analysis is very useful for simulation of nonlinear systems and the effective follow-up of market fluctuations. It makes feasible a level of accuracy that cannot be obtained through classical methods.

Another financial institution is currently examining the use of fuzzy engineering tools in connection to the control of *overdrafts*. As far as the larger customer accounts are concerned, the control of overdrafts is a steady business and should not be done one-tantum, (only once), as financial institution after financial institution are discovering.

As an example, prior to its merger with Chemical Banking, the former Manufacturing Hanover Trust Bank (MHTC) had done an *intraday risk evaluation* and found astonishing results. Just one customer, General Motors, was running at 2:00 P.M. a $2 billion overdraft.

Powerful models and networked computers are needed for management controls and real-time reporting. Knowing what is the exposure by customer is no easy business, requiring the following:

- Fuzzy engineering algorithms and heuristics able to *project on positions*
- Networked databases and *database mining* procedures
- *High-performance computing* for number crunching and interactive visualization purposes

As with open lines of credit to major clients, the real problem is being for or against risk-taking financial operations. For instance, we have to do off-balance sheet trades for hedges and in order not to miss a lucrative market. But we cannot afford to do so without the appropriate risk control, which operates in *real time*.

Why can't the legacy type operations every bank has, and pays dearly for, do the risk management chores? There are two reasons why this, which indeed has been tried and failed, is not a good idea.

1. Typically run on mainframes through Cobol programs, legacy type applications are low technology.

Low technology simply cannot answer risk management requirements, particularly those connected to global risk and new financial products. Exposure can become uncontrollable by the time the legacy software of old data processing provides information.

2. Due to bad habits and inertia, it takes ages to get something out of the classical data processing chores—and what finally comes out is too little, too late.

It would typically take 2 to 3 years to get some results from the legacy guys, and whenever they come they are of rather low value to the users. They will not answer the requirements of the marketplace. This is not the way *a profitable bank* works.

This experience, and the associated wave of dissatisfaction, has led the foremost financial institutions to the decision to reform and restructure information technology operations. Increasingly, they build *financial engineering* with rapid qualitative and quantitative support placed near the end users:

- Providing analytical but business driven solutions.
- Encouraging *change* in the culture of traders and investors.
- Providing the means to *take controllable risks*.
- Developing models able to handle *uncertainty* to achieve better results.

These are the issues behind the interest that leading-edge financial institutions show in the new mathematical tools at our disposal, fuzzy engineering being one of the best examples. But let's always recall that tools alone don't solve problems. We need insight, foresight, and an inquisitive spirit to get significant results.

5 IMPROVING THE SCOPE OF ANALYSIS THROUGH FUZZY SETS

Models are the means we use to handle an idealized abstraction. Inference based on fuzzy engineering models permits dealing with uncertainties, and as we have seen in section 3, handling *uncertain data* is an opportunity, provided we have the means to do so.

The theory of fuzzy sets, which underpins fuzzy engineering, provides a method of treating essentially subjective information—therefore, ill-defined and ambiguous. Such information is typical of human cognition and reasoning. Fuzziness defines the following state of mind:

- We may know what we really want to reach, but

- We cannot describe the process of a weighted decision in crisp terms.

In this sense, the fuzzy sets are *qualifiers*. Their proper place in financial analysis is as an intermediate layer between known modeling solutions and the systems architecture as a whole. The fact that we can express shades of grey, that is intermediate values, is important. As we have already seen, few real-life financial decisions can be described in yes/no answers.

Many applications in finance, business, and industry are missing the point that, in the majority of cases, both the data and the knowledge can be fuzzy. Hence the importance of having tools that help in

- Examining *qualitative* relation and
- Making possible *macroscopic* understanding.

These are, however, prerequisites to the efficient integration of information elements that will permit us to conceive how global financial markets work at any given point in time. The number one prerequisite is to appreciate that market data is inherently fuzzy.

What financial analyst, trader, or manager would not like to have a "rational" picture of the markets? But can we do it? The aim is usually to get structured knowledge of certain phenomena, hoping that the underlying structures:

- Will reiterate predictably or
- Can even be reproduced at will.

The facts of business life demonstrate that such hope is rather illogical and discards the fact that the interpretation of financial information tends to be a very subjective issue.

There are arguments of *alleged meanings* and of *unconfirmed reports* practically relating to how various questions are being treated. Sometimes trading and investment decisions are based on observed regularities that it is thought could be formulated as rules. But how often this really happens?

Concepts regarding market regularities have as a common background the fact that they conveniently forget about market imprecision, vagueness, and uncertainty. When we remember these constraints, we find that there are two ways of clearing our ideas about things, that is, of gaining an orientation:

1. By using more powerful tools that permit getting over a previous disorientation or lack of clarity.

2. By changing a pseudo-orientation, in which we ourselves were not convinced, into one which can be clarified by *defuzzifying* a situation.

Through practical examples, in Chapter 10 we will see how this can be accomplished. The way it has been introduced in section 2, the aim of defuzzification is to make a very imprecise, vague, or uncertain market perception somewhat more certain and clear.

- In Figure 9-1, for example, this has been done by creating an area under which inflation rates vary between 3 percent and 5 percent, at different levels of certainty.

- What in reality this means is "at different levels of possibility" rather than "certainty," but the latter is the term fuzzy engineering uses.

When we become conscious of this way of converting numbers into figures and of expressing them by means of visualization, we can search for in market variations a more focused manner. We also get a more accurate orientation and do so with a great chance of success.

Cash management is a good example of fairly complex financial requirements, which can create an appreciation of what new technology can achieve in terms of solutions. Due to the limitations of present tools and of available databases, cash management is usually done in a rather summary manner.* For instance, it takes place

- Only by currency and
- Only for reconciliation purposes by account.

One does not need to be a genius to see that this is totally inadequate, hence, the request many finance divisions pose for *improvements*. They want to see online available information in connection to both detailed and consolidated reporting, by:

- Customer identification
- Type of account

---

* See also the Manufacturers Hanover Trust example in Section 4.

- Account identification
- Currency
- Steady or transit funds
- Value date, and
- Accounting date.

They would also like to have this information *interactively*, and quite definitely before the closing of the market. This cannot be done through classical accounting because typically some of the accounts don't yet square out; fuzzy sets permit us to make available this information. But there is also another requirement.

In many financial institutions major customers, including corresponding banks, leave an amount of money in transit. Often these are significant sums transferred for a specific purpose, but not all customers are able to manage their balances in real time. Overnight, funds can be invested for a profit. Can fuzzy engineering contribute to deciphering the customer's behavior?

6 ESTABLISHING THE CUSTOMER'S PROFILE FOR RELATIONSHIP MANAGEMENT

Section 5 has outlined the criteria that financial institutions usually describe as being important for both detailed and consolidated reporting. Starting with the fundamentals, it will be proper to elaborate on each one of these seven issues and what it means in terms of organizational prerequisites and information technology support.

First and foremost, in the majority of financial institutions, the individual customer is not identified as such in the current legacy system. That is very bad because it deprives management of the ability to look into the customer relation at a time when *relationship banking* is supreme.

The lack of customer identification also makes it impossible to forecast customer behavior in connection to longer-term account handling and most particularly cash management, specifically,

- The *balances* the customer leaves with the bank
- The length of *time* credit balances stay with the bank
- The *currencies* the customer uses most frequently, and
- *Patterns* in the covering of debit balances.

Customer behavior can be effectively studied through fuzzy engineering, provided the associated data has the necessary detail. The fact that in many financial institutions customer details are missing is very bad. Paraphrasing an old proverb: "No money, no commerce," we can say: "No databases, no business."

The problem, however, *ends* at the IT level—it does not start there. At the very beginning comes *corporate strategy*, and the next prerequisite is *organizational work*. Thorough organizational perspectives should definitely precede the implementation of fuzzy engineering; otherwise, applications will be built on shaky ground, and this will be visible.

In other words, prior to applying advanced information technology tools, the management of the bank will be well advised to study organizational issues connected to the *basics* such as

- Appropriate customer identification and
- Type of customer account.

For relationship banking reasons, but also for cash management, each individual customer must be properly specified, classified, and identified. This is no easy task and, therefore, in the majority of cases the concept of an account as currently practiced seems to be awfully confused.

Many banks find it quite difficult to properly identify an *account*. There are *client accounts*, which are part of the set of *external accounts*. There are also *internal accounts*, and other accounts such as *profit accounts*.

It is difficult to see why things should be so messy, since in reality the whole issue is rather simple. At least, that's the experience expressed by banks that have tried to clearly define the concepts of

- Client and
- Account.

The prevailing confusion is even more surprising, as the disorganization that prevails in the majority of cases handicaps relationship management. It also suggests the wisdom of classifying accounts using a classification matrix.*

But there are technical prerequisites to the correct implementation of a Classification and Identification Code.** Let's keep in mind that the clear definition of *client account(s)* can only be made after the issues of *client definition and profiling* as well as *the type of an account* has been sorted out.

For fine-grain classification reasons, there should be well-defined subgroupings within each class. This will permit a much more accurate system than the usually current one, which supports only a two-way sort:

- Entry of funds
- Withdrawal of funds

Summary presentations like that are quite common. Hence, as the foregoing discussion suggests, what takes place

* See also the dual Classification and Identification system in D. N. Chorafas, *Handbook of Databases and DBMS* (New York: McGraw-Hill/Tab Books, 1989).

** It might seem that this is not necessarily related to fuzzy engineering and yet, as we will see in section 7, it is most closely connected.

today in many financial institutions is quite approximate—unfit for relationship management reasons.

Another deficiency of many current legacy systems is that they are based on *pre-advice*, not confirmed figures. With pre-advice the situation is fuzzy, and therefore it cannot be handled in a deterministic way the way legacy solutions try to do. There is a schizophrenic situation:

- While the current, quite elementary, organization stands on a *fuzzy basis*,
- The available information technology supports are deterministic, hence unfit for the prevailing environment.

Here is, therefore, an excellent ground for the implementation of fuzzy engineering in connection to pre-advice, with inferences made from historical data and estimates based on uncertainties. Examples of fuzzy predicates are:

- Not sure on time
- May be
- Quite sure

An application reflecting this frame of reference can be very helpful in optimization, for example, in placing money based on fuzzy estimates. Figure 9-2 suggests a classification of client behavior on a 0 to 4 scale that characterizes how fast the customer moves funds around.

- 0 identifies a client who moves funds out "very fast."

Even so, the client may have some delays; thus, the certainty of fast movement extends toward 1, which stands for "not very rapid withdrawal." Notice that 1 is a peak figure; the values of the corresponding possibilistic curve decrease toward 0 and 2.

FIGURE 9-2 Fuzzy classification of client behavior in funds switching, for cash management purposes.

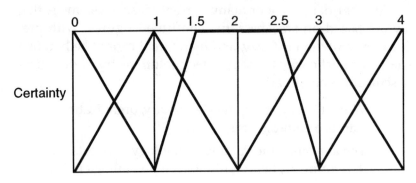

- 2 stands for "average speed of funds withdrawal."

In fact, as with all averages, this is an imprecise definition. In this case, values 1.5, 2, and 2.5 are just as likely. The distribution of the "average" curve extends from 1 to 3, which represents "rather slow funds withdrawal."

- 4 reflects the "slow funds mover," the clients who represent the better profits to the bank.

Notice also that the five possibilistic distributions in Figure 9-2 are crossing one another. This is normal since the concepts underlying the classification 0 to 4 of customer habits in terms of cash management is in itself fuzzy.*

7 USING A FUZZY SETS GRAPH TO JUDGE CUSTOMER BEHAVIOR

The example that led to the development of a fuzzy sets graph for cash management purposes primarily addressed the issue of

---

* We will see how to use these possibilistic distributions in order to judge customer behavior, through the example in section 7.

client profiles. If the precondition is the proper identification of customers, then profile analysis is necessary to judge who are the customers who leave significant balances and who remove their balance right away.

Any director of finance would say that in terms of deposits and withdrawals some customers are more inclined than others to leave their balances in the bank. But usually there are no tools permitting an accurate distinction to be made in this regard:

- Since there are no rules and no data in connection to client profiles,

- In the course of morning placements the finance division can only guesstimate possible positions.

- But the afternoon confirmation often involves a huge risk, and treasurers run for cover.

- Discrepancies and their coverage may oblige the bank to take expensive loans.

These vague estimates and subsequent discrepancies are due to the fact that the treasury usually only has access to the real figures in the afternoon of each day. As a result, during the day the director of finance has to operate with imprecise and uncertain balances.

Many banks feel that due to these facts there is an urgent need for customer profile analysis, which requires both data-based information and expert systems. The lesson is that

- Fuzzy adjustment to the current policy of deterministic placing is necessary, and

- Current tools don't permit such refinement. Hence, the risk remains.

To appreciate the dimension such a risk may take, we have to understand the fact that each day thousands of client orders to be executed involve significant amounts of money. Therefore, their handling should attract a great deal of attention.

Since we are talking of thousands of daily orders giving financial instructions, it is not humanly possible to optimize through recollections only. Yet this is what seems to be happening today in the large majority of cases using a printout as interface.

That is, of course, good documentation that there is no limit to the backwardness of the paper kingdom into which the EDPers and mainframers have led the financial institutions. Should this really be the case? Is there anything better that could be done?

To answer this query in a factual manner, let's look at Figure 9-3, which essentially reproduces the diagram we have seen in Figure 9-2—but with a difference. The difference lies in the two vertical bars at positions A and B.

- Customer A moves his cash balances rather fast, at least faster than the average.

In fact, his grading has a certainty value of 0.3 on the "not very rapid withdrawal" and a 1.0 value of the "average speed of funds withdrawal" scale.

Notice that this sort of evaluation would have been impossible with probability theory. If made at the same time for the same client, these two statements would have contradicted one another. But they do make sense with possibility theory.

- Customer B has a policy of slowly moving her funds out—but not as slowly possible.

Her evaluation bar identifies her condition at 3, "rather slow funds withdrawal," at a 0.3 level of the certainty function. Customer B's bar intercepts the "slow funds mover curve" at 0.8. The sum of these two certainty functions is 1.1.

FIGURE 9-3 Grading customers A and B on how fast they move their cash balances from the bank.

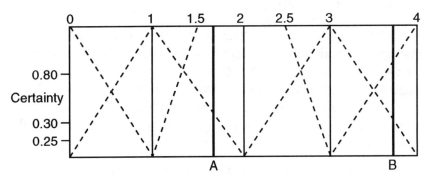

Once again, such a result would have been impossible with probability theory, where the sum should have been equal to 1. But with possibility theory such sum can be less than, equal to, or greater than 1—which speaks volumes about the power of expression of fuzzy engineering.

How should the customer A and customer B bars be positioned? This is a valid question, and a satisfactory answer to it passes through two types of prerequisites:

- A good solution to interactive information technology, of which we spoke in sections 4 and 5 and

- The appropriate classification/identification of clients and accounts, on which we focused section 6

Over time, say 6 months to 1 year, an expert system running on the computer can learn client behavior in terms of management of account balances, subsequently translating it into grades. The whole process should be automated, even if at the start knowledgeable bankers can do a first approximation of the classification and grading in question.

8 AUTOMATING SENSITIVE ASPECTS OF BANKING WORK

Cash Management is not the only domain that needs true automation rather than patchwork through Cobol and mainframes. Cash management, however, is central to many other financial operations, hence the need to bring this example further. Expert systems and models can help the efficient execution of financial functions in many ways. For instance, in the typical bank today,

- Between 15 and 20 percent of orders concerning cash position comes from fully manual customer instructions.

- These are taken over the phone or sent through telexes. They are typically badly formatted and take a lot of time for manual intervention.

This, too, is awkward and primitive, in no way reflecting what leading-edge financial institutions do. For instance, Bankers Trust, Citibank, Sumitomo Bank, Mitsubishi Bank, Banque de la Société Génerale de Belgique, and others use expert systems, not expensive people, to format the telexes.*

Clear-eyed financial institutions also employ incentives to induce clients into sending formatted orders. Because the larger and most important money orders come from large-scale correspondents, input automation can be negotiated.

At the same time, bank management must see to it that after the client input has been received it is handled online, and a cash position is arrived at. There should be no manual calculation made for the use of funds. Here, too, fuzzy engineering can be employed to advantage.

---

* See also D. N. Chorafas and H. Steinmann, *Expert Systems in Banking* (London: Macmillan, 1991).

Advanced models can be further used to optimize treasury functions. The aim should be to fully automate all inflows and outflows to the treasury, with parallel goals to:

- Use fuzzy engineering to best manage the uncertainty connected to the amount of funds (by source) and their usage and

- Balance Debit/Credit between different accounts (for instance, in various currencies) of the same client, in order to provide better service.

Let's not forget that many banks today, particularly those with international operations, deal in 20 to 30 different currencies simultaneously, even if five of them: dollar, yen, pound, german marks, swiss francs, make up more than 80 percent of the balances. It is therefore not easy to keep the customer cash position fully updated through classical data processing that reflects a 19th century culture.

Even if customer accounts were not taken into the equation—and they should be taken in—it is totally unfeasible to optimize 20 to 30 different balances in debit and credit in a non-integrative way. And it is also irrational, since advanced technology permits us to handle that job through financial engineering.

Limping on with legacy systems is silly business and works to the detriment of the bank. Hence, it should be stopped cold before it creates further frustration and damage. Stopping it, however, implies a tough management decision. It will not happen on its own accord. Top management should make it clear that

- There is plenty of purpose in doing experimentation, and knowledge engineering can help.

- A good example is the use of fuzzy engineering in studying patterns in bonds.

There are today in the market some 20 different types of bonds transiting through customer accounts and the bank's own treasury. In terms of *type of bond,* the following are considered to be the most important:

- Bullet
- Repayment at option of issuer
- Repayment by lottery
- Zero coupon
- Perpetual

A number of risk factors can be defined in connection to each of these bond types to be studied and analyzed through fuzzy sets. Among the most important factors that should be examined in detail but also have their handling automated are the following:

- Currency risk
- Company quality risk
- Interest rate risk
- Early repayment risk
- Country risk

Figure 9-4 reflects on the possible use of fuzzy engineering for calculating 5 different risks for bullet bonds. Notice that fuzzy sets is not the only way to study the decay curve of bonds due to early repayment. Since 1989, Wall Street firms use the Monte Carlo method* to estimate *Option Adjusted Spread* (OAS).

On Wall Street, the Monte Carlo approach is used for securitized mortgages. But both fuzzy sets and Monte Carlo can be employed to ascertain *core deposits* and their maturity. For instance,

- Client deposits and
- Currency deposits.

* Originally developed by Dr. John von Neumann for nuclear engineering studies. See Chapter 11.

FIGURE 9-4 Possible use of fuzzy engineering to calculate five different risks for bullet bonds ($100M represents capital and compound/interest for 20 years bonds).

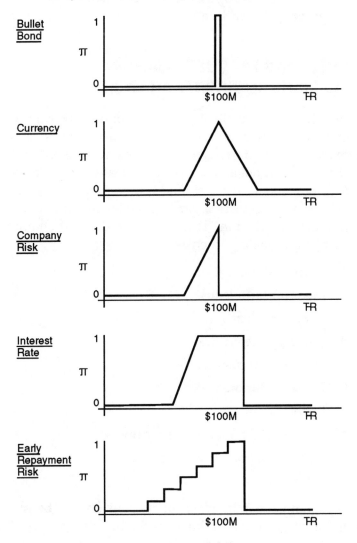

On average, a client may have a $100 million deposit. But what is *the core* that does not run out? How can we match customer funds? Can we do so by means of *sensitivity analysis*? This query is answered in section 9.

9 DEVELOPING THE CLIENT MIRROR AND DOING SENSITIVITY ANALYSIS

The need to know the client profile is not new. During the last 20 years the foremost financial institutions have developed a *client mirror*, which presents for each customer the *cost* and *benefit* to the bank. But not all constructs are really sophisticated.

Ideally, a client mirror should be computed on the basis of transactions and balances regarding a customer's relation with the financial institution. This should reflect all channels in which a client is dealing, such as:

- Cash position
- Medium-term loans
- Long-term loans
- Trading in securities
- Securities in custody
- Forex operations
- Export credit
- Commercial paper/underwriting
- Commercial paper/discounted
- Letters of credit

These and other financial operations should be mapped into the client account and linked to the bank's cost control system. Such linkage cannot possibly be deterministic; therefore, fuzzy engineering should be employed for integrative reasons. This is particularly true in connection to those operations involving *risk*.

Ideally, the customer mirror should provide a very accurate view of the customer relationship. It must permit the account manager to know the profit and loss with every important client of the bank, as well as to experiment on the account for optimization reasons.

Today we have the technology to do much better than in the past, through *client profiling*. Some banks are doing so through expert systems that analyze past account behavior. For instance, for cash management reasons an expert system identifies:

- Currency most used
- Debit or credit balances by currency
- Amount of client order
- Value date (by client order)
- Credit rating

To effectively manage its client accounts—and the associated cash—the bank may well require even more information, such as, *time and type* of cash in deposit, *payment pattern* to cover debit balances, and pattern of *moving out* of credit balances.

This has to be done in detail both by *client* and by *currency*. At the same time, it is wise to convert in real time the client account into one balance at preferred currency in order to estimate the mass of money being invested.

Algorithms and heuristics are therefore necessary permitting us to convert in real time DT/CR into a base currency, making it feasible to know the balance by client and in total. It is then possible to add *value dates* by client, account, currency, and DT/CR.

Another type of implementation that makes sense within the overall perspective of money management is *sensitivity analysis*. Practiced for the last few years, sensitivity analysis is a new subject—but it is spreading. It is being used, for example, in evaluating a portfolio of loans and investments.

In this connection, we should consider *country risk* as one of the sensitivities, identifying as critical factors political stability, interest rate fluctuations, exchange rate fluctuations, and so on.

In a recent sensitivity analysis project, four foreign exchange fluctuations were identified with the following sensitivity factors at the top of the list:

- Market sentiment
- Gross national product (GNP)
- Unemployment
- National debt
- Current account
- Possible country risk
- Balance of trade
- Safe haven
- Velocity of circulation of money
- Liquidity
- Behavior of local stock market
- Behavior of main stock markets in the world

Reuters gives statistics on some of these factors, and these can be exploited in real time. Other information is available in public databases and the bank's own databases. But if the bank's IT keeps working in batch, management will never get any results.

In other terms, as long as the old procedures and the people who brought them remain in charge, and the obsolete culture prevails, the situation is not going to change. Neither client mirrors nor sensitivity analyses can be done in any meaningful sense. The analytical approaches outlined in this chapter can only be implemented through advanced technology.

In conclusion, fuzzy engineering can help in forecasting future balances by client, currency, DT/CR, and so on, as well as in sensitivity analysis studies. In essence, this is what the bank needs in order to provide a more sophisticated service to its clients. The basic elements boil down to databases and mathematical models combined into one agile system.

New departures are necessary. Patches cost time and money, making bad things worse. Only a thorough reorganization can streamline the dataflow, revamp the algorithms and the heuristics, assist the professionals and the managers. There are absolutely no technical reasons preventing us from doing things right; but there are *political reasons*, which is why they are being done wrong.

10 Case Studies on How to Apply Fuzzy Engineering

1 INTRODUCTION

The subject of this chapter is case studies on the implementation of fuzzy engineering. A case study is usually done as a microcosm of another much more detailed or larger real-life case. As with every model, the case study permits us to abstract and idealize, while keeping close to reality. It also makes analogical reasoning feasible.

To serve its purpose as an emulator of real life, a case study must be a representative project. This is the way in which the cases in the present chapter have been selected. The implementations that took place in the macrocosm of these cases present events that are

- Realistic enough and able to retain the attention of committed learners, but

- Simple enough to allow experimenting with new ideas and fuzzy engineering tools.

The studies we will see in this and the following chapter—including their principal factors and the way fuzzy engineering has been applied—are fairly well-documented and able to be worked out in a nearly complete manner. Most importantly, the solutions that are elaborated are not hypothetical. They come from banking and finance, and they are doable.

In the background of all the implementation examples on fuzzy logic we will be examining are formal principles of approximate reasoning, with precise reasoning viewed as a limiting case. Central about these applications is the fact that unlike classical financial analysis

- The cases are modeling the imprecise modes of reasoning that play an essential role in our ability to make rational decisions, and

- They take place in an environment of uncertainty where we have to infer an approximate answer to a number of challenging questions.

As can be inferred through the case studies we will examine, there are two main reasons why classical financial analysis, and the logical systems on which it rests, cannot cope with the problems we will attack in these studies:

1. The tools used in traditional financial analysis do not provide a system for representing the meaning of propositions connected to the trading of financial instruments, when such meaning is imprecise.

2. Neither can legacy approaches represent the leading factors symbolically in a representation language such as a semantic network.

By contrast, as we will see through practical examples, fuzzy engineering effectively addresses these problems. The answer to a query is deduced through a propagation of *constraints*, a concept already introduced in Chapters 8 and 9.

Within the constrained environments we will see in the cases we study, the models we develop will deal with *dispositions*, that is, propositions that are preponderantly but not necessarily always true. This quality makes feasible numerous applications in fields ranging from finance to engineering, as in the case of learning the driver's behavior and pattern.

2 A GRADING PROCEDURE INVOLVING UNCERTAINTY AND THE DEFUZZIFICATION CONCEPT

This simple case study is taken as example of how fuzzy engineering is implemented in a financial environment. The goal is to demonstrate the way in which the concept of fuzzification can be applied. The chosen method is to start at a conceptual level and then proceed with the implementation in a step-by-step way.

For reasons of continuity, we will use the same grading scheme, from "0" to "4", that we used in Chapter 9 with the classification of client behavior in funds switching. But we will also bring this example a notch further by demonstrating how the fuzzy set evaluation should be done.

Suppose that a given college follows a grading system for test evaluation that ranges between "0" and "4." Grade "4" is at the top of the scale, but the grading itself is not crisp; it involves a certain degree of fuzziness as the individual instructors' temperaments and grading habits vary.

Students who receive in the horizontal scale a grade from "0" to "1" are considered to have flunked the examination. The result is worse the nearer it is to "0," the worst case being reflected by "Level 1"—which is the highest possibility of the certainty function π,* indicating the student has flunked the exam.

- Grades averaging around "1" are low.
- Grades averaging around "2" are median.
- Those averaging around "3" are high.
- As stated, the grade of excellence is "4."

---

* Which, as already stated, are also known as necessity, truth, belief, or possibility function.

FIGURE 10-1 Fuzzy sets to calculate degree of membership to different classes of college grades.

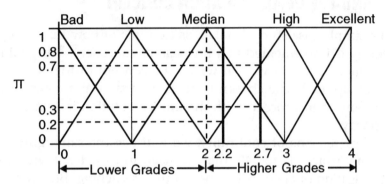

Notice that in each case in Figure 10-1, the center point of the respective curves (1,2,3) has a certainty function equal to "1." The extremes under the curve have a belief function of "0."

As the careful reader will observe, the possibility distributions of the bad, low, median, high, and excellent grades overlap with one another. This is a good practical example of fuzziness: The student being graded might belong to a certain degree, to the one, the other or both distributions. For simplicity purposes, in Figure 10-1 these distributions have been taken to be symmetric, as in the example that we have seen in Chapter 9. Let's, however, repeat that the possibility distribution does not need to be symmetric. This is done only to simplify the presentation.

Regarding each grading curve, the possibility π increases toward the center point and decreases in the direction of the limiting values, or *boundary conditions*.* For instance, limiting values 1 and 3 for central point 2 have a possibility (certainty) value equal to zero. This is only partly applicable at the two extremes of the graph:

* See also the discussion in Chapter 9.

- The curve of excellence starts with grade "3," with certainty equal to "0," and

- Ends at grade "4," with the possibility function equal to "1."

With this background in mind, two teachers are grading a given student. The one gives him a grade of 2.7 and the other of 2.2. As shown in Figure 10-1, both grades are input functions, each represented by a bar. They will be combined into a fuzzy result through a *predicate box*.

Once the inputs are known, to reach the output function we need to define the matrix in the predicate box, which helps combine the grades of teacher A and teacher B. Its structure is shown in Table 10-1. In a block diagram form, the combination of the two inputs through the predicate box and the fuzzy result obtained as output are exhibited in Figure 10-2.

To appreciate how the predicate box matrix works, let's return to Figure 10-1 and fuzzify the grades according to the bad, low, medium, high and excellent curves already established:

TABLE 10-1 Predicate matrix combining the inputs of Teachers A and B

	Teacher A				
	Bad	Low	Medium	High	Excellent
Teacher B					
Bad	o				
Low		o			
Medium			0.55*		
High				0.45*	
Excellent					o

* Mean of the respective belief function values given the grades by the two teachers.

FIGURE 10-2 Input and output functions, predicate box combining the teacher's grades.

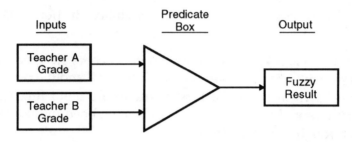

- Teacher A's 2.7 grade cuts the high curve at 0.7 and the medium curve at 0.3.

- Teacher B's 2.2 grade cuts the high curve at 0.2 and the medium curve at 0.8.

In this particular case, for each teacher, the sum of the two certainty functions is equal to 1, but as already noted this does not need to be so. It may be less or more than 1, which would have been the case if the curves were not symmetric but skew.

In Figure 10-1, none of the bad, low, or excellent curves are intercepted by the two grades. Hence, the entries at the intersection of the three columns is 0.

- Medium grade certainty functions have been 0.8 by teacher A and 0.3 by teacher B. *The mean is 0.55*, and this is the entry to the predicate matrix.

- High grade certainty functions have been 0.7 by Teacher A and 0.2 by Teacher B. *The mean is 0.45*, which is entered into the predicate matrix of Table 10-1.

This is a simple example with 2 graders. If, for instance, there were 5 graders, the system would enter *a virtual 5-dimensional matrix*, using cuts of that matrix to present in 2-D two

FIGURE 10-3 Defuzzification of the degree of membership to the medium and high membership sets.

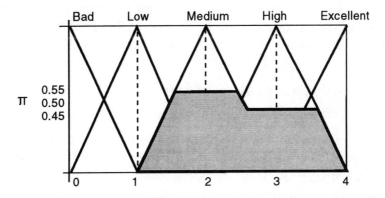

entries at a time. It is, however, advisable not to use too many inputs to a predicate box since this makes the system complex in terms of estimating and testing.

Fuzzification and defuzzification results are shown in Figure 10-3. After having used the fuzzy entries, we can define an area that is practically crisp. In this sense, the grey area *defuzzifies* the obtained fuzzy grading results. This area

- Is limited by the two medium-grade and high-grade curves and
- Is cut at the level of 0.55 belief function for the medium grade and 0.45 for the high grade.

Defuzzification is essentially an integral over the area the predicate matrix has helped to define. As such, it demonstrates what has been established in the subjective grading process. *If* the two teachers were reliable in their judgment, *then* in the longer run the performance of the graded student is to be found in the *shaded domain* of Figure 10-3.

3 CAPITALIZING ON THE POWER OF DEFUZZIFICATION

The shaded area we have seen in Figure 10-3 represents a non-fuzzy subset of the universe of discourse. Its establishment has been made possible by the fact that in fuzzy logic *the predicates may be crisp.*

- *Crisp predicate* examples are equal, mortal, and father of.
- *Fuzzy predicate* examples are unequal, ill, and fired by.

Fuzzy logic also permits the use of fuzzy quantifiers such as most, many, several, few. These can be interpreted as fuzzy numbers that provide an imprecise characterization of the cardinality of one or more fuzzy or nonfuzzy sets.

Using this perspective, the shaded area in Figure 10-3 is a nonfuzzy set and may be viewed as a second-order fuzzy predicate. This view represents sufficiently well the meaning of propositions containing possibilities, thereby making it possible to manipulate grading results based on fuzzy logic.

Precisely because fuzzy logic provides a method for representing the meaning of both nonfuzzy and fuzzy predicates, the possible variation of the student's grades can be constrained. Theoretically the variation may be in the whole area of 1 to 4, but the extreme values have a zero possibility, while values next to them:

- 1.1, 1.2, etc.
- 3.9, 3.8, etc.

have a very low possibility. This can be easily understood through visual inspection of Figure 10-1 and Figure 10-3. Notice, however, that all values in the medium curve

- From 1.55 to 2.32

have the same 0.55 possibility, which establishes a sort of *confidence interval.* Correspondingly, all values in the high-grade curve

- From 2.56 to 3.58

have the same 0.45 possibility. The possibility between values 2.32 and 2.56 starts at 0.55 and decreases to 0.45, as shown in the chart of Figure 10-3.

It is just as important to take notice that the 0.55 and 0.45 averages have been obtained through simple addition of the two grades, followed by division by 2. Had there been 5 teachers (hence a 5-D solution space), the process would have been quite similar: addition of their grades and division by 5—a simple *arithmetic mean.*

If the type of application requires it, it is possible to use *relative weights* for each grader. In other words, some implementors may choose to employ weighted averages rather than simple arithmetic means.

The last reference helps to further document that the method is generally flexible and adaptable. It can handle subjective judgment well, but let's always recall that the results are neither better nor worse than the judgments that enter into the input—unless we are able to purify them through iterations. This is not only realistic, it is precisely the way decisions are made in business.

The careful reader will also appreciate that this type of logical handling cannot be achieved through the financial analysis tools used in classical studies. At the core of this statement is a fundamental distinction about the nature of

- *Qualitative* and
- *Quantitative*

evaluations, which have been already introduced in Chapter 8, and about which we talk in the next section with the example of using equities as a collateral.

Another basic question often posed with this type of implementation regards the necessary amount of processing power. Simple applications like the one we just saw run very easily on a personal computer. The cycles necessary for more complex real-life applications generally depend upon the following:

- The volume of database pumping
- The number of rules involved
- The amount of defuzzification which needs to be done
- The necessary response time

For interactive financial applications, the response time should be subsecond, and this helps define the power of necessary number crunching. Networked work stations and high performance computers (super-computers) are the advisable solutions. Mainframes are an aberration.

Machine cycles are needed not only for processing reasons but also cross-database access in a heterogeneous environment. High performance computing is necessary and today this is the case with any information technology implementation, most particularly by the major financial institutions. We also need cycles to handle at high speed visualization and visibilization chores in interactive reporting.

4 QUANTIFICATION, QUALIFICATION, AND FUZZIFICATION IN TRADING

The fuzzy engineering implementation highlighted in the grading case study (in section 2) is fully applicable to the financial world. But prior to looking at practical examples, we need to clarify some other issues that will permit us to better appreciate how the method works.

The model we construct will be more accurate if we properly appreciate the fundamental distinction existing between *quantification* and *qualification,* as well as where between these two notions the concept of *fuzzification* lies.

As we have seen since the beginning of Chapter 1 when we spoke of insight and foresight in finance, we use computer models to better understand the process we are working on, emulating complex real-life situations in order to make predictions. If subsequent market results agree with these predictions, we conclude that there is indeed quantitative proof that the model we have made may be on the right conceptual track.

- Analogical reasoning, and therefore simulation, rests on this simple notion.
- A qualitative description will necessarily be judgmental, hence more or less fuzzy, but
- The essence of quantitative verification also underpins the test of a hypothesis, which we saw on numerous occasions.

Quantitative agreement means that real-world data is closely in line with the hypothesis we have created to help analyze rather obscure situations. By contrast, a qualitative agreement tells us something has been detected but not precisely measured.

Qualitative agreement essentially deals in *qualities* rather than quantities, but as we have seen with the cases in sections 2 and 3, order of magnitude quantities could also be present. The difference between quantitative and qualitative agreement is similar to that prevailing between

- The precision of numbers and
- The fuzziness of ideas and concepts.

Because numbers can also be fuzzy,* the quantitative and qualitative appreciation of a situation need not be that different. By contrast, when numbers are crisp, the two may be worlds apart.

* Or may come from a noisy environment, as is the case with financial time series.

---

1. *Quantitative understanding* is hard edged and precise.

This state of affairs characterizes sciences like physics and chemistry, which are relatively well settled, but few business processes fall into this class. A possible exception is *accounting*—because accounting standards get legislated—where both data and the method must be *crisp*.

Established in 1495 by Luca Paciolo, a Franciscan monk and teacher of mathematics, double entry accounting will soon be 500 years old. Most importantly, the way to treat the general ledger is specified by law. Notice, however, that accounting laws (for instance, assets depreciation) are not the same in all countries or in the same country over a period of time.

Hence, in terms of globalization of financial instruments and other resources, accounting rules can be fuzzy, though country by country they may be crisp. This is a good example of the overlap existing between *fuzzy notions* and *crisp rules*.

2. *Qualitative understanding* is typically fuzzy, reflecting much ignorance about what is really happening.

Such ignorance is due to the vagueness and uncertainty characterizing, for instance, market environments and their behavior. Predictions about where the market is going, many actuarial calculations in insurance, and the grading of collateral in connection to loans are qualitative, not quantitative events.

The interplay between quantification, qualification, and fuzzification characterizes the new world of financial trading which capitalizes on *discontinuities*. "Sometime during the 1970s, the longest period of continuity in economic history came to an end," suggests Dr. Peter Drucker. "At some time during the last dozen years, we moved into turbulence."

- Propelled by the dynamic economies and by technology that keeps advancing, the rules of the financial games keep changing.

- If we do not adapt to these changes and equip ourselves with the appropriate tools, we are out; we can no
more be valid players.

That's how not only companies but whole industries and
markets disappear. In the late 1960s and early 1970s, the watch-
makers of Switzerland were so good at their craft, and so widely appreciated, that they owned a remarkable 65 percent of the
world market for all types of timepieces. By 1980, the Swiss
share of the market plunged below 10 percent.

Why this sharp discontinuity? The Swiss did not suddenly
forget how to make excellent clocks and watches. Neither did
they overprice their works of art making everyone want to opt
out of their products. What they were guilty of was failing to
see the future.

The same is true with trading and *financial instruments* at
large. A financial instrument is cash but is also evidence of
ownership in equity or debt. It is a contract that meets obligations and rights, which however may be fuzzy. Nobody said
that contractual obligations are always crisp, or that they can
ever be immune to *credit risk* and *market risk*—which we must
carefully study—hence the need for competitive tools.

5 THE EVALUATION OF COLLATERAL FOR EQUITIES

The basic concepts that section 4 has outlined must be kept in
perspective as we discuss the evaluation of *collateral equities*.
Not only do different evaluators have different opinions which
are, in principle, fuzzy, but the value of the equities themselves
can vary as a result of market reaction. This is true even if the
value of a given portfolio was established in the most precise
way.

Taking as a frame of reference stocks that have been placed
as collateral, it is evidently unsafe to apply an across-the-board
average number as percent of current market value (for instance

60 percent, 70 percent or something similar). In any given market, stock prices can vary as a result of fluctuations in:

1. Stock market trends (bull, bear, drifting)
2. The company's stock value
3. The national economy
4. Political stability
5. Prevailing volatility
6. Market liquidity
7. Interest rates
8. International trade and the world economy*

These are among the key factors influencing a given stock's collateral value. With the exception of items 2 and 8, these factors are just as well applicable to bonds, and all of them can be treated through qualitative analysis reflected in fuzzy sets.

The introduction of this chapter spoke about dispositions. A *disposition* can be viewed as a usually-qualified proposition, which is a different way of looking at the implementation of fuzzy quantifiers. The following statement is an example:

"Bonds are *usually* good investments."

The message provided by this statement and its importance in evaluation procedures stems from the fact that most of what is usually referred to as commonsense knowledge may be viewed as a collection of dispositions. Hence, the development of rules of inference can be enhanced by means of commonsense knowledge.

Furthermore, the financial examples we will see from section 6 onward may be viewed as an extension of multivalued logic, dealing with approximate rather than precise modes of reasoning:

* In section 6 we will use these eight factors to develop a fuzzification model.

- The chains of reasoning in these case studies are short in length.
- Rigor does not play as important a role as it does in more classical mathematical models.

In the financial markets, everything, including truth, is a matter of degree. The greater the expressive power we have available, the better able we are to go beyond classical two-valued logical systems.

As is the case with the statement, "Bonds are usually good investments," one of the important issues in fuzzy logic relates to inference from qualified propositions. This is of central importance in the management of uncertainty and in the formalization of common sense reasoning. Dr. Lotfi Zadeh makes the distinction between

- Probability-qualification and
- Usuality-qualification

Zadeh associates to this issue the role played by fuzzy qualifiers. For example, the disposition: "Usually Dobermans are black" may be interpreted as: "most Dobermans are black" or, equivalently, as: "It is likely that Dobermans are black."

In this example, *likely* is a fuzzy predicate that is numerically equal to the fuzzy quantifier *most*. Equivalently, in both the cases of bonds and of Dobermans, *usually* qualifies a proposition (bonds or Dobermans).

- What is the relation between fuzzy predicates and the evaluation of equities given as collateral?
- Whether they appreciate it or not, banks that use a fixed percentage rate to evaluate collateral essentially apply fuzzy concepts, but in an average way over which they have no control.

What they express in an "average" manner is their uncertainty which oscillates between good and bad collateral, thus greatly reducing the security which they are taking. As we will see in the next section, there is a better way of doing the evaluation job in pricing securities given as collateral.

6 MORE ACCURATE WAYS FOR PRICING COLLATERALS*

Some people may say that as far as stock market trends and fluctuation in value are concerned, crisp data is available. For instance, if we wish to analyze market behavior, we could use the time series of the Dow Jones Index as our reference.

- But don't some of the same financial analysts who make that statement also suggest that stock market data are full of noise?

- If so, can fuzzy engineering provide a better, more dependable methodology than time series from the New York Stock Exchange?

To answer this query, Figure 10-4 presents the fuzzification of the Dow Jones Index. This is one of the two inputs we will consider in the present example.

While the input to the predicate box has been, for the sake of simplicity, purposely limited to only two factors, when many factors exist the methodology requires sorting them by degree of

- Importance and/or
- Precedence.

* This section focuses on stocks, while the next sections address bond-related issues.

FIGURE 10-4 Fuzzification of the Dow Jones Index considering ranges of the last 20 years and possible maxima, using today's perspective.

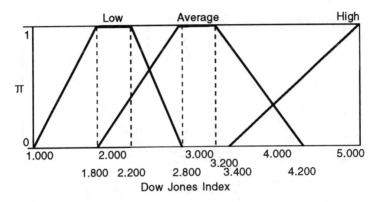

In other words, one of the rules in fuzzification is to decide which inputs to combine first, and which inputs should be grouped with one another. As an example, the following are logical groupings of the 8 factors we have considered in section 5 are:

- 1 and 2 into a Master Factor
- 3 and 4 into an Economic Factor
- 5, 6, and 7 into a Market Sentiment Factor

The outputs of 1 and 2 can be combined with 8; then this output and those of 3 and 4, as well as 5, 6, and 7 can be combined in pairs. Notice that factors 3, 4, 5, 6, and 7 could also have been grouped together into one 5-dimensional predicate box.

To continue this example on a simpler platform, we will proceed with the calculation of only the market factor. We can fuzzify the value of the company's stock which, say for example, has been moving in the time frame we have considered for Dow Jones, in a range of $20 to $130, with $60 to $100 as the band in which the stock value dwells most frequently.

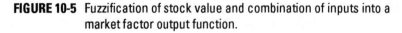

FIGURE 10-5 Fuzzification of stock value and combination of inputs into a market factor output function.

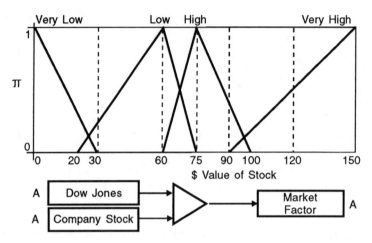

This is shown at the upper half of Figure 10-5. The second half of the figure shows the two inputs to the fuzzification box, and the output market factor. Let's now examine how the output function should be estimated.

The best way to explain the bigger system is to start by noticing that inputs and output have been labelled A. This stands for *absolute* value. During the study it was felt that both the

- Absolute (A) value and
- Relative (R) value

of stock market movements as reflected in the Dow Jones index and the company's stock value should be determined and fuzzified. The A and R market factors should be studied each on its own merits and then combined. Since the calculation of the R inputs and output is similar to those of A, we will not review them in detail, besides making this statement of difference.

7 VISUAL PROGRAMMING AND PRACTICAL RESULTS

A crucial part of this implementation is the preparation of the predicate matrix. For absolute values, this has been elaborated with Dow Jones index and stock price as inputs. The form is shown in Table 10-2, but grading values have not been included.

As knowledgeable readers have most likely appreciated, this has been an exercise in visual programming. The IF... THEN...ELSE rules compiled by the shell to reflect the predicates that have been entered into this matrix are presented in Table 10-3.

- Significantly, these expert system rules have not been written by the analysts. They have been automatically generated by the system.

- The next step, which is automatically taken, is to compile this rule base (knowledge bank) into C language, producing a run time code.

These two steps exemplify a major contribution to the automation of programming chores visual programming makes

TABLE 10-2   Predicate matrix combining the absolute value of Dow Jones index and stock price variation.

	Dow Jones		
	Low	Average	High
Stock Price			
Very High			
High			
Low			
Very Low			

TABLE 10-3 The knowledge bank of the fuzzy engineering expert system automatically generated by the shell after the predicate matrix was set.

IF (aDow Jones IS low) AND (aCompany Stock IS very low)
    THEN (aMarket Factor IS pessimistic)

IF (aDow Jones IS average) AND (aCompany Stock IS very low)
    THEN (aMarket Factor IS pessimistic)

IF (aDow Jones IS average) AND (aCompany Stock IS low)
    THEN (aMarket Factor IS pessimistic)

IF (aDow Jones IS high) AND (aCompany Stock IS very low)
    THEN (aMarket Factor IS pessimistic)

IF (aDow Jones IS high) AND (aCompany Stock IS low)
    THEN (aMarket Factor IS pessimistic)

IF (aDow Jones IS high) AND (aCompany Stock IS average)
    THEN (aMarket Factor IS pessimistic)

IF (aDow Jones IS low) AND (aCompany Stock IS low)
    THEN (aMarket Factor IS indifferent)

IF (aDow Jones IS average) AND (aCompany Stock IS average)
    THEN (aMarket Factor IS indifferent)

IF (aDow Jones IS high) AND (aCompany Stock IS high)
    THEN (aMarket Factor IS indifferent)

IF (aDow Jones IS low) AND (aCompany Stock IS average)
    THEN (aMarket Factor IS optimistic)

IF (aDow Jones IS low) AND (aCompany Stock IS high)
    THEN (aMarket Factor IS optimistic)

IF (aDow Jones IS low) AND (aCompany Stock IS very high)
    THEN (aMarket Factor IS optimistic)

IF (aDow Jones IS average) AND (aCompany Stock IS high)
    THEN (aMarket Factor IS optimistic)

IF (aDow Jones IS average) AND (aCompany Stock IS very high)
    THEN (aMarket Factor IS optimistic)

IF (aDow Jones IS high) AND (aCompany Stock IS very high)
    THEN (aMarket Factor IS optimistic)

feasible. The analyst can concentrate on the conceptual and creative part of the problem and not have to spend time and effort in writing a code—that is the computer's job.

Visual programming approaches are the smart banker's tool kit. But how many are using them? How many of us appreciate that the world of financial analysis can be simple or very complex—and it all depends on how well prepared we are to face the challenges?

In 1917 George F. Baker, president of First National Bank, invited Jackson Eli Reynolds to join his inner circle. The proposal came out of the blue, and Reynolds, a corporate lawyer and Columbia University professor, responded with a spontaneous burst of laughter.

"Have I said something funny?" the 77-year-old Baker asked. "It sounds to me," Reynolds responded, "as I am expecting a telephone call any moment from Paderewski asking me to play a piano duet with him." "Banking is not as hard as piano playing," Baker assured him.*

Banking is not as hard as piano playing, provided we know how to play. If we don't, the risks we take can blow up and bring us to the abyss because partners in the financial markets behave like one another and become a tightly knit system. Trading in off-balance sheet financial instruments, for instance, is in essence a one-partner risk.

The only sound approach to the risks we are taking is to address the issue of exposure instrument-by-instrument and client-by-client, classifying the bank's customers by rating—in a similar fashion to that which we have followed with stocks. We can effectively use Standard and Poor and Moody's as a basis of creditworthiness for the computation of credit limits.

The methodology suggested in these paragraphs is no different than the one we have applied already. To better appreci-

---

* James Grant, *Money of the Mind* (New York: Farrar Straus Giroux, 1992).

ate how this approach works, let's continue on the stock rating case study that was introduced in section 6.

For the fuzzification of relative values, rather than making the possibility curves, which we saw at the beginning of this chapter, it was felt that for Dow Jones and stock price variations it was better to work with percentages qualifying changes either way of a current value as one of the following:

- Indifferent (change is too small)
- Important
- Very important
- Impressive
- Very impressive

In the cases of absolute and difference, the market factor has been calculated. The fuzzy set graph of the absolute market factor is shown in Figure 10-6. Notice that there is a:

- Pessimistic,
- Indifferent, and
- Optimistic

FIGURE 10-6 Fuzzification of absolute market factor, as output of the Dow Jones Index and stock market price.

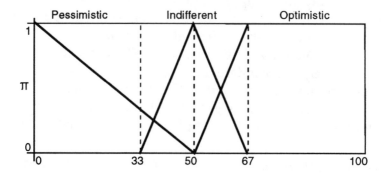

FIGURE 10-7 Defuzzification of variable: market factor.

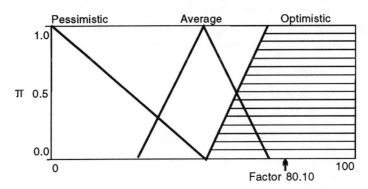

characterization. This is the combined qualification of Dow Jones movement and changes in the value of the company stock. A direct output from the computer, Figure 10-7 shows the defuzzification as a result of an 80.10 rating.

This result is real-life based on an ongoing valuation. The way it stands, it defines an optimistic stock market situation which can be expressed in this way: In terms of being bullish about this stock, the chances are just a little better than 4 out of 5. As every manager and professional knows, an accurate estimate of the prevailing situation in the marketplace is necessary in order to make tough decisions: "4 out of 5" is accurate but not precise. At the same time, a characteristic of tough decisions is being able to change one's mind on the basis of available evidence, reversing actions already taken and having confidence in the course chosen.

8 A FUZZY SYSTEM FOR BOND EVALUATION

Experience from daily practice teaches that for trading and investment purposes the emphasis should be on accuracy, not precision. Which factors can provide an accurate picture of the dependability that can be placed on a corporate bond?

Taking only bullet bonds of AAA companies* as a frame of reference in order to simplify the problem, the following nine factors were defined during a working meeting on bond evaluation as impacting on the price of the bond:

1. Company Profitability
2. Assets and Liabilities
3. Cash Flow
4. Dow Jones Index (absolute value)
5. Company Stock (absolute value)
6. Interest Rate
7. Market Liquidity
8. Market Volatility (for bonds)
9. Currency of Investment and Exchange Rate

The first three inputs are combined through a predicate box into an "A&L+Revenue" output factor, as shown in Figure 10-8. Input factors 4 and 5 have already been established through the case study on stocks.** We will see how to compute the inputs, predicate box, and output for the "A&L + Revenue" factor by the end of this chapter.

Interest rate fluctuations can nicely be expressed in a graph very similar to the one we saw in section 2 of the grading by two teachers (Figure 10-1). In fact, it will be wise to use two or more economists forecasting interest rates, leading to a defuzzification set as the one in Figure 10-3.

A similar consideration can be made regarding *liquidity* and market *volatility*. Market Volatility could be divided into

* Otherwise, among the top factors would have been bond repayment plan and quality grading of the issuer.

** It should be recalled, however, that this is an example of the method. A real-life application will provide a much more thorough examination of the input factors in reference, and of their interconnection.

FIGURE 10-8 Step-by-step combining of primary factors into a collateral evaluation.

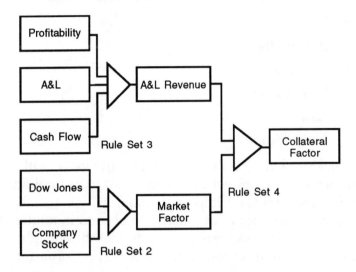

three factors to be combined through a predicate box with the following inputs:

- General market volatility
- Market volatility for the class of bonds to which the present one belongs
- Observed market volatility for this specific bond

As investment decisions get increasingly globalized, but each investor also watches a base currency (typically the currency of country of origin of the firm), it is appropriate to also consider *foreign exchange risk.*

This can be done nicely through radar charts,* representing in six dimensions the value change of a given currency against

* See also D. N. Chorafas and H. Steinmann, *Implementing Computer Networks in Financial Institutions* (London: Macmillan, 1989) and D. N. Chorafas, *Simulation, Experimentation and Expert Systems* (Chicago: Probus, and London: McGraw-Hill, 1992).

six other currencies, with time as the seventh dimension. Such changes can be automatically fuzzified through a threshold scale:

- High
- Rather High
- Average
- Rather Low
- Low
- Insignificant

Percentage change rather than absolute value will be the better metric. This, however, is a hypothesis to be carefully analyzed in terms of real-life implementation.

With this setting, what remains to be seen in a little more detail, in order to make this case study realistic enough, is the estimation of inputs, output, and predicate box for factors 1, 2, and 3. Inference from propositions of this type is a main concern of fuzzy engineering.

As suggested earlier, this is an example of implementation. The following formula shows the way the assets and liabilities estimate has been simplified by taking only the *acid test*:

$$\text{Acid test} = \frac{\text{Current Assets (CA)}}{\text{Current Liabilities (CL)}}$$

Up to a point, the more detail we put into the model, the better it reflects realistic conditions. No doubt, in real life two other inputs have to also be considered in order to examine A&L in all its aspects:

- Medium Term A&L
- Long Term A&L

Subsequently, current, medium, and long-term assets and liabilities should be combined through predicate boxes into one

FIGURE 10-9 Fuzzification of the acid test of current assets over current liabilities.

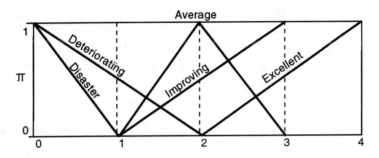

A&L output, to be used as an input to the integrative factors 1, 2, and 3 (of which we have spoken) the same way the acid test input is used in this example. Figure 10-9 describes the fuzzification of the acid test, taking as the basis that

- $\frac{CA}{CL} \leq 1$ is a disaster*
- $1 < \frac{CA}{CL} < 2$ is poor
- If $\frac{CA}{CL}$ moves from 2 towards 0, the situation is deteriorating.
- If $\frac{CA}{CL}$ moves from 1 to 3, the situation is improving.
- If $\frac{CA}{CL}$ goes from 2 to 3, the liquidity situation is excellent.

"Disaster," "poor," "deteriorating," "improving," and "excellent" are fuzzy concepts. They are essentially qualitative expressions often used by financial analysts, traders, and investment managers. But they are also a good point of departure in implementing fuzzy logic in the way we have seen in this and the preceding two chapters.

* The company is illiquid and must deposit its balance sheet.

9 WAYS AND MEANS OF ESTIMATING CASH FLOW

Continuing with the implementation example we established in section 8, *cash flow* has been estimated on the basis of what it exactly covers in terms of running expenditures. On that basis, possibilistic curves similar to those for bond evaluation have been plotted in a way resembling Figure 10-9. The premise is that:

- If cash flow covers only variable expenses, the situation is *bad*.
- If it covers variable expenses and depreciation (VE+D), the situation is *poor*.
- If it covers 150% of VE+D, it is *fair*.*
- If it covers 200% of VE+D, it is *good*.
- If it covers 300% of VE+D, the company is a *cash cow*.
- If it covers 500% of VE+D, it is a *terrific* cash flow.

Notice that, up to a point, analyses of this type have since 1980 been done through spreadsheets. Hence, they are well known but rather deterministic. Fuzzy engineering offers the possibility of being much more sophisticated than the use of spreadsheets permits.

Of course, we can be much more detailed in the cash flow estimates. Better yet, we can apply any procedure in this domain that the bank currently uses. This statement is also valid for what appears to be a deterministic approach, but our methodology and the results we obtain are of greater assistance by

- Detecting those elements involving vagueness or uncertainty and

* Percentages rather than more detailed expenses such as overhead, R+D, and marketing have been chosen, since this is an example.

- Expressing them by means of predicate boxes, in a way similar to the foregoing examples.

Cash flow analysis is not the only domain that can be approached by means of converting deterministic procedures into fuzzy engineering. We can do the same with the estimation of *profitability*, taking as a basis the known metrics of

- Revenue,
- Variable cost, and
- Fixed cost.

Or, if we wish a finer classification, we can add semi-fixed costs as well as overhead.

The following algorithms were chosen as the basic structure for a profitability evaluation. First, fuzzification was attempted in connection to the input factors in the revenue equation, according to the following rules:

- If revenue does not cover variable cost, the financial situation is a *disaster*.
- If revenue equals variable cost only, the situation is *bad*.
- If revenue equals variable costs and fixed cost (VC + FC), it is *poor*.
- If R = 1.1 (VC + FC)* or better, it is *good*.
- If R > 1.3 (VC + FC), it is *excellent*.
- If R > 1.5 it is *fantastic*.

Evidently, return on assets and return on equity would have been two other input factors to consider. They have not been included into the case study but should be part of a real-life application. The same is true of overhead, semi-fixed costs, costs of debt, and other issues.

* Assuming that all other costs, including overhead, are less than 0.1 (VC+FC).

TABLE 10-4 Weighting factors connected to the CA&CL, cash flow and profitability inputs.

Inputs	Relative Weight
CA & CL	1.00
Cash Flow	0.75
Profitability	0.50

Evidently, other analysts may place different weighting factors or none at all.

The flexibility of the method is further demonstrated by the fact that weighting factors can be associated to each input, if so desired. It was, for example, decided to associate the weights identified in Table 10-4.

With three input variables, the development of the predicate matrix is more complex than the examples we have earlier seen. One way to approach the task is to consider each factor of one of the input variables stable and vary the other two in that column.

- This is what is attempted in Table 10-5, with Assets and Liabilities the steady issue on a column-by-column basis.

- Subsequently, a predicate matrix of two input variables was developed.

In this particular case, the predicate matrix considered cash flow and profitability, integrating with the preceding (first) matrix into the predicate box. This is another example of how to establish a two-input predicate matrix.

Table 10-5 also brings into perspective issues characteristic of the *output factor*. Figure 10-10 concludes the integration of the inputs by presenting the fuzzy sets of the *collateral facilities* output curves.

TABLE 10-5 Characteristics of A&L states leading to predicate matrix with three input variables.

Assets and Liabilities				
Disaster	**Deteriorating**	**Poor**	**Improving**	**Excellent**
Cash Flow	*Cash Flow*	*Cash Flow*	*Cash Flow*	*Cash Flow*
Bad or Poor	Poor or Fair	Fair or Good	Good or Cash Cow	Cash Cow or Terrific
Profitability	*Profitability*	*Profitability*	*Profitability*	*Profitability*
Bad or Poor	Poor or Average	Average or Good	Good or Excellent	Excellent or Fantastic
Output Factors: Collateral Facilities				
State Chapter 11	Feel Bad	Can Sleep	Feel Good	Very Optimistic

- The grading scheme in the graph ranges from 0 to 4.
- Three different values: 1.5, 2, and 2.5 have a belief function equal to 1 in the "Can Sleep" curve.
- The other curves are quite similar to those we have already used.

FIGURE 10-10 Output function for collateral facilities, integrating the input from A&L cash flow and profitability.

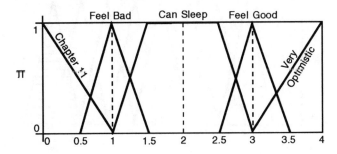

The collateral facility resulting from this predicate helps define the percentage level of a credit to be given to a company's bonds deposited as collateral. As will be appreciated from Figure 10-11, the ratios can range from 20 percent to 90 percent, depending on the input functions.

The *defuzzification* shown in Figure 10-11 suggests a 90-percent level, to which management may apply further reserve requirements. But such calculation is never fixed forever. If the system operates online, which should be the case, then the level of reserve requirements will be steadily changing in accordance with the outlined conditions.

This last reference shows the flexibility of the method, which permits fairly accurate evaluation of collateral values, but also permits further integration of reserve ratios, which for whatever reason have not been mapped into the model. *Simplification* is one of the often advisable options, provided we know that is has taken place—and what it means in real terms.

As has been demonstrated, the mathematical tools are available. What still needs to be done is to establish the appropriate management procedures. Organizational issues are not just important; in many cases they can make or break an application.

FIGURE 10-11 Defuzzification of variable: collateral factor.

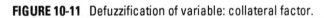
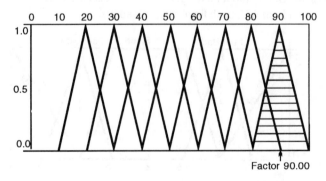

TABLE 10-6 Compilation into a knowledge bank of the predicate matrix defining the collateralization output.

IF (A, L + Revenue IS Chapter 11) AND (aMarket Factor IS pessimistic)
THEN (Collateral Fac IS no value)

IF (A, L + Revenue IS feel bad) AND (aMarket Factor IS pessimistic)
THEN (Collateral Fac IS 20ies)

IF (A, L + Revenue IS feel bad) AND (aMarket Factor IS indifferent)
THEN (Collateral Fac IS 30ies)

IF (A, L + Revenue IS optimistic) AND (aMarket Factor IS pessimistic)
THEN 0.200000* (Collateral Fac IS 30ies)

IF (A, L + Revenue IS can sleep) AND (aMarket Factor IS indifferent)
THEN (Collateral Fac IS 40ies)

IF (A, L + Revenue IS feel bad) AND (aMarket Factor IS optimistic)
THEN 0.200000* (Collateral Fac IS mid50ies)

IF (A, L + Revenue IS feel good) AND (aMarket Factor IS indifferent)
THEN (Collateral Fact IS mid50ies)

IF (A, L + Revenue IS can sleep) AND (aMarket Factor IS optimistic)
THEN (Collateral Fac IS 60/70ies)

IF (A, L + Revenue IS optimistic) AND (aMarket Factor IS indifferent)
THEN 0.200000* (Collateral Fac IS 60/70ies)

IF (A, L + Revenue IS feel good) AND (aMarket Factor IS optimistic)
THEN (Collateral Fac IS 80ies)

IF (A, L + Revenue IS optimistic) AND (aMarket Factor IS indifferent)
THEN (Collateral Fac IS 80ies)

IF (A, L + Revenue IS optimistic) AND (aMarket Factor IS optimistic)
THEN (Collateral Fac IS 90ies)

Finally, let's again bring into perspective the fact that all that is involved in the system's work is the setting of the graphics and of the predicate matrices. The shell will automatically generate the rule base, as shown in Table 10-6, and from there will generate the C code.

11 Using the Monte Carlo Method in Financial Analysis

1 INTRODUCTION

The *Monte Carlo* method has been used in solving problems in physics and engineering since World War II. Originally known as *Random Walks**, the method was revived and renamed** by von Neumann, Ulam, and others to help investigate military and atomic energy problems. The method outlived the more restrained notation of Lord Rayleigh or that of unrestricted random sampling.

Around the end of last century, the mathematician John William Strutt Rayleigh (1842–1891) was watching the way a drunkard walked in the streets of London. Each of the drunk's steps was supposed to have an equal probability of going in any direction.

- The mathematician wondered how many steps the drunkard would have to take, on the average, to get a specified distance away from his starting point.

- The pattern was stochastic and irregular, and therefore it was called the problem of *Random Walks*.

---

* Not to be confused with the random walks some financial analysts use in connection to time series.

** After the roulette in the principality in the south-east part of France.

The most attractive feature of the method is that it often affords a direct and simple model of the problem studied. As an example, let us take a diffusion problem.

A detective wants to know about the histories of numbered ten dollar bills stolen in a certain robbery. A bill is passed from one person to another, even back to the previous owner by random choice. The distribution f(t) of the bills in the population is governed by its diffusion equation:

$$\frac{\partial \phi}{\partial t} = \frac{\partial^2 \phi}{\partial x_1^2} + \frac{\partial^2 \phi}{\partial x_2^2} + \frac{\partial^3 \phi}{\partial x_3^2} + \cdots$$

We could find a solution by analytical methods, but this might be difficult when realistic boundary conditions are introduced. For instance, members of the underworld do not deposit bills in the bank, but others do.

Alternatively, we could get a solution by taking *n* bills and working out a typical history for each one, throwing a coin to see which person in a community receives a particular bill, following each bill through a succession of, say, 200 transactions. We could repeat this for a number of bills, and find, by single counting, *the distribution f(t) of the n bills* in the community at *a time t*, to which the analytic expression is an approximation. However, this would be a tedious approach. Through the use of the Monte Carlo method

- We can set up a model characterizing the problem under study,
- Program the sequence of events by deterministic rules when they arise, and
- Toss a coin when the determining factors are either obscure or, indeed, subject to probabilistic processes.

In this way, idealization of the problem in order to cast it into a known mathematical formulation can be minimized. As far as the Monte Carlo method is concerned, empirical functions taken from observational data are just as easy to handle as mathematical functions fitted on top of the data.

2 PROBLEMS CONNECTED TO THE CONSTRUCTION OF STOCHASTIC MODELS

In constructing a model of a system, we strive to use variables whose values can be obtained without too much difficulty. It is, however, just as true that some of the expressions built up out of even very simple variables may themselves become quite complex, a statement particularly valid when probability concepts are involved.

For example, consider a composite financial product that contains two parts. The composite product does not do well in the market because, presumably, one of its two parts fails to attract market attention, but it is not very clear which one.* From studying sales figures in product life cycles, we know the probability of failure of each item as a function of time. Hence,

- What we try to guesstimate is the life curve of each of the component items.

- What we want to know is the life curve of the product that contains both of these elements.

If g(t) represents the life curve of one of the items, and h(t) represents that of the other, then the life curve of the products is a function of these two component parts, and it is written:

$$F(t) = f[g(t)nh(t)]$$

---

* In the late 1980s, for instance, Shearson Lehman introduce a new financial product composed of three parts, one of which was not appreciated by the market, but it was not immediately clear which one.

Assuming functions g(t) and h(t) are known, function f(t) must be made explicit before we can experiment toward a possible solution.

In some cases, f(t) can be derived by mathematical analysis, for example when g(t) and h(t) are normal probability density functions. But in other instances, it is not possible or practical to evaluate such a function by classical mathematical means.

Taking an example from industry, this is the case with terms appearing in queuing and replacement models. Such expressions, however, can be evaluated by Monte Carlo, which permits us to obtain

- Approximate evaluations of mathematical expressions
- If these formulas are built up of one or more probability distribution functions.

Such a procedure can be combined with analytical and/or iterative approaches, making it possible to derive a solution to problems that cannot be effectively approached through more classical techniques.

As stated in the introduction to this chapter, the method we call Monte Carlo is a new use of older procedures such as random walks and unrestricted random sampling. What the latter essentially means is selecting items from a population in such a way that each item has an equal probability of being drawn.

- The new element Monte Carlo brings is using random sampling to determine some probabilistic property of a population of objects or events.
- One of the earliest and best-known uses of Monte Carlo has been in connection to studies of the decay of atoms, has random characteristics.

Remember the example of the drunkard we saw in the introduction. How can the probable distance of zig-zag walking be estimated without observing a large number of drunkards in similar circumstances? An extended number of observations would be impossible or impractical, but since the drunkards move at random, we can simulate the patterns of their walks by means of random numbers.

This approach will approximate the actual physical situation. From a large number of these simulated trials, we are then able to estimate the probable distance for any n irregular zig-zag phases.

In other problems, we can do the same thing through random sampling. Stochastic sampling has been precisely developed to solve this problem and it constitutes an essential part of the Monte Carlo technique.

In a way, the concept predates Lord Rayleigh. An ancient and simple example of random walks is the determination of π' by throwing a needle on a checkerboard and counting the number of times the needle falls across the line.

In mathematics, Laplace's equation can be solved by taking the random walks as starting at a point (x,y,z), noting the potential at the point at which each one crosses the boundaries, and adding them together. This is the potential at (x,y,z).

One of the better applications examples is the determination of the width of a door, the only measuring device being a two-meter standard with no subdivisions. This has applicability to finance, for instance in guesstimating the *fair value* of securities.

Fair value is indeed a fuzzy concept, but so is the evaluation of the collateral of securities and the estimation of the drunkard's walks. In Lord Rayleigh's calculations, random walks did permit an analytic solution. This is obtainable and is given by:

$$d = a \cdot \sqrt{n}$$

where d is the most probable distance of the drunkard from the lamppost, after a large number of irregular phases of his walk. The distance is equal to the average length a of each straight track the drunkard walks, times the square root of the number n of phases of the walk.

More generally, from a large number of simulated trials we may estimate the probability of being at a specified distance from a goal or point of origin (like the drunkard's lamppost). Or we may estimate the decay of loans in a pool of mortgages that has been securitized (see section 4) and resold to investors.

These are all practical applications. Another popular domain of Monte Carlo implementation is futures, options, swaps, and generally off-balance sheet financial instruments.

The drawback is that Monte Carlo simulation requires a great many machine cycles.* Therefore, many banks now use high-performance parallel computers. Some of those who employ client-servers have developed an alternative strategy: They use steadily Black-Scholes or binomial approximation for portfolio pricing by models—and run Monte Carlo simulation periodically to validate the results of the other methods.

3 CONCEPTS AND CHALLENGES IN IMPLEMENTING MONTE CARLO

Monte Carlo procedures permit us to elaborate problems similar to those we have seen through realistic functions. One of the better examples with implications to finance is *transition probabilities*, or Markov chains, which can be handled by biasing the random walks.

A very simple case is tossing a coin when the probability of heads or tails is biased not by a defect in the coin but by the outcome of the previous toss, for instance tails making tails more likely in following tosses.

A little more complex case is the algorithm underpinning *the genetic algorithm*, which we have studied in Chapter 5. Also in

---

* Also, it does not handle all cases, an example being American type options—as some banks suggested during the research.

---

nature, the survival of the fittest is an application of transition probabilities, where the chances are loaded toward the fittest.

As one of the examples in section 2 suggested, through Monte Carlo we are able to obtain synthetic data for the life span of a product or system, if we know only the life curves of its components. Consider the case of an electronic system with three component parts. The life curve of each component is given in Figure 11-1. The mean and the standard deviation of the life of the three components (in hours) are as follows:

$$\bar{x}_1 = 400 \quad s_1 = 80$$

$$\bar{x}_2 = 670 \quad s_2 = 200$$

$$\bar{x}_3 = 800 \quad s_3 = 115$$

Let's assume that parts belonging to these three populations will be selected at random on the assembly line. By using

FIGURE 11-1 Reliability curves of three components characterized by normal distribution.

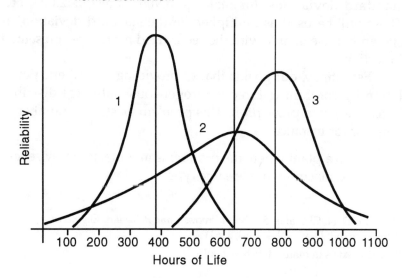

Monte Carlo, we can simulate this stochastic selection and subsequently compute the anticipated life of the system.*

Two alternative approaches to the problem exist. One
requires the plot of the cumulative curve of each of the three
distributions. In order to select at random the sample from
which to compute the systems' probability of failure, the
researcher should construct another vertical scale, divide it into
n equal distance, say $n = 100$, and then use a table of random
numbers.

Locating the value of the table on the ordinate and using
the cumulative curve as a parameter, we can easily find the
hours of life for a part belonging to the corresponding population. This can be repeated until the optimum size of a random
sample from every distribution is obtained.

The better alternative is to use a table of *random normal
numbers* (RNN).** It is better in the sense that it is more straightforward. Assuming a population of normal distribution, with
mean $\mu = 0$ and with standard deviation $\delta = 1$, the table of random normal numbers gives the random variation in units of
standard deviations; for instance 0.905 1.562 −2.003, etc.
These will be used as multipliers of the standard deviation, as
shown in the example with the securitized mortgages presented
in section 4.

Essentially, our goal is that of providing a synthetic population by combining three heterogeneous statistical distributions in a given proportion. This problem exists in a number of
cases, as for instance

1. In a plant where the product is manufactured by sever-
    al machines of the same type.

* See also D. N. Chorafas, *Statistical Processes and Reliability Engineering*
(Princeton, NJ: D. van Nostrand, 1961)
** Which exists in many statistical books.

In this case, the distribution of the quality of the item produced will often be heterogeneous, on account of individual differences between machines and their operators. Other background reasons may be variations in the quality of raw materials or semimanufactured goods.

2. In connection to securitized financial products which are composite of underlying assets each with different conditions and maturities.

These may represent not just three (as the example we saw in Figure 10-1) but many underlying distributions. What's more, we may not have the time, means, or even the will to sort them out. But we need to know about their heterogeneity to predict what happens next.

Any heterogeneous distribution raises the question: "What has caused the heterogeneity?" It is often possible when considering what we know about the process that leads to the observed values to dissect the observations into two, three, or more groups, each corresponding to a normal curve—or more likely being approximated by a bell shape. But is it a sound practice?

First of all, such dissection should never be purely formal. A *justified reason* should be demonstrated for making it. The fundamental question must be: Is it meaningful to dissect observed values into several groups on the basis of criteria other than the one and only property we have considered?

For instance, in the example on manufacturing, our first guess might have been that the property causing heterogeneity is *machines*. But in reality it may be *time*, which itself needs to be analyzed with regard to different criteria:

- Wear, because of delays in maintenance
- Change in shift, and hence in operators
- Fatigue due to night hours, and so on

The message is that both in finance and in manufacturing heterogeneity is often caused by a false formulation of the problem and/or an erroneous identification of the variables. This leads to a one-dimensional investigation instead of a multidimensional approach, which may be much more appropriate.

If one criterion is stochastically dependent on another criterion, and the characterization of the distribution is only done according to the first criterion, the outcome will often be heterogeneous on account of variations of the second or third criterion.* Hence, we must be very careful in our analysis—that is where one of the major challenges lies with the implementation of the Monte Carlo technique.

The other key challenge is in the assumption of dealing with a normal distribution, which is a hypothesis underpinning all statistical techniques. The tables we have available, like RNN, are based on this hypothesis, but real life does not always wish to comply with it. That is why fuzzy engineering—which makes no bell curve assumptions—can be a better alternative in a number of cases.

4 USING MONTE CARLO IN A FINANCIAL ENVIRONMENT

How can the Monte Carlo method be applied in a business environment? To start with a practical example, say that we are evaluating 10 pools of mortgages, each composed of only 3 mortgages,** which each come from a subpool.

The subpools respectively have 20, 25 and 30 year lives. That is heterogeneous, but they have other characteristics of

* If the second criterion is included, the process becomes an analysis of variance or a regression study.

** This is a hypothetical case, of course. A real pool would be composed of a three- or four-digit number, but 3 was chosen to keep the example simple.

homogeneity (for instance neighborhood), which lead to pooling them. We wish to find the worse case in life cycles:

- Each of the subpools comes from a known population, at least as far as its standard deviation is concerned.
- The three standard deviations are respectively 3, 5, and 6 years, which means that the last two are practically truncated.
- The normal curve is, of course, an approximation, but this being said, the mean in years is 10, 12.5, and 15.

As shown in Table 11-1, three sets of random normal numbers are selected. Since the random numbers are in units of standard deviation, they need to be converted into years. This is easily done by multiplying the RNN by the value of the corresponding standard deviation and adding it to the mean.

- First, the smallest value of the three random times in the row is taken as the corresponding life of the pool.

This helps to show when components of the pool start being repaid. Therefore, the stratum underpinning the securitized products starts wearing off.

- Then, in the next column the average life of the pool is calculated to help construct the life curve of the pool.

The second step is the one most frequently followed in practice, but as can be seen in Table 11-1 column 8 (the averages) looks like an overestimate when compared to column 7 (the minimum of the three times).

Averages typically aren't worth much. The notion behind them is that of the fellow who thinks that if he has his head in an oven and his feet in a refrigerator, on average he should be feeling alright. If averages can serve at all, it depends, of course, on the reasons why the investor buys the securitized mortgages:

TABLE 11-1 Calculating the life cycle of a mortgage pool in years.

Subpool 1

(1) RNN	(2) Life of Mortgage 10+3 (1)	(3) RNN	(4) Life of Mortgage 12.5+5 (3)	(5) RNN	(6) Life of Mortgage 15+5 (5)	(7) Minimum of Columns (2), (4), (6)	(8) Average Life Span (2)+(4)+(6)
-1.633	5.1	-0.542	18.2	-0.250	16.5	5.1	13.2
1.114	13.3	0.882	16.9	1.265	22.6	13.3	17.6
1.151	13.4	-1.210	6.5	-0.927	9.5	6.5	9.8
-1.939	4.3	0.891	16.9	-0.227	13.6	4.2	11.6
0.385	11.1	-0.649	9.3	-0.577	11.5	9.3	10.6
-1.083	6.7	-0.219	11.4	-0.291	13.3	6.7	10.4
-0.313	9.1	0.084	12.9	-2.828	0.0	0.0	7.3
0.606	11.8	-0.747	8.8	0.247	16.6	8.8	12.4
0.121	10.4	0.790	16.4	-0.584	11.5	10.4	12.7
0.921	12.7	0.145	13.2	0.446	17.7	12.7	14.5

- *If* the investor is an insurance company and the security is purchased to back up pension funds and annuities,

- *Then* the minimum time is very relevant because it indicates that no matter what the averages say the investment will slim much earlier.

If the sample is large enough to be considered representative of the population under study, then the distribution plotted against time can give a realistic projection of future events. Let's, however, keep in mind the fundamentals.

From Table 11-1 you can see that the mortgage with the minimum mean life is the one dictating the effective life span of the system as an indivisible entity. This example indicates the need for a *balanced life cycle* for component mortgages, a process not all investment banks observe. Hence, investors will be well-advised to examine it by experimenting through Monte Carlo on their own computers.

To help you develop your own Option Adjusted Spread (OAS) model through Monte Carlo, a word should also be said as to how a random selection of items from a normal population can be made. Though we have used as an example normal distributions, the method for obtaining a random selection is general and applies to any distribution:

- Since items should be chosen in such a way that each has an equal probability of being selected,

- The procedure must be such that the probability of selecting an item in any interval along the time scale is equal to the proportion of items falling in that interval.

This means that we cannot take a random sample of values along the horizontal axis (absissa) of Figure 11-1 because, if we did, we would have the same probability of drawing an item at the tails of the distribution as in the center. Consequently, we must select values at random along the vertical scale (ordinate)—as briefly stated in section 3 through an example.

- This is practically what the tables of random normal numbers are doing.
- But it is always good to understand the background processes in order to design experiments.

In many financial problems, the Monte Carlo method suggests itself as a good solution. Although it is not very precise, it is adequate for the kind of work on hand. It is also comprehensive and fairly simple. Moreover, once a library of random walks has been constructed, different problems can be solved by running the same walks through the computer.

These notions are in the background of many applications whose domains are securitization. Mortgage-based financing is one example; asset-backed financing is another.

The following two sections address problems and opportunities with Monte Carlo within the broader perspectives of securitization. Since the problem and the method we use to solve it are interlinked, section 5 introduces the procedures connected to mortgage-backed financing, and section 6 shows how to use Monte Carlo in the development of a marketable financial product.

5 UNDERSTANDING THE BUSINESS OF SECURITIZATION

Lewis S. Ranieri's contribution to the constellation of financial products has been the securitization of mortgages.* In the early 1980s, as a top trader at Salomon Brothers, he bundled home loans together into

- Widely traded securities,
- Which we backed by the loans.

---

* This statement does not contradict what is said in section 6 because what Ranieri essentially created was a mass market.

Within less than 10 years this created an $800 billion market, which flourished by buying billions of dollars' worth of mortgages from thrifts and selling these mortgage-backed financing (MBF) products to different institutional and other investors.

Home loans are not the only securitized products, of course. Pools of securitized auto loans were introduced in 1989. A year later, these pools exceeded $20 billion.

The securitization of company loans is another example, though asset-backed financing (ABF) is a trifle compared to MBF.

Whether MBF, ABF or any other type, securitization involves turning an illiquid asset with a cash flow into a tradeable security. This brief definition, however, does not reveal the amount of financial engineering that must be involved in this process.

- It is precisely the sophistication of the instrument that has attracted knowledgeable investors to the interesting fixed and floating rate products available.

- Securitized assets tend to be sold to banks, insurance companies, asset management firms, and industrial corporations—that is, investors who are quite knowledgeable and apt to ask lots of questions.

The problem for firms addressing the securitization market is that as investment managers become more familiar with the concept, they push for advanced modeling techniques, which permit them to *control their exposure*, and thus that of their clients.

Most particularly, some investment companies that buy bonds to cover pensions and annuities do not like *prepayment risk* in their bonds. Yet no matter what other advantages they present, as section 4 has documented, the prepayment risk is present and must be properly identified.

Prepayment means that an investor could well receive his or her principal back in, say, seven years instead of fifteen. In section 4 we have seen an example of how Monte Carlo can assist in identifying such risk. This example demonstrated how much faster securitized mortgages may be prepaid.

Since more than 10 years with MBF investments have made such risks known, investors increasingly want to see documentation on the expected life of a pool. They are not satisfied only with the quality of the product, which can be good since with mortgages the risk is widely spread. *Time* is a resource that counts a great deal in facing future commitments.

MBF and ABF are not the only implementation domains. Cash flow studies are another, and so are fair price evaluations. In fact, cash flow studies and MBF have much in common. Figure 11-2 shows how the Monte Carlo method can be put to advantage in studying cash flow requirements in connection to mortgage-backed financing.

- In Figure 11-2A are shown the projected cash flow needs of a given investor over a 30-year period.

- To cover some of these requirements, the investor buys securitized home loans, the salesperson promising the decay curve I have shown in Figure 11-2B.

- Using Monte Carlo simulation, the institutional investor finds that, given the characteristic statistics of the loan, after a 12-year income period there is an accelerated cash flow decay, as shown by curve II.

The reason investors are interested in MBF is that, other things being equal, securitization tends to offer a better controlled approach to risk management. The advantage for the financial institution is the possibility of restructuring and selling actual and potential loan assets in order to alleviate balance sheet constraints. It is surely more advisable than the sale of parts of the business.

FIGURE 11-2 Customer requirements analysis for securitized products: mortgage-backed financing.

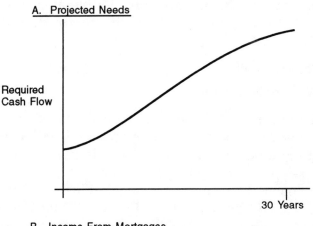

A. Projected Needs

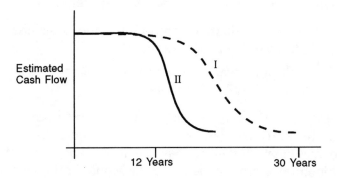

B. Income From Mortgages

As lenders try to cut costs and meet international capital standards, more and more shift the risks of their corporate and consumer loans, leases, and mortgages to investors by selling securities backed by those and other assets. For their part,

- Investment banks emphasize a brokerage role.
- This implies intermediation and fees, without expanding balance sheet and off-balance sheet risk.

It is precisely the investment banks that use Monte Carlo and other methods* to analyze pools of mortgages and structure them into securitized securities. Rating agencies, too, employ such tools for proof that the structure is default-free under both

- Best-case and
- Worst-case scenarios.

As time goes by, experience is gained and competition increases; more complex models are being developed featuring a number of sophisticated constraints. The existence of such constraints make optimization a key tool in financial engineering.

To be done right, securitization requires high-performance computers. Home loans cannot be effectively evaluated either on a manual basis or through mainframes scanning the tapes of legacy systems. Modern financial analysis requires

- A thorough evaluation of mortgages and other assets, prior to choosing them as a security.
- This calls for advanced tools to exploit databases and speed up this type of analysis.

For example, *stock option pricing* models have been implemented at the Northeast Parallel Architecture Center (Syracuse, NY). The mathematical theories have been Black-Scholes option pricing, binomial approximation, and the Monte Carlo method.

Minimal configurations of the Connection Machine (CM-2) and Maspar (DECmpp-12000) were used to compare financial instruments prices, historical market data, and other databased information. The response time has been 2 percent of that needed on the 30 MIPS Sun 4—which through analogical reasoning

---

* Such as Black-Scholes and binomial approximation.

means 8 percent of the time required by an IBM 3090/600 main-frame with vector processor.*

The successful bank typically uses rocket scientists and knowledge engineers to map the chosen methodology into rules and to automate the process as well as to provide for fast execution to beat competitors in the market.

6 MAKING HOME MORTGAGES A MARKETABLE PRODUCT

The first packages of mortgages sold in a *secondary market* dates back to the 1930s. But this market did not really start moving until the 1970s, when the Government's National Mortgage Association (Ginnie Mae) came to life and got into the act. By 1983 three government-sponsored agencies packaged mortgage loans:

- National Mortgage Association (Ginnie Mae)

- Federal National Mortgage Association (Fannie Mae)

- Federal Home Loan Mortgage Corporation (Freddie Mac)

Among them, they created a securitized market for home mortgages that grew 30 to 40 percent per year. Then, as we saw in section 5, it exploded.

The principle is that a home mortgage must be *depersonalized* in order to become a marketable bond. This means that it has to be *pooled* with the mortgages of other home owners.

- By the laws of probability, only a small fraction of mortgages in a pool should default.

* In terms of costs, this mainframe has a price tag of about $8.5 million. The Maspar costs $125,000. The price-performance ratio is evident to everyone who knows how to read.

- Pooling is based on statistics along the lines of the examples we have seen in section 4.

- But traders and investors trust statistics only when they are explained to them.

Bonds based on mortgage pools entitle the bearer to a pro-data share of the cash flow from the pool. Pools typically hold mortgages producing financial paper that must be fairly homogeneous in the following areas:

- *Mortgage level*—For instance between $100,000 and $200,000

- *Interest rate*—Say 10 percent to 12 percent

- *Life expectancy*—For example 15, 20, or 30 years

Theoretically, this would mean that a bond from this pool would entitle its holder to an interest rate of, say, 10 percent per year on his money plus his share of the repayment of principal from the homeowners for the next 20 years. Practically, however, it does not work that way.

As we have seen through practical examples, the major flaw in the outlined logic is that the repayment may come much faster. Homeowners often choose to pay a mortgage prior to its maturity. What this means in terms of cash flow has been demonstrated in Figure 11-2.

- This makes the buyer of the bond unsure of how long the security she purchases may last.

- She doesn't lose her capital, but she may receive such capital at a most inopportune time, for instance as interest rates are falling.

In this sense, while mortgage-backed financing helps create a sound security that can be traded, such trading is handicapped by the uncertainty the buyer faces in terms of the bond's life cycle.

There are, quite evidently, return-on-investment problems associated with life-cycle uncertainties. If we do not know when the cash will come back to us, we cannot calculate the yield in any meaningful way.

Therefore, not only mortgage-backed financing but all securitized issues can only flourish if this deficiency is corrected and, as we have seen, the way to go about it is through mathematical analysis. The aim is to make securitized assets resemble other bonds by giving mortgage-backed securities a *realistic maturity* that is factual and documented.

Another basic reason we are so interested in establishing the effective *life cycle* prior to packaging the mortgages for sales is *pricing*. Given their lifecycle uncertainty we must consider the following questions:

- At what price are mortgage-backed bonds attractive?
- What should the premium over treasuries be to overcome buyer resistance?
- Can mortgage-backed financing be repackaged to offer features not available with other bonds?
- Can the repackaging take care of some of the uncertainty associated with repayment?

As every trader and salesperson knows from experience, prospective investors ask questions similar to these anyway. It's much better if they have been analytically studied in advance, so they can be answered. But effective implementation requires know-how and competitiveness:

- The investors' assets are that they have the *capital*, but
- The challenge they pose is that they want to know about the *risk*.

A financial institution that wishes to move quickly to securitize and market must be certain its packaging procedures are well accepted. These are the rules of the game. To win, the vendor must not only make sure the project is done correctly, but also within a *short time frame* and have features that make the market tick.

7 EXPLORING THE BUSINESS OPPORTUNITIES THAT ARE PRESENT

In order to discuss the tools we need in a meaningful way, we have to understand the process. The best way of explaining securitization is by means of an example. Say that a consumer finance company sold a large number of receivables from auto loans into a special purpose vehicle called Hire Purchase, then issued $400 million of floating rate notes to pay for the purchase.

Let's assume that these bonds carry a AAA risk rating due to an extra $100 million the company has put aside. This is supposed to stand as a sort of guarantee of payment for holders of the regular notes, sugarcoating the issue to better its market appeal.

To cover the $100 million exposure, however, the company issues $100 million of subordinated paper. Its holders will not be repaid until all investors in the $400 million floating rate notes have been repaid.

- Interest on the 5-year notes is 0.65 percentage point over the prevailing London interbank rate.
- But the average life of the notes is 3.9 years. Thus note holders may have their principal repaid before the 5 years are up.

This is one example of how investors can access AAA rated securities while receiving the sort of interest normally associated with much higher risk.

What is motivating the issuer to pay a higher rate? In its fundamentals, the interest paid by a mortgage bond over and above the treasuries' risk-free rate must compensate for two factors:

- The risk the investor takes with mortgage-backed financing
- The repayment uncertainty connected to the security's lifecycle

The repayment uncertainty is calculated through an *Option Adjusted Spread* (OAS), which we spoke about in section 4. As explained, it can be computed through Monte Carlo. The goal is to be able to approximate as close as possible the right premium for the repayment risk—that is its *real value*.

As the nature of securities trading changes, rocket scientists have taken hold of the mechanics of financial product planning and started carving up securities instruments into bits and pieces. Then they reassemble these bits into new investment instruments as the following paragraphs help document.

One of the business opportunities rocket scientists have exploited is the tendency of borrowers to repay their loans when by all logic they should not. One of these borrowers is the government:

- The ingenuity of the method is in determining beforehand which of the loans the government is most likely to repay.
- There may be an enormous windfall to the bond investor when the repayment comes, provided new lucrative investments are available.

Something similar happens with *below par bonds*. For instance, bonds based on mortgage loans that pay only 6 percent when the going rate is 12 percent make up for the interest difference by trading well below par. When such loans are repaid immediately, the lender realizes a huge profit as the bonds are paid at par.

Another opportunity to make profits is with the lottery system in some bonds. Theoretically at least, lottery numbers are pulled at random—but when some basic facts are known, probabilities of making a profit can be precalculated.

- Monte Carlo simulation has been successfully used for this purpose, to predicting windfalls.

- The same is true of probabilities with some types of mortgages when home-owner mobility, behavior, and greed can be guesstimated.

One example is the so-called "cashy upmarket property." This may be government financed, but in a suburb that turned upmarket, where pools and jacuzzis are being built. Like the other extreme of the financially distressed neighborhoods, cashy properties are good candidates to early conversion. In other terms,

- Extremes in the mortgage market help document that the market is inefficient; there goes the efficient market theory.

- Windfalls may also come from studying and then exploiting the inefficient behavior of home owners with mortgages.

In deciding when to pay off debts, the mortgage taker is not much smarter than the government. Sometimes homeowners with 6, 8, and 10 percent mortgages insist on paying them off, even if the prevailing rate at the time is 12 or 15 percent.

Since with mortgage-backed securities home loans underpin the bonds, those with 6, 8, or 10 percent interest are priced below par value. Hence, there is a potential profit in buying them with a view to repayment at par when the homeowner pays the debt ahead of time.

This may sound incoherent when compared to what was said in section 5 about the cash flow risk to insurance companies due to early repayment. The difference is that some investors are more interested in long cash flow life cycles and others in fast recovery of capital with significant gains. Both need a great deal of simulation and experimentation to optimize their investments.

8 DEVELOPING VALID MODELS FOR SECURITIES PRICING

One of the most competitive model-building efforts in the financial market concerns security pricing. A valid approach is necessary to valuate securities, and this is often done by using the Monte Carlo technique.

Given the multiplicity of options embedded in many securities offerings and the time horizon over which they can be exercised, one of the most practical option valuation approaches is stochastic simulation analysis:

- Cash flows are generated over a wide spectrum of market environments.

- These are subject to multiple options such as cap, floor, reset frequency, and prepayment activity.

The overall impact of the multiple options is measured by calculating the average spread to the funding cost that the investor can expect to earn over the remaining life of the security. The approach is similar to an analysis connected to the fixed rate mortgage option.

As these real-life examples document, there is plenty of scope in financial engineering, as well as good profits to be made. One of the models used in this connection consists of three components:

- Interest rate dynamic algorithms
- A cash flow generator
- A price spread estimator

The interest rates dynamic model generates monthly and yearly rates as well as index rates. It uses drift parameters, a long-term equilibrium rate, annual rate volatility, and other factors that enhance predictive capabilities.

The goal of the cash flow generator is to produce monthly cash flows of different interest rate scenarios. With the price-spread estimator, cash flows are discounted at the funding cost rate plus a spread needed to obtain a price:

- The spread can be determined through a numerical iteration for different specified prices.
- The relationship between price and spread is exploited through stochastic sampling, using Monte Carlo.

Similar approaches are followed when we examine ways and means for turning the liability of early bond repayment into an asset. This is doable, provided we carefully pick the bonds more likely to be repaid or, alternatively, we invest in the right financial instrument, such as principal-only bonds (PO).

Rocket scientists and security analysts on Wall Street have invented a very fine distinction in repackaging homeowner loans to create mortgage-backed securities through bifurcation.

- Interest-only obligations (IO), and
- Principal-only (PO).

The trick is to split a pool of home mortgages into a sub-pool of interest payments and another subpool of principal payments. Subsequently, the issuer is selling the rights to the cash flows from each pool as separate investments.

The American, European, and Japanese homeowners may not know it, but their interest payments might be destined for a German investor and their principal payments for an insurance company in the United States. More sophisticated yet, some rocket scientists may shuffle around the IO and PO and repackage them together to create composite mortgage-backed securities that could not exist in any other manner. Product design of this type rests on two premises:

1. By increasing the number of financial products, securities houses tempt the buyers and capitalize on their thirst for profits.

2. By inventing securities that do not exist in the real world, financial products tend to fall outside the rules of accounting regulation.

For instance, because they are not required to be listed on balance sheets, they offer the buyer company an opportunity to grow outside the regular supervision, by writing such purchases off-balance sheet (OBS).

The dual attraction of a calculated homeowner probability to repay the mortgages and off-balance sheet recording has been a potent factor in increasing the lure of new investment instruments. Not only mathematics but also demographic studies have been instrumental in this connection, as the latter help document that the probability of early repayment is affected by the following factors:

- The size of the home loan
- The length of time this loan is outstanding
- The neighborhood in which the house is located

Astute securities analysts and rocket scientists were the first to discover that *mortgages and mathematics have much in common*, and by using the latter they can learn a great deal about the former.

This type of analysis capitalizes on data collected by the investment bank's research department. Financial analysts chart how homeowner behavior changes in terms of holding mortgage loans. The reason may be fluctuations in the interest rate.

Once they are satisfied that one group of homeowners is more likely to behave irrationally than another, they bet on the inefficient group.

The business opportunity and the complexity of the calculation go together. They both arise out of the option a homeowner has to repay a loan. This has led to the perception that mortgages may be the most mathematically oriented securities in the market, and Monte Carlo proved to be a good technique in facing the challenges.

12 Can We Reach the Goal of Managing Complexity?

1 INTRODUCTION

As the preceding chapters—particularly those on nonlinear solutions—have shown, in simple dynamic systems it is possible to predict an oncoming catastrophic change in behavior. This can be achieved by using data taken before the catastrophe and subsequently experimenting on the underlying trends.

Provided we know how to use the appropriate tools, the current state of the art permits insight and foresight, though such predictions may not reach detailed specifications on what form the post-catastrophe behavior will take.

- What is feasible is to know the period of the unstable motion suspected of triggering the catastrophe.

- This has been approached from different viewpoints, the goal being to help develop a model through which realistic experimentations can be done.

As ways and means for a solution, we have spoken of nonlinear equations, genetic algorithms, fractals, fuzzy engineering, and Monte Carlo, as well as high-performance computers and databases. There is a range of powerful tools from which to choose.

What we have not yet discussed is the overall methodology needed to attack complex problems and the procedures the able execution of such methodology would suggest. These are cornerstone issues in reaching our goal of managing complexity; hence, they have to be elaborated.

Hindsight available through mathematical approaches suggests that forecasting procedures might be disrupted by changes in solution spaces (attractors). However, in usual practice and to a first approximation these disruptions have been ignored in simple dynamic approaches. This is indeed irrational, because

- *If* information elements observable from a dynamic system with chaotic characteristics may be sufficient to forecast a catastrophe,

- *Then* understanding the appropriate method that has to be taken in real-life situations is critical for problems involving complexity.

The problem is that years of experience with simplifications has led to abstractions that help to hide irrelevant detail. Such a strategy did not develop randomly. It was chosen because it often permits us to focus on concepts and terms appropriate to the task at hand, particularly when we model nontrivial environments.

In order to obtain significantly better results in connection with the study of complexity problems, we need to enumerate the processes to be simulated for a given application, the factors each process involves, and the levels of detail they require. What sort of simplifying assumptions about objects and surfaces must we make without altering the system and its environment?

Problem sizing can allow us to match the complexity of simulation to the application, and to do so in a principled way.

It will also make it possible to follow a stepwise path for increasing simulator sophistication, such as:

- Representation requirements
- Available processing power increase

But prior to making our artifacts more realistic, we must understand the processes to be modeled and their interaction. This is where *complexity theory* comes in.

Of particular importance to this effort is the ability to characterize the relationship between systems, processes, their components, and their representation. That is a prerequisite not only for mapping but also for establishing the appropriate measures, which, when handled in an able manner, will lead toward problem solution.

2 COMPLEXITY, ADAPTABILITY, AND BEHAVIORAL PATTERNS

The comment is often made, and has been reflected in this text, that data of financial time series is noisy. But in the chapters on fuzzy engineering we also said that an alternative hypothesis is that the data of financial time series is *not* really noisy—it is fuzzy—and we have the tools to work with such situations.

Other issues are also quite important. In a time series of financial data, a complex pattern may involve bifurcations. The concept of forecasting bifurcations by exploiting chaotic dynamics has the advantage of requiring no external manipulation of the system, and therefore warrants a fair amount of investigation. The same is true of a number of other subjects we have examined.

If we apply fuzzy engineering to financial time series, we may well find that elements seemingly caused by noise often come from the vagueness and uncertainties created by disconti-

FIGURE 12-1 Uncertainty in market trends is often misinterpreted as noise in the time series, while the reasons are different.

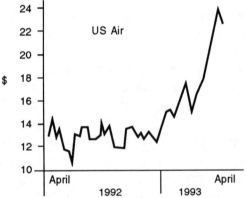

nuities and changing patterns. This is shown in Figure 12-1 with stock market data from United Airlines and USAir.

- How are the time series behaving in the different sciences, particularly in natural systems?
- Can a study of biology, for instance, provide some guidance?
- What can we learn about patterning that is applicable to finance?

These are queries that physicists, biologists, engineers, and other professionals with a penetrating experience in the natural sciences pose to themselves. When they do so, invariably the question of *patterns* attracts a significant amount of attention.

Patterning is a very useful tool in all sciences, and finance is no exception. Most often, we do not think of orderly patterns as being complex because we can describe them with very little information. But other appearances can be deceiving:

- The typical case is that disordered or random patterns seem to be quite complex.
- But often this is not so, as their statistical properties can also be described with limited information.

It is only the patterns at the phase transition between order and disorder that are hard to describe, and it is these that are really *complex*. Hence, the methodology we chose must be able to work at the *edge of chaos*. This has been underlined since Chapter 1.

Is there a pattern from biology on which we can capitalize, or at least explain what has just been said? If we study evolution, one of the first queries we should pose to ourselves is whether it works by small or big steps. What's the pattern? The answer must be focused, and this requires stratifying the world in which it applies:

- Current evidence suggests that the pattern of biological evolution is to work in small steps.

- By contrast, the pattern of thinking is to work both in big steps and in step-by-step fashion.

Admittedly, both the query posed and the answer given are tricky because they deal with *systems of complexity*. One very interesting issue in terms of behavior and patterning is to examine the changes that take place in the total range, preferably doing so in well-defined segments that within themselves have a greater homogeneity.

Figure 12-2 gives an example of applying dichotomies to a larger process by sectioning the structure of the human nervous system and its constituent parts. The division into two sets of organizational levels is, of course, artificial, motivated by the fact that it permits a better focus:

- The one set covers the nervous system from a complex whole to neural networks, with units of measurement from a meter to a millimeter.

FIGURE 12-2 Segmenting seven levels of organization into two groups to better handle the issues of complexity.

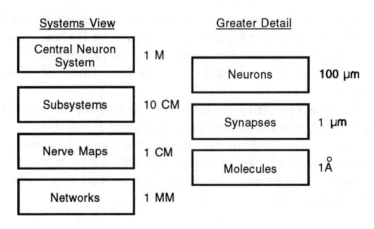

- The other set goes from neurons to molecules, and the units of measurement varies from microns to Angströms (Å).

Seen in its entirety, through a wide range of metrics that vary in a wide order of magnitude from meters to Å, the nervous system is immensely complex. We can make the study somewhat more specialized, and better manageable, by dividing the nervous system into the brain, spinal cord, maps, networks, neurons, synapses, and molecules.

In both structure and process, there are significant differences among these components. Such differences regard size of cells, number and length of neurons, number of other cells contacted by each synapse, and so on, as well as diameters of fibers and number of neurons in the chain.

- Why is this biological example so important?
- It is so important because financial organizations, as well as markets, can be approached in a similar way.

We must first define the functions going on at each of the several echelons we are aiming to study, then deal with comprehension and control of various degrees of structure. Subsequently, we must correlate these states and show how they work together—in a way similar to that which has been shown in Figure 12-2.

Since organizations are made of people, to study their complexity we must understand the stages of decision-making among managers, traders, investors, and financial analysts. This behavioral and patterning study, too, can be approached in a modular manner:

- Establishing purposes and goals as well as the *emotions* involved in peoples' interaction
- Reflecting on the behavioral role played by successive higher echelons of the system

- Understanding subsystem adjustments, from their reason for being to the pattern they take

- Modeling how information can influence reflexes at each organizational level

Righting reactions occur in response to signals, and this is as true of brain activities as it is of financial markets. Are we able to study behavior in a comprehensive sense?

While we might expect that the complexity of a system will not increase if it adapts to a changing environment, we would like to know which level of complexity makes adaptation really possible and which kinds of elements are involved in it. Such understanding practically underpins any valid methodology— and this is a fundamental message.

3 THE PROCESS OF LEARNING AT THE EDGE OF CHAOS

To better understand the process of learning, we must study the evolution of the mammalian brain and of other natural systems. Whether we are active in

- Financial markets,

- Physical sciences, or

- Sociology and demographics,

we do not study subjects relating to learning only to understand its background elements. We also examine them in behavioral terms through analogical reasoning, all the way from perception to cognition, reaching into decision processes.

Complex market behavior is influenced a great deal by social aspects that often go unnoticed. Its study poses a broad set of questions dealing with the origin and sustainability of behavior.

- Learning is a fundamental issue in the process of self-adaptation.

- In any domain, learning is closely associated with the structure and function of specific systems because it helps define their response.

People and processes capable of learning are continually refining original ideas and past experience in light of what they find by working in their specific fields. They learn as they strive for pragmatic results.

This is why we are so interested in describing the behavior of learning systems by means of tools we borrow from advanced scientific fields. In physics, in engineering, in humanities, in economics—generally in most disciplines—dealing with learning processes is practically indivisible from studying notions at the edge of chaos. If we are careful in analyzing the foundations of learning processes, we will see that:

- Learning proceeds by *demolishing old ideas* and concepts, making old tools redundant or unwise.

- Learning, then, structures a new environment that is more flexible and efficient than the one we knew before.

Therefore, we can benefit a great deal by analyzing, comprehending, and applying the methodology of learning. This methodology and the notion of self-organized criticality leads to the following changes:

- Abandonment of crumbling concepts and structures
- Avalanches in new ideas and know-how
- A growing sense of synthesis

But what else is complexity in addition to the message these three bullets convey? As Murray Gell-Mann underlines, "It is premature to say there exists a rigidly defined science of complexity, but research is coming up with a whole set of candidate metaphors for adaptive systems that look quite promising."

From physics to ecosystems and economics, there is an emergence of concepts in science characterized by networks where *the nodes are smart,* and the component parts are constantly adapting to each other. This is quite similar to what we said in section 2 about the organization and structure of the nervous system.

One of the issues taught by the nascent science of complexity is that there exist some yet unknown—and therefore mysterious—factors that make life and mind possible. They do so through a certain kind of balance between the forces of order and those of disorder. To learn more about these factors, we should use the following strategy:

- Look at systems in terms of how they behave.
- Pay relatively less attention to how they are made.

Scientists of a multidisciplinary orientation who have chosen this strategy find that order and chaos lie at the two extremes. As we have seen since Chapter 1, right in between these two extremes is a phase transition we have called *the edge of chaos,* where we find *complexity.*

We might as well call this limiting situation the *edge of learning.* In it we find the conditions that have been underlined earlier in this section:

- Abandonment of past concepts and structures, hence disruption
- Followed by a sense of synthesis, or back to order

True enough, there seems to be a still-not-well understood connection between complexity and phase transitions like the one that has been studied in cellular automata. No one really knows if the models we now elaborate hold true in the real world, particularly in relation to complex organizations—but chances are that they might.

The crucial element in all this transition is *behavior*. Not only in science but also in organizational theory, the behavior of the components of the system that finds itself at the edge of chaos never quite lock into place, yet neither do they dissolve into turbulence. These systems are

- Stable enough for storing and processing information,
- Yet in the middle of a transition that steadily transforms them.

If they are adaptive enough, even at the edge of chaos they can pull themselves together to perform complex processes necessary for reacting to the world. This is precisely what is meant by being spontaneous and keeping alive.

4 IS CHAOTIC BEHAVIOR A PREREQUISITE TO RENEWAL?

One of the first things that Stuart Kauffman discovered a couple of decades ago about his genetic networks is that if the connections were too sparse, the networks would basically just freeze up and sit there. If the connections were too dense, the networks would churn around in chaos.

By contrast, in between these two states the networks produce an interchange of edge of chaos and stable state cycles, which helps in promoting renewal. Can we translate this finding into organizational behavior?

Drawn within an organizational setting, the graph in Figure 12-3 exemplifies this reference by means of some disintegrating (or disintegrated) structures whose connection to reality has been too sparse. This contrasts to the renewal mechanism made feasible through diversity and dynamic behavior within a system. Another similar paradigm is that of autocatalytic behavior.

FIGURE 12-3 Complexity can also be seen as interfacing between dynamic components and crumbling structures—characterizing a process of renewal.

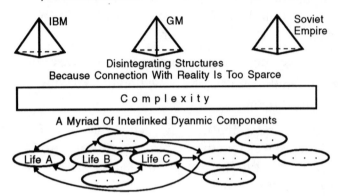

Whether at the national, the corporate, or the molecular level, it is quite clear that the over-rigid, over-centralized approach to organization does not work well. In the long run, the system becomes

- Too stagnant,
- Too locked into itself,
- Too overcontrolled to survive.

Both of the big computer companies, IBM and the so-called BUNCH*, and the big three automakers in Detroit grew so large and so rigidly locked in to certain ways of doing things that they could barely recognize the growing challenges:

- The challenge to the rigid mainframes and their main-framers comes from personal computers, local area net-works, and the flexible client servers into which they combine.

* Burroughs, Univac, NCR, Control Data, and Honeywell. Burroughs and Univac have formed Unisys.

- The challenge to the Detroit automakers comes from the novel and cost-effective designs by the Japanese competition, as well as the very short time-to-market requirements.

New solutions, like the wholesale change from mainframes to client servers and the observance of rapid time-to-market criteria call for toughness, quickness, competence, and freedom from political cant. They also require significant force of personality.

In his heyday, Dr. Robert McNamara personified these characteristics. Says Michael R. Beschloss* "[Robert McNamara] was geniusly attracted by the [Kennedy] family's toughness, rationality, intellectual curiosity. . . . He was grateful for deliverance from the anti-intellectual, illiberal realm of automobile men and their wives he had endured for fifteen years."

Rigid and overcentralized organizations like those represented by the motor industry and the mainframe industry have become inefficient and arrogant. Arrogance and inefficiency kill initiative, leaving no room for the imagination and the will needed to respond to challenges. Hence, they lead to self-destruction.

- Evolution thrives in systems that give rise to flexibility.
- A steady change transforms and upgrades, but does not destroy the organization.

We can learn a great deal from the autocatalytic model. It has a number of parameters such as the catalytic strength of the reactions and the rate at which food molecules are supplied. In an early learning mechanism of this type, Farmer, Packard, and Kauffman had to set all these parameters by hand, essentially by trial and error.

---

* *Kennedy vs. Kruhchev* (London and Boston: Faber and Faber, 1991).

- One of the first things they discovered was that nothing much happened in the model until they got the subject parameters into a certain range.
- Thereafter, the autocatalytic process took off, gained momentum, and developed quickly.

This behavior, the researchers suggest, is strongly reminiscent of a phase transition, though it is still not so clear how it relates to phase transitions in other models, such as learning or change in organizations. There are, however, reasons to believe that

- These findings are independent of any particular field,
- Whether or not there exist inherent dynamically adaptive characteristics.

One of the basic reasons behind this statement is that specific instances of dynamic systems are generic in nature and can be mapped through processes by referring to state transition graphs, without attaching any meaning to the states themselves. Such generic systems evolve in order to solve constantly changing tasks with which they are confronted.

This is why the mapping of the edge of chaos and the development of learning mechanisms is so important. While the interdisciplinary approach to these issues is still in its beginnings, studying the underlying processes is rewarding both in the short and in the long term—as it helps reveal how nature works and regulates itself, capitalizing on millions of years of evolution.

5 PATTERN FORMATION IN AN ENVIRONMENT OF COMPLEX BEHAVIOR

Closely associated with the learning issues treated in sections 3 and 4 is that of pattern formation, most particularly, the emergence of new, sometimes unexpected *macrostructures*, which are often due to a number of *microinteractions*. The latter may regard molecules, neurons, networks, industries, and the whole financial system.

One of the areas worthy of specific attention, because of what we can learn in terms of methodology, concerns patterns involved in the formation of *cooperative structures* evolving over time. Another interesting field concerns the process of selection of one from many possible potential candidate structures through the process of adaptation. A number of questions came up in this connection:

- Can we learn by analogical reasoning from the way new macro- and microstructures form?

- Can pattern formation theories in physics and biology help our understanding in economics?

- What are the possible candidate patterns of trade, industry, and the financial markets?

These are some of the critical questions asked by advanced systems projects run at, among other research organizations, the Santa Fe Institute. Mathematicians, physicists, biologists, engineers, and economists devote a great deal of their time and activities to providing answers to these queries.

Pattern formation can be of assistance in understanding and learning because an integral part of the answers we are after have to do with interacting processes, for instance those characterizing behavior—from the realms of nature to economics.

Market players and market makers must decide on their actions with a view to possible future benefit—but also in reaction to other agents. They formulate strategies based on expectations, but in doing so they may be faced with complex and possibly ill-defined problems that are far beyond the power of normal human intelligence to solve completely.

- Due to the increasing number of ill-defined systems, factors, and situations, market players are often forced to act inductively.

- They form conceptual models, transfer experience from other, similar problems, generalize from limited data, and try to learn as they go.

Patterns can be instrumental in this learning process. This is particularly true when, as learning and mutual adaptation take place, new market structures emerge. As a result, there is a continual formation and reformation of institutions, behaviors, and technologies that both comprise and underpin the economy. The result is the drive toward the following goods:

- Understanding and modeling the apparent messiness of the real world.

- Developing simulators for theoretical and applied experimentation.

- Changing from a narrow focus of closed compartmentalized disciplines to real interdisciplinary approaches.

- Visualizing through behavior patterns and trends, then asking a totally new set of questions.

Visualization through *visibilization* (the ability to perceive graphically very small and very large images) and *visistraction* (mapping basically abstract concepts into graphs) can be seen as a means of stimulating individual understanding. It also helps in research collaboration through interdisciplinary interaction.

The emphasis placed on adaptation, evolution, and emerging phenomena has in the background this need to visibilize and visitract, hence the attention being paid to the study of brain patterns as well as of neurobiology and nonlinear dynamics—all with their associated computational theory.

The varied but interconnected background of these reference fields is necessary for the study of evolutionary systems with behavior characterized by learning and adaptation. Finance is a good example in this context because it is *an evoluting system* with many autonomous agents operating on the trading networks. Other examples come from manufacturing.

- The fact of focusing on the process more than on the product does not change the need for rapid development and tailoring. If anything, it underlines it.

- Mass marketing is a process with many of the characteristics we are discussing, but the same is also true of tailor-made products and customized marketing approaches.

At the beginning of the mass marketing era in the United States, there were plenty of commentators who warned that customers would never want mass-produced. Then Henry Ford introduced the assembly line, and people accepted standardized goods because they were brought within the economic reach of so many.

Looking back, we see it did not take very long before mass marketing became *the* standard, but as affluence increased and tastes changed at a different level and different pace by strata, this process reversed itself:

- Sophisticated customers opted for differentiation in human-made products.

- Astute producers responded by carving out segments they could tailor to specific niches that they could serve economically.

- The same thing now happens with financial products after a first phase of global standardization.

Important market niches exist for sophisticated customized financial products provided that personalization can be done rapidly at low costs. But neither customization nor short time-to-market are achieved through mainframes, Cobol, and EDPiers. They are done through the skills of rocket scientists who

- Apply chaos theory, fuzzy engineering, and other non-traditional financial analysis tools,
- Use visual programming to compress software development timetables, and
- Employ high-performance computers to make great power available at affordable cost.

All this is necessary to personalize the financial services that a financial institution offers to high net worth individuals or other well-defined investor groups. In a way, the many different types of products the leading mutual funds offer are—though yet not fully personalized—a precursor to this future trend.

6 NEW STRATEGIES IN FINANCIAL TRADING AND IN PERSONALIZED INVESTMENT SERVICES

Since without automation the cost of personalization of financial investment services will run high, research is needed on ways and means to provide flexible and adaptable computer-based processes rather than relying mainly on manual procedures.* The goal of well-tuned financial research projects should not be to exploit very broad, all-inclusive domains, but rather to focus on pockets of predictability.

"What it means is that you are being bombarded with all kinds of financial data: exchange rates, bond prices, interest rates, and so on," Norman H. Packard explains. Market patterns must be developed at subsecond speed, not next year. Through

---

* See also D. N. Chorafas and H. Steinmann, *Expert Systems in Banking* (London: Macmillan, 1991).

the mathematics of complexity theory we can treat information streams, provided we appreciate that

- At any given moment, products and services for that instant represent points in the solutions space,

- But over the longer run these points evolute and distribute themselves throughout the solution space in a detectable pattern.

One of the interesting lessons we have learned from simulating physical systems on computers is that complex behavior need not have complex roots. Indeed, sophisticated and interesting behavior can emerge from collections of simple components. This is more or less true throughout financial trading and investments, and is fundamental in the personalization of services.

The greatest challenge financial managers face is that they cannot plan for tomorrow by studying what happened yesterday. Let's repeat once again what Peter Drucker said to make the message clear: "Sometime during the 1970s, the longest period of continuity in economic history *came to an end*. At some time during the last dozen years, we moved into *turbulence*."

Even in relatively stable financial environments, it is effectively impossible to cover every conceivable situation. Therefore, inflexible approaches and hierarchical systems are forever running into combinations of events they do not know how to handle. They tend to be backward and fragile, and they all too often grind to a halt through indecision.

These negatives are immensely magnified in turbulent market environments. Furthermore, as technology continues advancing and the foremost financial organizations capitalize on it, the rules of the game keep on changing. The problem of many traders and investment managers is that it is not enough to merely keep up with change, even if they are ready to do so.

- The most important *survival skill*, which sophisticated customers appreciate, is the ability to *anticipate change* and identify new opportunities.

- If we can figure out what changes are in store for the marketplace, we gain extraordinary leverage against our competition.

Therefore, the financial institution that wants to be one of the first into the new trading and investment territory cannot wait for large amounts of evidence. Nor can it afford to continue poring over the numbers in the old linear ways in hopes of seeing the events lying ahead.

What is needed is the risk mixture of *rationality* and *creativity*—the latter being given the upper hand. This can make the difference in terms of competitive advantages. Rationality and creativity have always been thought to have contrasting characteristics. These are served, correspondingly, by the left and right hemispheres of the brain. Should there be a preference?

In the World War II years, Dr. Niels Bohr gave the answer. When he saw one of his assistants being too rational but not so creative he would say: "You are not thinking. You are only being logical."*

For reasons of traditionalism, both our educational system as a whole and large organizations, as a matter of long-standing policy, prize rationality much more than creativity. Yet

- Rational approaches focus on facts, and

- Facts reflect on issues of *the past.*

Creativity, by contrast, focuses on *the future.* Its engine is imagination and an inquisitive spirit that must be supported by means of well-focused research activities, as we will see in the following sections.

* Otto Frisch, *What Little I Remember* (Cambridge: Canto/Cambridge University Press, 1979)

7 STREAMLINED OR OVERLAPPING RESEARCH INTERESTS?

The analysis of complex issues in the financial markets resembles a structure of overlapping research interests among people, themes, and programs, as suggested in Figure 12-4. The more advanced the programs, the more they will have characteristics and attributes of complex systems, with nonlinear functions, multivariate representations, polyvalent goals, constraints, and fuzziness.

The analysis of the form, structure, and behavior of these systems must consider non-equilibrium and multiple equilibria conditions as well as pattern forming, adaptive approaches, evolving methodologies, and co-evolving possibilities. In principle, such systems will be

- Self-organizing and
- Self-destroying.

FIGURE 12-4 Complex financial studies resemble a collection of overlapping research interests.

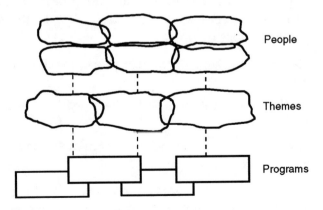

Many will develop and operate on a rugged landscape. All worth talking about will have memory and exhibit information processing functions. Hence, they will be able to distill incoming data streams.

The methodology behind the issues of self-organization and self-destruction—and the pattern to which it leads—should be evaluated in a multidimensional manner. In economics and finance, for instance,

- Both endogenous and exogenous shocks play an important role in astute modeling of fluctuations.

- Both can lead to market destabilization and therefore chaotic conditions.

- Both require the measurement of parameter values that might conflict with one another.

This is particularly true as today's economies are no longer based on long-cycle agriculture and bulk manufacturing but, rather, on high-technology industries and increasingly sophisticated service sectors. In both these examples, short time-to-market is crucial.

High-technology industries, financial services, and other service sectors share the condition that *most of their costs are up-front* due to large R&D investments as well as to the steady renewal of their infrastructure.

- The more market a product or process is able to capture,

- The lower its unit costs and its overhead per unit will be,

- But also the clearer its positioning against the evolving market forces has to be.

Old organizational concepts are not made for this environment. Many of the complex systems we are concerned about show positive feedback rather than the stabilizing negative feedback. Learning can improve this situation, underlining the need for advanced understanding of markets to take advantage of the opportunities that are created—but learning is handicapped by the old structures.

There are plenty of examples to document what has just been written, and a good many have to do with learning the methodology as well as what makes the market tick. In a rather depressed market for airline stocks in April 1993, AMR (owner of American Airlines) became a strong favorite of investors following

- Dramatic cost-cutting in 1992 and
- Expansion into investment management services.

Investment banks and their clients who jumped onto this false bandwagon forgot to take the proverbial long hard look at the U.S. economy at large and the blues of the airline industry in particular. Not surprisingly, a month later airline stocks retreated.

A similar behavior pattern exists with financial products. That is why traders and investment managers must improve their skills. They should be spending less time reacting to existing problems, increasing, instead, the time they spend anticipating new opportunities. This is where the science of complexity comes in.

In lieu of relying on an old methodology with misinterpreted trends and undercurrents, traders, financial analysts, and investment managers should keep an open mind. Rather than traditionalists, they should be mavericks who always ask *why* things have to be done the way they were.

Creative minds enjoy playing with a problem until it is solved. This requires the tools we have studied in this and the preceding chapters, the ability to make intuitive judgments, and the courage to act on them.

8 STUDIES IN FINANCE THAT ENHANCE COMPETITIVE ADVANTAGES

Research and development on systems behavior, particularly that of large aggregates, is key to our ability to manage complexity. The studies that need to be done in this domain during the next 10 years will be both fundamental and fairly costly. Where will the money come from to finance them?

Since 1955, the U.S. Government has spent more than $1 trillion on research and development of nuclear arms and other weaponry. According to the National Science Foundation,

- This amount represented 62 percent of all Federal research expenditures, while

- Untold dollars went into related efforts, like the civilian space program's $90 billion race to land men on the Moon.

Out of all this military research came the hydrogen bomb, the neutron bomb, nuclear-powered ships and submarines, laser weapons, spy satellites, intercontinental rockets, stealth warplanes and the precision armaments—but with few notable exceptions the industrial fallout has been limited.

In contrast, out of civilian research came new market potential. Examples are products such as nylon, teflon, television, and microwave ovens. Civilian and military research, however, reinforced one another in domains such as passenger jets, weather satellites, and computer chips—that is, the huge industry that propelled computers, communications, and software at the forefront of the economy.

But in terms of the 1990s and beyond, the requirements posed by the First World's markets are no longer what they used to be. There is a whole new ball game under way with 24-hour trading, the productization of debt, off-balance sheet financial instruments, and real-time response to market opportunities.

Two guidelines can help in responding in an able manner to an increasing number of challenges as the component parts of the economy become more complex, nonlinear and unpredictable with current tools.

- To improve upon the prevailing limited visibility, we need huge amounts of research, comparable to what military and civilian projects attracted during the post World War II years.

- Flexibility and adaptability are basic prerequisites in managing change; otherwise, organizations will not be able to meet the more demanding goals of the coming years.

As the preceding chapters documented, one of the issues most organizations fail to appreciate regarding the management of change is that with highly dynamic systems *we are more interested in the process than in the outcome of the process—the product.*

It is precisely because this understanding is most important in the new competitive environment that emphasis must be placed on advanced techniques and our ability to analyze complex processes. If the focal point is behavior rather than structure, can we map in real time the pattern of this behavior?

How far can we use the methodology and tools from the physical sciences in reaching this goal? One of the basic differences with the physical systems that have been extensively studied during the last 40 years* is that financial markets make up an aggregate vastly more complex than that of other chaotic processes.

Many traditional-thinking bankers, economists, and financial experts are rather skeptical about complexity studies until they see hard evidence in the form of successful long-term pre-

---

* In blue ribbon labs like Los Alamos, Lawrence Livermore, Argonne, and Brookhaven.

dictions. If this is the way they think, they deceive themselves not only because the methodology underpinning very advanced studies is still in the formative stages, but also—if not primarily—because complexity theory only permits short-term predictions.

Not everything that is wrong is on the side of the traditional bankers. What not all rocket scientists have yet realized is that part of the difference between physical and financial complex systems is in the major role played by psychology. Financial analysts:

- Read the same papers,
- Watch the same ticker tapes,
- Respond to similar rumors, and
- Act according to normal *human emotions.*

What many brilliant financial analysts miss is that it is *not sufficient* to calculate on a mathematical basis the probability of an event happening. This one track approach starts at school where analysts are not being taught that *lust* and *greed* make the world go round.

The market is an aggregate of behavior motivated by emotions, including hope, greed, and fear. When the different traders, salespeople, and investors act as a herd, the market may obey one type of rules; by contrast, when they act more independently a different set of rules dominates. Both behaviors can be analyzed in an effort to predict the financial future.

Complex market entities that depend on the behavior of many diverse individuals create a kind of challenge which, as we have seen, can be handled through nonlinear mathematics and ingenuity. Quite often, the difference between things we can forecast and those we cannot is the number of degrees of freedom they possess.

9 ORGANIZATIONAL PREREQUISITES IN MANAGING COMPLEXITY

Economic theory concerning financial markets has changed through the years. As we have seen, most recently we have come to view the market forces in terms of a transition state between chaos and equilibrium. But in addition to markets, organizations also look inherently unstable.

Processes characterized by decay are those with a status quo mentality. Yet these are the same processes that provide conditions for comfortable living—as long as they last.

- Moribund organizations look backwards to the best of their history and change as *little* as they can.

- Those destined to survive want to change as *much* as they can, and their guide is the future.

In times of great discontinuity with past practices, the status quo is no way to survive. If we wish to enjoy more of the economic opportunities and less of the risks, we need to understand changes better.

The more we realize where changes are heading, the better positioned we are to use them to our own advantage. The organization that welcomes change can ride the wave of it instead of just reacting to it. As a result, it can position itself in the market ahead of its competitors.

Let's never forget that we are entering an age of increasing complexity when the future is there to be shaped, and when the only prediction that will hold true is that *no predictions will be good for very long.*

- To survive, we have to be thinking the unlikely and even doing the unreasonable.

- This can be done successfully if we better understand the changes around us.

- When we take the initiative, we end up suffering less and profiting more from the process of change.

As cannot be repeated too often, the changes taking place in the financial markets are *discontinuous* and are not part of a linear trend. That is why their pattern can be confusing or at least disturbing, particularly to those who do not appreciate it.

- Whether organizations and markets are poised at equilibria or at the edge of chaos, the key question is how predictable they are.

- Organizational theory has vacillated over this point, viewing movements toward restructuring sometimes as salutary and sometimes as unsettling.

The duality of this argument and its impact on both markets and organizations should not be forgotten. Forty years ago at the University of California, Los Angeles, I learned from my professors that organizational life more or less resembles one long continuous line.

But in four decades things have changed tremendously, requiring us to alter *our mental images* and *our rules*. Forty years ago a company saw the future as largely predictable, to be planned for in a more or less rigid manner. Nothing like that is true anymore.

Today in organizations there is a curious application of chaos theory where initial conditions subjected to a few changes can in fact make a big difference—the butterfly effect. This is particularly true if these small inputs go unnoticed or we are unclear about initial conditions.

- *Discontinuous change* requires a different way of thinking if it is to be dealt with successfully.

- It also calls for new organizational structures able to respond to new requirements in a rapid and flexible manner.

Fast response cannot be made through hierarchical, pyramidal structures in which the nerve pulses take a long time to travel. Even making a decision to change course will take a great deal of effort, and implementation will most likely involve very significant delays. It is simply not possible to make a U-turn with a battleship.

Even the classical concept of a decentralized approach to organizational management is no more an answer to the requirements imposed by a highly competitive environment. Figure 6-4 clearly made the distinction between *decentralized* and *federated* organizational approaches. The latter, it was said, have a major advantage:

- Federation is a sort of inverse delegation, with the power flowing from the periphery to the center rather than vice versa.

- This approach permits operation in small units but capitalization on larger resources available in the federation.

In conclusion, living in a complex, highly competitive environment requires structures and systems with a very different kind of organization from the one we have been accustomed to. Instead of being designed from the top down, living systems always seem to emerge from the bottom up from a population of much simpler autonomous components.

If a paradigm from biology can be of help, a cell consists of proteins, DNA, and other biomolecules. A brain consists of neurons, an ant colony of ants, an economy of firms and individuals. The more dynamic the interaction of these autonomous components, the greater the adaptation, the competitive advantages, and the capacity for survival.

Index

Absolute value, 298, 306
Accounting, 292
Acid test, 306
Adaptability, 190
Agents, 150, 151
Airline industry, 137
Algorithmic approaches, 188
Algorithms, 250, 277
Amplification, 92, 93
Analog differential analyzers,
   159
Analogies, 75
Analysis
   fundamental, 97
   technical, 97
Aristotle, 101, 228, 254
Arrow of time, 79, 208
Arthur, Brian, 150, 151
Artificial life, 158, 167, 173
Asset-backed financing (ABF),
   320, 329
Associative memory, 259
Attenuation, 92, 93
Autocorrelation displays, 197
Automation, straight-through,
   214
Averages, 325

Baker, George F., 231, 301
Bankers Trust, 10, 191, 193, 213,
   214, 216, 224, 272
Banque de la Société Géneral de
   Belgique, 272
Bellman, Richard, 3, 128
Below par bonds, 337
Ben-Gurion, David, 137
Beschloss, Michael R., 355
Bifurcation, 23, 24, 25, 92, 93,
   109
Binomial approximation, 320
Black, Fischer, 229
Black-Scholes model, 320
Bohr, Niels, 362
Bonds, 334
Booms, 231
Boundary conditions, 253, 284
Bubbles, 8
Burroughs, 354

Cairns-Smith, A.G., 53
Calculation of confidence, 105
Carnot, Sadi, 11, 77, 78, 82
Cartesian coordinate system,
   106
Cash flow analysis, 308, 309

Cash flow generator, 340
Cash management, 263, 272
Causal concepts, 233
Causal knowledge, 235
Causal relations, 259
Certainty, 254
Certainty factor, 221
Change, 9, 13
Chaos, 14, 15, 16, 25, 26, 87, 204
Chaos theory, 3, 8, 11, 12, 15, 25, 31, 34, 35, 91, 98, 179, 185, 203
Chaotic attractors, 107
Chaotic behavior, 19
Chaotic systems, 14, 15, 51
Chemical Banking, 259
Chicago Board of Trade, 180
Citibank, 10, 272
Classification and Identification Code, 266
Classification, fine-grain, 266
Classification procedures, 148
Classification tool, 149
Clausius, Rudolf, 78
Clearing House Interbank Payments System (CHIPS), 230
Clearing houses, 53
Client mirror, 276
Client profiling, 277
Collateral equities, 293
Community intelligence, 162, 165
Company loans, securitization of, 329
Complex systems, 59, 70
Complexity, 351, 352, 366, 369
Complexity, algorithmic, 191

Complexity, real-world, 48, 89
Complexity theory, 7, 44, 60, 68, 70, 72, 84, 85, 95, 128, 345
Computer memory, 210
Computers, high-performance, 204
Computers, massively parallel, 168
Conceptual and analytical skills, 60
Concurrent engineering, 68
Confidence intervals, 253, 288
Connection Machine, 204, 332
Constraints, 145, 225, 282
Control parameters, 24
Core deposits, 274
Cowan, George, 45
Creativity, 362
Credit cycle, theory of the, 231
Crisp, 63, 64
Crisp rules, 292
Cross-correlations, 193
Cross-overs, 129, 140
Cumulative exposure, 200
Customer identification, lack of, 265
Customization, intensive, 214
Cybernetics, 173

Danzig, George, 127
Data flow, 43
Data, multiple variable, 194
Data stream filtering, 213
Data streams, 190, 191
Database mining, 213, 259
Databases, 210
    networked, 259
Dawkins, Richard, 176

DECmpp-12000, 332
Defuzzification, 228, 253, 287, 304, 312
Degrees of freedom, 74, 75
Democritos, 101
Derivatives, 198
Descartes, 228
Dimensioning, 75
Discontinuities, 103, 104
Disposition, 294
Diversity, 6, 46
Dow Jones Index, 296–99, 303
Drucker, Peter, 292, 361
Dynamic linear systems, 95
Dynamic problems, 48
Dynamic systems, 16, 34, 41, 53
  modeling of, 12

Ecological approach, 173, 174
Econometric analysis, 28
Econometrics, 28
Economic model, 151
Economic theory, 369
  classical, 147
Edge of chaos, 33, 36, 43, 74, 136, 221, 347, 352
Einstein, Albert, 16, 100
Electrical Power Industries Research Institute (EPRI), 185
Energy, 102
Entropy, 77–81, 84
  in organization, 80
  negative, 83
  per unit time, 80
Equation, quadratic, 97
Equation, time-dependent quadratic, 108

Equations
  deterministic, 179
  nonlinear, 12, 179
Ergodicity, 86
Error, 172
Euclid's geometry, 61, 121
European Exchange Rate Mechanism (ERM) crisis, 22, 23
European Monetary System (EMS), 111
Evaluation, 214
Exchange rates, 198, 211
Exposure and risk, 192

Fair value estimate, 145, 319
Farmer, J. Doyne, 85, 178, 179, 180, 182, 245, 355
Federal Home Loan Mortgage Association (Fannie Mae), 333
Federal Reserve, 53
Federated solutions, 183, 371
Feedback, 171
Feedback loop, 37, 173
Feedback processes, 172
Feedback signals, 173
Feigenbaum, Mitchel, 3, 12, 21, 212, 213
Feigenbaum's number F, 213
Financial Accounting Standards Board (FASB), 229
Financial analysis, 10, 162
  classical, 282
  non-traditional, 94, 96
Financial analysts, 3, 11, 22, 31, 104, 106–108, 137, 204, 341
Financial data analysis, 259

Financial engineer, 250, 260
Financial instruments, 293
Financial investment services,
    personalization of, 360
Financial markets, 27–29
    networked, 185
Financial products, customized,
    359
Financial research, 202
Financial services architecture,
    216
Fitness surface, 40, 41, 131
Flock coherence, 166
Flow dynamics, 30, 31
Fluctuations, aperiodic, 11
Force of liveliness, 100
Forecasting procedures, 344
Foreign exchange risk, 305
Fractal dimension, 109, 112, 118,
    121
Fractal distribution, 110
Fractal geometry, 119, 120
Fractal theory, 113, 245
Fractals, 3, 106, 110, 112, 117,
    122, 203
    random, 122
Fuzzification, 283, 287, 290,
    309
Fuzziness, 66, 217, 261
Fuzzy adaptive control, 258
Fuzzy Associative Memory
    Organizing Units Systems
    (FAMOUS), 233, 234, 238,
    258
Fuzzy cognitive model, 233, 238,
    239
Fuzzy concepts, 307
Fuzzy data, 237, 250

Fuzzy engineering, 3, 148, 149,
    204, 218, 223–27, 229, 230,
    240, 245, 279, 281, 282, 283,
    308, 345
Fuzzy engineering algorithms,
    259
Fuzzy engineering functions,
    243, 245
Fuzzy engineering models, 233,
    240, 241, 258
Fuzzy financial information, 251
Fuzzy functions, 226
Fuzzy inference, 259
Fuzzy logic, 113, 220, 222–24,
    243, 282, 288, 307
Fuzzy notions, 292
Fuzzy predicates, 267
Fuzzy rules, 241
Fuzzy sets, 117, 227, 232, 237,
    238, 240, 244, 261, 274
Fuzzy sets graph, development
    of, 268, 269

Galilei, Galileo, 228
Gell-Mann, Murray, 34, 36, 52,
    89, 101, 351
General Motors, 259
Genetic algorithms, 42, 128–32,
    137, 143, 146–48, 152–55,
    204, 244–46, 320
Genetic regression trees, 149
Geometry, 119
Gibbs, J.W., 83
Globalization, 216
Goldman Sachs, 229
Gould, Stephen Jay, 140
Grading system, 148
Grammar model, 46

Harvard University, 208
Hawking, Stephen W., 79
Heisenberg, Werner, 102, 251
Herodotus, 119
Heterogeneous distribution, 323
Heuristic approaches, 188
Heuristics, 250, 259, 277
High-performance computers, 290
High-performance computing, 259
Holland, John, 128, 133, 147, 151
Homologies, 75
Honeywell, 354
Hosei University, 61
Human capital, 216
Human genome project, 153, 155, 156
Human memory, asymmetry of, 209
Hutton, James, 31
Huygens, Christiaan, 100

IBM, 354
Imprecision, 255
Induction, 217
Inference method, 238
Information, 78
Information elements, 43, 217
Inheritance, 54
Initial conditions, 251, 252
Intel, 103, 204
Interactivity, 242
Interest rate dynamic model, 340
Interest rate fluctuations, 304
Interest-only obligations (IO), 340

Intraday risk evaluation, 259
Intrinsic time, 17–19
Iterations, 252

Kauffman, Stuart, 38, 46, 51, 74, 353, 355
Kemptborne, Peter J., 196
Kinetic energy, 100
Knowledge
    common sense, 225
    deep, 225
    macroscopic, 62, 65, 66
    microscopic, 63
Knowledge engineering, 42
Knowledge engineering constructs, 68
Knowledge engineers, 333
Knowledge management, object-oriented, 259
Koch's snowflake, 119, 122

Laboratory for International Fuzzy Engineering (LIFE), 61, 224, 233, 234, 236
Langton, Chris, 158, 166, 167, 175, 177
Laplace, Pierre Simon, 102
Layering, 64
Learning, 350, 351, 365
Learning, process of, 350
Legacy system, 181, 273
Leontief, Vassily, 127
Leptokyrtosis, 196
Leptokyrtotic, 196
Leptokyrtotic models, 197
Life cycle, 325
Linear modeling techniques, 117
Linear models, 127

Linear programming (LP), 127
Linearity, 21
Lipsitz, Lewis, 16
Liquidity, 304
Liquidity predictor, 179
Living organisms, 177
Living systems, 32, 102, 103
Local fitting, 244
Logic
    default, 225
    non-monotonic, 225
Logical system, 60
Logistics equation, 42, 205, 212
Lorenz, Edward, 3, 12, 21, 72, 73
Los Alamos National
    Laboratory, 158
Lottery selection, 145

Macroscope, 61
Macrostructures, 356
Mainframes, 290
Mandelbrot, Benoit, 3, 5, 21, 117,
    118, 121, 122
Mandelbrot fractals, 114
Mandelbrot Set, 114
Mandelbrot's fractal theory, 204
Manufacturers Hanover Trust
    Company (MHTC), 259
Market behavior, complex,
    350
    mapping of, 189
Market customization, 38
Market interactions, mapping
    of, 161
Market patterns, 360
Market psychology, 92, 148, 161,
    163
Market volatility, 192, 195, 304

Markets, 38, 39
    efficient, 205
Markov, Andrei A., 175
Markov chains, 160, 320
Markov Modeling, 175
MasPar, 204, 332
Massachusetts Institute of
    Technology, 10, 21, 187–91,
    193–95, 197, 198, 200, 201,
    238
Mathematics, 89, 90, 91, 92
    nonlinear, 103, 185, 213
    possibilistic, 227
Mathematics of complexity, 183
Mathematics of nonlinear
    dynamic systems, 98
Matter, 102
    inanimate, 177
McGill, Jim, 178
McGinnis, Patricia, 10, 192
McNamara, Robert, 355
Memory system, 206, 207
Menger sponge, 123
Metalevel, 62
Microinteractions, 357
Mies van der Rohe, Ludwig, 10
Miller, John H., 148
Mitsubishi Bank, 272
Modeling, 96, 159, 176, 187, 193
    financial, 242
Modeling by the abstraction of
    concepts, 235, 236
Models, 157, 160, 162, 261
    advanced, 273
    autocatalytic, 355
    econometric, 161
    mathematical, 220
    nonlinear, 203, 212

Models of economic evolution, 47
Modern Portfolio Theory, 188, 204
Molecular biology, 153
Molecular evolution, 154
Momentum, 100
Monte Carlo method, 274, 315, 317, 318, 320–22, 324, 327, 328, 330, 332, 337–40
Moody's, 301
Morgan, J.P., 232, 233
Mortgage-backed financing (MBF), 231, 320, 329, 334, 335
Mortgage-backed securities, 340
Mortgage pools, 334
Mortgages, 333, 334–42
Mutations, 129, 132
  order-based, 145, 146
  position-based, 145

National Mortgage Association (Ginnie Mae), 333
National Science Foundation, 366
National Security Agency, 175
Natural selection, 139, 140
Natural systems, 176
NCR, 354
Near certainty, 113
Network knowledge, causality of, 234
Neumann, John von, 47, 172, 315
Neural networks, 238, 240, 242, 246
Newton, Isaac, 100, 228

Newtonian mechanics, 49
Nikkei Average, 189
Nikko Securities, 224
Noise, 86, 223
  dynamic, 88
  white, 87, 88
Nonlinear approaches, 25
Nonlinear dependence, 189, 198
Nonlinear dynamics, 23, 26
Nonlinear effects, 205
Nonlinear equations, 94
Nonlinear function approximator, 242
Nonlinear mathematical methods, 178
Nonlinear problems, 5
Nonlinearity, 3, 4, 34, 50
Northeast Parallel Architecture Center, 332

Observation noise, 88
Off-balance sheet (OBS) deals, 143, 145, 341
Operations Research (OR), 127
Option Adjusted Spread (OAS), 274, 327, 337
Options, 198, 199
Order, 9, 13
Organization model, hierarchical, 71

Pacemakers, intelligent, 19
Paciolo, Luca, 292
Packard, Norman H., 178–80, 182, 355, 360
Panics, 8, 230
Parallel computation, 170
Paris CAC-40, 189

Pattern formation, 357
Patterning, 347
Patterns, 347, 258
  transactional, 170
Perot, Ross, 161
Phase or mode locking, 32
Phase transition, 356
Planning, 214
Plato, 254
Poincaré, Henri, 11, 12
Polynomials, 244
Possibilistic logic, 249
Possibility, 220, 221
Possibility distribution function,
  257
Possibility distributions, 284
Possibility theory, 242, 243, 249,
  250, 253, 271
Predicate box, 185
Predicate matrix, 310
Predicates, 288
Prediction algorithm, 207
Prediction Company, 178, 183
Prediction theory, 217
Predictions, 5, 6, 292
Prepayment, 330
Prepayment risk, 329
Principal-only (PO), 340
Probabilistic approaches, 21
Probability, 220, 221
Probability theory, 249, 253
Problem sizing, 344
Problems, nonlinear, 12
Processes
  logical, 221
  physical, 221
Product innovation, 216
Product strategy, 216

Program trading, 148
Protagoras, 150
Pythagoras, 118, 119

Qualification, 290
Qualifiers, 261
Qualitative agreement, 291
Qualitative description, 291
Qualitative understanding, 292
Quality databases, 233
Quantification, 290
Quantifiers, fuzzy, 288
Quantitative analysts (Quants),
  97
Quantitative understanding, 292
Quantitative verification, 291
Quantum mechanics, 251
Quarks, 101
Queries, non-crisp, 213

Radar charts, 305
Random normal numbers
  (RNN), 322, 324
Random processes, stationary,
  86
Random sampling, 318
Random walks, 197, 315, 318
Randomness, 21, 254
Ranieri, Lewis S., 328
Rationality, 362
Raveche, Harold J., 68
Rayleigh, John William Strutt,
  315, 319
Real-time systems, networked
  distributed, 213
Reasoning, analogical, 75–77,
  224, 357
Reasoning by analogy, 158

Reference signal, 171
Regression analysis, 105
Relationship banking, 181, 182, 264, 265
Relative value, 198
 fuzzification of, 302
Relativity, theory of, 100
Research and development on systems behavior, 366
Return on Equity (ROE), 216
Reuters, 278
Reverse delegation, 183
Reynolds, Jackson Eli, 301
Risk, 196
 degree of, 232
 securitization of, 232
Risk Adjusted Return on Capital (RAROC), 224
Risk analysis, 148
Risk management, 56, 58, 183, 232, 260
Risk management tools, 191, 193
Risk rating, 150
Robustness, 32
Rocket scientists, 8, 37, 333, 340, 341, 368
Ruelle, David, 12, 14, 21, 24, 30, 69

S matrix, 251
Salomon Brothers, 328
Samarov, Alexander, 196
Santa Fe Institute (SFI), 10, 21, 147, 150, 152, 158, 162, 163, 166, 168, 176, 187, 188, 195, 209, 210, 238, 357
Schemata, conceptual, 67
Schön, Donald, 9

Securities, 336–39
Securities analysts, 253, 340, 341
Securitization, 332
Self-similarity, 117
Sensitivity analysis, 98, 278
Sensitivity dependence, 111
Sensitivity factors, 210, 278
Shannon, Claude E., 80, 83
Sierpinski triangle, 123, 124
Simplification, 312
Simulation, 42, 159
Simulators, 163, 188
 mathematical, 160
Sloan, Alfred, 71
Socrates, 254
Solution space reconstruction, 43
Standard and Poor's 500, 189, 301
Stochastic systems, 128
Stock returns, 198
Strange attractors, 30, 106
Structures, cooperative, 357
Sumitomo Bank, 272
Supercomputer, parallel, 204
Swarm Simulation System (SSS), 169, 170, 176
Swarms, 158, 160–65, 167, 168, 170, 173, 177, 178
System prediction, 11

Technology transfer, 214
Terano, Toshiro, 61, 63, 233, 240
Thermodynamic degradation, 83
Thermodynamics, 11, 80, 81
 second law of, 77, 81
Thermostatics, 81

Theory of complexity, 44
Theory of relativity, 100
Thinking
  discontinuous, 26
  interdisciplinary, 72
Thinking by analogy, 166, 187
Time, 17, 142
Time series, 43, 104, 210
  chaotic, 99
  financial, 345
  long-memory, 204
Time variance, 205
Time's arrow, 144
Time-to-market, 40
Tolstoi, Leon, 69
Trading centers, 53
Transition patterns, 166
Transition probabilities, 320
Transition probability concepts,
  175
Tribus, Myron, 81, 82
Truman, Harry S, 222
Turbulence, 24, 30

Uncertainty, 113, 217, 250, 251,
  254, 255, 257, 292, 345
  degree of, 217
Uncertainty factors, 221
Uncertainty principle, 102
Unisys, 354
Univac, 354

Untermyer, Samuel, 232
U.S. Naval Surface Warfare
  Center, 19, 21

Vagueness, 218, 250, 257, 292,
  345
Valuable swaps, 142
Value, 142
Vamos, Tibor, 254
Visibilization, 90, 358
Visions, 6,
Visistraction, 90, 358
Visual programming
  approaches, 301
Visualization, 90, 105, 114, 195,
  358
Volatility, 192
  dynamic, 194
  higher, 199
Volatility modeling paradigms,
  203
Volatility spillovers, 190, 202
Vona, Carmine, 214

Workstations, networked, 290

Yamaichi Securities, 224

Zadeh, Lotfi, 3, 295
Zooming, 64